PRINCE PHILIP

Other books by the same author

King of Fools
The Princess Royal
Five for Hollywood
The Trial of Rock Hudson

PRINCE PHILIP

His Secret Life

JOHN PARKER

St. Martin's Press
New York

PRINCE PHILIP: HIS SECRET LIFE.

Copyright © 1990 by John Parker. All rights reserved. Printed in
the United States of America. No part of this book may be used or
reproduced in any manner whatsoever without written permission
except in the case of brief quotations embodied in critical articles or
reviews. For information, address St. Martin's Press, 175 Fifth
Avenue, New York N.Y. 10010.

Library of Congress Cataloging-in-Publication Data

Parker, John.
  Prince Philip : his secret life / John Parker.
    p.   cm.
  ISBN 0-312-06444-6
  1. Philip, Prince, consort of Elizabeth II, Queen of Great
Britain, 1921-   . 2. Great Britain—Princes and princesses—
Biography. I. Title.
DA591.A2P37 1991
941.085′092—dc20   91-21820
[B]   CIP

First published in Great Britain by Sidgwick and Jackson
Limited.

First U.S. Edition: October 1991
10 9 8 7 6 5 4 3 2 1

Contents

PRINCE PHILIP'S GREEK AND DANISH ANCESTRY

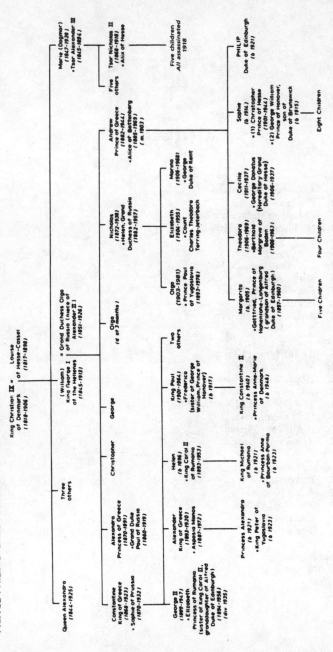

PRINCE PHILIP'S GERMAN ANCESTRY

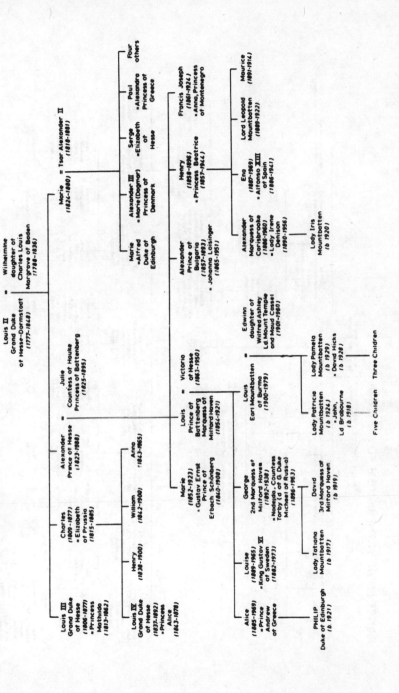

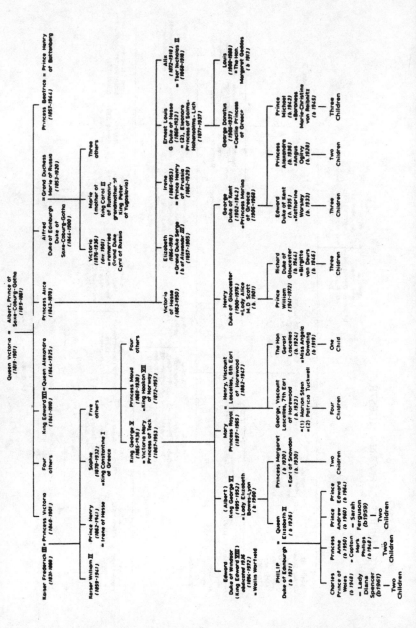

PRINCE PHILIP IN THE BRITISH ROYAL FAMILY

PART ONE

Chapter One

A Precarious Dynasty

Prince Philip's casual denial in March 1963 of his Greek nationality brought an angry response from the Parliament of his country of birth. It was an off-the-cuff remark. A small boy asked him during a visit to Sydney, Australia, 'Are you Greek?'

'No,' Philip replied. 'I was born in Greece but I am not a Greek.'

The following day, hurt feelings were displayed in the Greek Parliament and leading newspapers demanded that the 'cold English prince'[1] who had assumed British nationality should be reminded that if he wished to renounce his Greek origins and his royal Greek blood, he should also remove the nation's flag from the right-hand corner of his coat of arms.

Such minor exchanges of unpleasantries have been typical in both public and private discussion of Prince Philip's background. The truth is, of course, he has not a drop of Greek blood in his veins. He comes from a strong line of royal German–Danish–Russo stock and if there has been confusion in the minds of some, it is due in part to the smokescreen set up around him in the 1940s when he became suitor to the Princess Elizabeth. He was described variously, from 'Prince Who?' to 'Phil the Greek', and no wonder. At the time of their courtship, he was a penniless, stateless and virtually unknown prince earning £11 a week, whose father had died bankrupt after twenty indolent years of banishment and whose mother was, as the diarist Sir Henry 'Chips' Channon described her, 'eccentric to say the least'.[2] Although there was no secret about his attempts to gain British naturalization, some of the detail of his pedigree was 'edited' through fear of post-war sensitivity over his Germanic connections. Far better to latch him to the coat-tails of his famous uncle and acclaimed hero, Earl Mountbatten of Burma, and to the Greek dynasty into which Philip was born.

King George VI was advised by his ministers that another imported royal with relatives who had recently fought on the side of the Nazis

3

might not be palatable to the British public so soon after the concentration camps had been opened to the outside world. Therein lies a story which will be examined fully in later chapters; at the time it was sufficient for King George to delay the announcement of his daughter's engagement for almost a year and for Buckingham Palace to provide a mere cursory, almost reluctant review of his ancestry which actually did not do justice to his lineage.

Behind Prince Philip lies the complex story of the European ruling families whose political involvements and romantic meanderings have left a dubious imprint on the twentieth century. He became an oddly pivotal figure, both in childhood and in later years, linking the dispossessed with the still reigning monarchs, the discredited with what tenuous power survived.

On his father's side lay a royal pedigree stretching back into the Kingdoms of Denmark, Sweden and the Imperial Court of Russia. His mother's ancestry was set in the ruling houses of Germany, though already interlinked through marriage with her husband's family. Prince Philip's Greek birth was a mere accident of location: his Danish-born grandfather had moved to that country in the 1860s to fill the vacancy for a king which the Greeks had been touting among the offspring of the crowned heads of Europe. The family had no previous Greek connection, and, in trailing their crown, a stipend and the tenancy of a barn-like palace from one monarch to another, the politicians from Athens who so desperately wanted a new Royal Family had rather devalued the throne of Greece.

In the hothouse of Balkan intrigue, rivalry, treachery and local wars which had caused several other eligible princes to reject the Greek occupancy, the new Royal Family suffered a precarious tenure which, before and after Philip's birth, forced them into dramatic exile, greatly reduced circumstances and brought about the break-up of his parents' marriage. From this turmoil emerged a young Prince who would be groomed by his Battenberg uncles to capture in name the proudest throne in the world.

In 1947, the year of Philip's bethrothal to Princess Elizabeth, Mountbatten embarked on an exercise in self-aggrandizement which Lord Beaverbrook described as verging on the fanatical: the tracing of his family tree back to a starting-point in the Dark Ages – although Lord Lambton has since tarnished the glittering image by claiming the Mountbatten branch was the byproduct of an adulterous affair, and Lord Louis and Prince Philip result from an assignation on the wrong side of the blanket.

Lord Louis called his book of ancestry 'The Mountbatten Lineage: The Direct Descent of the Family of Mountbatten from the House of Brabant and the Rulers of Hesse, prepared for private circulation by

Admiral of the Fleet, the Earl Mountbatten of Burma, KG, PC, GCB, GCSI, GCIE, GCVO, DSO, LLD, DCL, BSc.'[3] The history took eleven years to complete, with the aid of eminent genealogists, and in it Mountbatten proudly proclaimed his family to be a branch of one of the oldest traceable families in European history. His remaining hope was that the British Royal Family of Windsor would, upon Princess Elizabeth's marriage, assume the family name of Mountbatten, which Philip had taken as his own. In this, as we will see, he was thwarted first by Queen Mary and then by Elizabeth herself.

Mountbatten's family tree, now deposited in the British Museum, helps shed some light on the many branches of Prince Philip's intriguing family history, as closely woven as the threads of a fine carpet and interlocking with almost every royal house of Europe.

For the sake of simplicity, a suitable starting-point to Philip's story – and a clue to the origins of some of his strongest character traits, such as his opinionated, arrogant outspokenness – is to be found at the arrival in Athens in 1863 of his grandfather: an event that provides us with the beginnings of an illuminating excursion, albeit brief for the purposes of this book, through the fading dynasties of Europe.

In that year, the Greek National Assembly, encouraged by the protecting powers of England, France and Russia, began its concerted effort to find a new king. The last incumbent, King Otto I – the only ruler Greece had seen since in 1829 the country won its freedom from 400 years of Turkish domination, and himself 'imported' from Bavaria – had been dethroned in 1862 after a bumpy thirty-year reign which he began at the tender age of seventeen. The Greeks liked him, but the protecting powers were uneasy about his nationalistic views and had him removed.

Otto's turbulent time in a politically volatile country were hardly any recommendation for a successor. Queen Victoria's second son, Alfred, the then Duke of Edinburgh, was among those who refused the Greeks' kind offer. The protecting powers together added £12,000 a year to the Civil List payment Greece was offering its new King (it was the lowest-paid monarchy in Europe) and for good measure Britain threw in a bonus of the Ionian Islands, including Corfu, which had been a British protectorate since the turn of the century. With that, the Greeks had more success when a delegation was sent to Copenhagen for discussions with King Frederick VII of Denmark.

It is in Denmark that we find Prince Philip's immediate ancestors on his father's side. In the first half of the nineteenth century the Danes were a fairly unsophisticated nation whose prosperity had evaporated with the Napoleonic Wars, their naval fleet decimated and their maritime trade ruined. Frederick VII became a popular national hero after these trying times because he gave his people a democratic constitution. Privately he was a reprobate, a womanizer and renowned drunk, who used his royal privilege with relish. Twice married and twice divorced,

5

he set up home with a common hatmaker. He was feared by his family and staff during his rampages and was a mischievous dabbler in international affairs.

Frederick promptly saw the Greek monarchy as an opportunity for Prince William, son of his nephew and heir Prince Christian. William, a mere eighteen years old and a cadet in the Navy, was reluctant to take the job, however. 'Do I have to?' he asked the King. 'It is a far-off land and I really want to continue my naval career.'

Prince Christian supported his son. He too was unimpressed by the Greek offer and went immediately to seek an audience with the King.

'I will not have my son taken to Greece . . . my boy will not be forced into going there,' he said.

Frederick flew into one of his angry rages: 'Very well. If you do not allow him to go, I'll have you shot.'4

Prince William was sent for and the King made his position clear: he would like the young man to accept the throne of Greece. He went for a walk in the palace gardens and returned an hour later after struggling alone with the thoughts of being taken from his family and his naval friends. His father, though heir to the Danish throne through marriage to the King's daughter, was a poor man of irreproachable character, totally reliant for his income on the military pension he received from the Crown, and could do nothing further to help. William agreed to go.

The Greek delegation was overjoyed. They had done well. With the boy monarch came a royal lineage which could be traced back to 1448.* More than that, the Greek throne would soon be directly and prestigiously linked to the throne of England by the marriage of their new King's sister Alexandra, to Edward, Prince of Wales,† and, although as yet unknown, his younger sister, Princess Dagmar, was to become Empress of Russia when she married Tsar Alexander III.‡

William presented himself to the Greeks and formally accepted the title. He would thenceforth be known as King George I of the Hellenes – although to his family and relations he remained Willy (pronounced 'Veellee') – and on a dismal October morning he appeared before his relatives dressed in the uniform of a Danish admiral, tall, erect and looking older than his years. He saluted his King and his father and kissed the womenfolk; then he set off in a convoy of carriages, bearing

* Through the marriage of King George I of the Hellenes (as William of Denmark became) to Grand Duchess Olga, granddaughter of Tsar Nicholas I Prince Philip's family includes among its ancestors and descendants sixteen kings of the House of Oldenburg and three from the House of Schleswig-Holstein-Sonderburg-Glücksburg-Beck, seven tsars of Russia and eventually six kings of Sweden.

† Alexandra thus became great-grandmother to Princess Elizabeth and great-aunt to Prince Philip.

‡ On her marriage Dagmar took the name Marie Feodorovna.

his entourage of advisers and diplomats, on the journey to a new life and to establish a new dynasty.[5]

George I was a natural leader. Descriptions of him have been echoed in the next century when almost identical characterizations have been drawn of his grandson, Prince Philip. His son Prince Christopher wrote, 'George I was a born ruler, for he had a force of character and was not afraid of showing it, felt strongly on all subjects and never hesitated to express his opinion, no matter what the cost.'[6]

In 1866 King George's search for a Queen took him to Russia, where he had met by chance the Grand Duchess Olga, daughter of the Grand Duke Constantine and granddaughter of Tsar Nicholas I.* She was fifteen years old, a beautiful child with classically delicate features, and was still in the schoolroom of the Grand Duke's palace. George asked for her hand and, the following year, she arrived in Athens in a little dress of blue and white – the Greek colours – travelling in a carriage in which she also brought her family of dolls. She was shy, nervous and knew neither Greek nor English, just her native Russian, which few others in the palace spoke, and a smattering of German through which she communicated with her husband.

For the first year of her married life, Olga went back to the schoolroom in the huge palace of Athens to become fluent in the two languages required to enable her to converse more fluently with both her husband and her subjects.

So now the Greeks had a King in his early twenties and a Queen in her mid-teens. Their main residence was the vast palace built in 1849 by King Otto – a stark and draughty stucco-marble monstrosity constructed on a high hill overlooking the city of Athens. Members of the family, in their later writings, remembered it as an uncomfortable building, the facilities of which were minimal. There were long, gloomy galleries and many unused rooms. The huge reception hall with stone pillars and a classical staircase was used only on State occasions.

Despite its unwelcoming air, however, that palace became a well-arranged domestic paradise in which the young King and his younger bride, virtual strangers when they married, became anchored by a loving devotion to each other and, over the next twenty years, produced eight children. The first-born was Constantine, the heir presumptive; Prince Philip's father, Andrew, the second youngest of five sons, was born in 1882. His younger brother Christopher painted in his memoirs an idyllic picture of a happy and contented family although they lived a comparatively frugal existence. The daily dread of the royal children was being 'hiked out of bed at six o'clock' and thrust into a tub of cold water. They used to cycle and roller-skate through the corridors and around

---

* Olga was also cousin to Tsar Alexander III, whom King George's sister Dagmar was to marry.

7

the ballroom to keep warm in winter. The wind would whistle through the corridors, whipping in and out of the lofty rooms which were so large that the fireplaces provided little heat; oil lamps hung from the ceilings or were set on tables and gave out a strong odour that wafted through the palace on the wind.

All this was in stark contrast to the lavish lifestyles of their various relatives abroad, as the children discovered when they were taken by their mother or their aunts on holidays across the Black Sea to Russia or Denmark and, as they became older, to England. The Russian branches of the family displayed their wealth at a time when revenues were at their peak, while the peasants starved and plotted their assassinations. Their palaces shone with gold and silver and treasures of incalculable value. Chinese porcelain – part of a collection presented to Catherine the Great by the Emperor of China – was in daily use. The women were afire with jewels, each competing with the next in their displays of finery, with emeralds as large as pigeon eggs.

Family gatherings were frequent in any one of their related countries but a popular meeting point was Fredensborg Castle, one of the country homes of King George of Greece's father, Christian IX, who had by now ascended the Danish throne. They were all there one summer when, on a sunny afternoon, George went for a stroll with Edward, Prince of Wales, and Tsar Alexander III of Russia. They were joined by a stranger who began talking with them as they walked through the park.

When they reached the gates, the man turned and said, 'I have enjoyed walking with you – may I ask your names?'

'Certainly,' said George. 'I am the King of Greece, this is the Prince of Wales and this is the Emperor of Russia.'

'Oh yes,' said the stranger. 'And I am Jesus Christ.' He walked away in disgust.[7]

Apart from their palace in Athens, the Greek Royal Family had two other homes, one at Tatoi, fifteen miles from the capital, which George had bought on his arrival in Greece. It was a more homely family estate and farm. The second was a holiday home on the island of Corfu, called Mon Repos, where they often met Wilhelm II, the German Kaiser, who came each April to a small estate he had bought from the Emperor of Austria. He had obviously heard that the Athens palace was short of modern installations and bathing facilities, since he invariably brought gifts of soap and perfume for the Greeks. Through these visits, the Kaiser became a close relation; his sister Sophie met and married Crown Prince Constantine, heir of King George and Queen Olga.*

---

* Another link in the chain. This meant the King of Greece, brother of Queen Victoria's daughter-in-law Alexandra, had now become father-in-law to Queen Victoria's granddaughter.

Athens and the Greek islands became a regular stopping-off point and holiday area for the British Royals. Queen Victoria had long since written, 'How charming Olga of Greece is! So handsome & so dear & charming. She has none of the bourgeoiserie of the rest of the Russian family including our own dear excellent Marie.'[8]* Queen Victoria was less enthusiastic when her royal relations from Greece and other parts of Europe were together *en masse*. Using a phrase introduced in 1889 by her son-in-law Prince Louis of Hesse-Darmstadt, Victoria talked of the 'Royal mob', than which she 'disliked nothing more'. Once, when she had received a description of the family get-together scenes at Fredensborg, she wrote, 'That Mob of Royalty & that noise must have been dreadful & and rather strange to romp & carry one another as they do.'[9]

The true Mob descended annually at Gmunden in Germany, where, littered around the Traunsee, stood the summer villas of the Queen of Hanover, various Württemberg, Hessian and Danish cousins, two or three archdukes from Austria, and a grand duchess from Tuscany.

It was from Gmunden that, in the spring of 1893, Queen Olga was inspired to act as matchmaker for her nephew, 28-year-old Prince George, from England and the German Princess May of Teck – the future British King George V and Queen Mary. Olga had become George's second mother while he was posted to the Mediterranean station during his naval service, to which he was devoted. Shortly before his engagement to Princess May, then aged twenty-six, George stayed at the Hellenic Court in Athens and, during long walks, Queen Olga gave the future King some advice over whether or not he should seek May's hand. Olga herself had first met the Princess on one of the family gatherings at Gmunden but much had happened since; in accordance with the wishes of Queen Victoria, May had become engaged in 1891 to George's wayward and unstable elder brother, Prince Eddy – Albert Victor, Duke of Clarence, the elder son of the Prince of Wales and, had he lived, England's future King. Eddy, who in 1891 was in his twenty-eighth year, was not long for this world. The tall, thin, sickly young man with a long neck and a strange oval face set with haunting eyes, had brought nothing but grief upon his parents through his illnesses, his unruly antics and his much-discussed affairs with lovers of both sexes. On Queen Victoria's instruction that he should get married, he had pursued a couple of German princesses who refused his advances before he became engaged to Princess May, whom he barely knew, in December. A wedding was hastily arranged for the following February. In January 1892, however, Eddy caught a chill during a bad winter when

* Marie was the daughter of Tsar Alexander II and first cousin of Queen Olga of Greece. She married Victoria's son, Alfred, the first Duke of Edinburgh.

a thick, polluted fog enveloped London. He took to his bed with a high fever and fell into a wild and violent delirium; he died on 14 January.*

It was against this background that his brother Prince George sought the counsel of Queen Olga. He had been urged by Queen Victoria to marry quickly to ensure the succession of a third generation, and after George had made an unsuccessful approach to his cousin Princess Marie,† daughter of the Duke and Duchess of Edinburgh, Victoria came back to her original thought: George should marry his dead brother's fiancée, Princess May. During the spring of 1893, he had long talks with Queen Olga in Athens. She advised him to propose to May immediately.

---

* As we now know, his death was to become surrounded by rumours linking him to the Jack the Ripper murders, to a male brothel which he frequented in the Whitechapel area and to a mad homosexual lover who died in St Andrews Hospital, Northampton. Some writers have attempted to prove that Prince Eddy was deliberately put to sleep by Palace physicians to cover up an impending scandal of mammoth proportions, while others have said that he did not die in 1892 at all but was hidden in a locked chamber in total madness until he passed away in 1930. As yet, the history books remain unaltered in the record of his death.

† Princess Marie later married King Ferdinand of Romania.

Chapter Two
Philip's Parents

The Greek family's deepening involvement with their British cousins took a step closer with the arrival at the Athens Court of Prince Philip's mother, the demure and shy Princess Alice of Battenberg. She came into their realm in 1901 at the age of seventeen, and she was noticed by the tall, handsome young cavalry lieutenant Prince Andrew of Greece while they were both visiting Darmstadt, her family's German home.

Alice brought her strong German lineage to Prince Philip's family tree and it makes either an impressive contribution or a scandalous one, depending on whether students of genealogy take Lord Lambton's version of events or Lord Mountbatten's. Lambton claims that the immediate Battenberg ancestors of Prince Philip and Lord Mountbatten were the result of an adulterous affair in the Hesse family in 1820 when Princess Wilhelmina separated from her husband, Grand Duke Louis II of Hesse and the Rhine, and lived openly with her lover, Baron Augustus Senarclens von Grancy.[1] The Mountbatten Lineage naturally does not mention the Baron and claims the Grand Duke as the father of Prince Alexander and Princess Marie of Hesse, whom Lambton says were fathered by the Baron. Either way, it provides a dramatic tapestry, tinged with scandal, as we journey back into the mid-nineteenth century when the offspring of the German ruling families were appearing in plentiful numbers.

At Darmstadt, the first son of Grand Duke Louis II inherited his father's title in 1848 and became Grand Duke Louis III. His younger sister Marie married Tsarevich Alexander II when she was barely fifteen, eventually becoming Empress of Russia, and his younger brother Prince Alexander followed her to the Russian Court to become a colonel in the military at the age of eighteen. More scandal followed – this time acknowledged, but politely and romantically dealt with in the Mountbatten Lineage. Prince Alexander pursued a gallant soldierly role and a busy amorous career among the beauties of the Russian Court and

11

could have married well. Instead, he fell in love with a commoner, a Polish orphan who was his sister's maid-of-honour, named Julie Hauke. The Courts of Russia and Darmstadt were scandalized; Prince Alexander was refused permission to marry as anger raged in both quarters. 'You cannot possibly marry this commoner,' the Grand Duke wrote to his brother. 'It is unthinkable. How can we take a plain Frau Hauke into the family?' Julie, however, discovered that she was pregnant and the lovers eloped from the Winter Palace at St Petersburg to marry in Breslau.[2] Instant banishment from Russia followed, but resentment at Darmstadt gave way to partial forgiveness. The Grand Duke, while forbidding Prince Alexander's new family to use the title of Hesse, created Julie the Princess of Battenberg, a dusty old title which had lain dormant for years. Any children from the marriage would thereafter also take the title Battenberg – not Hesse – and thus was created the Battenberg line which leads directly to Lord Mountbatten and Prince Philip.

Grand Duke Louis wanted the family out of the way. In July 1853 they were packed off to the Austro-Hungarian Empire of the Habsburgs where the Prince was given rank of brigade commander in a far-flung garrison at Graz, there to join another banished Royal, Archduke John of Austria, who had married a postmaster's daughter.[3]

Eventually Alexander and Julie, who had five children, were able to return to the German fold with their Battenberg princes and princesses. There was now a new court at Darmstadt: in 1877 Louis III died without producing an heir and was succeeded by his nephew, Louis IV of Hesse, who was married to Queen Victoria's second daughter, Princess Alice.

It is difficult not to lose track amid this plethora of German and Russian aristocracy interlinked by Queen Victoria's matchmaking. However, a simple route to the next development in the Battenberg branch comes through the marriage in 1874 of Prince Louis of Battenberg – Alexander and Julie's eldest son – to his cousin Victoria, the eldest of seven children born to the Princess Alice and Grand Duke Louis IV of Hesse. By now, the Battenbergs had established themselves as a favoured family, closely allied, through the marriage of Queen Victoria's daughter into the Hesse family, to the British Royal Court, though German nobility still tended to look upon them disdainfully.

Prince Louis of Battenberg was an ambitious young man but, like his father, something of a rebel. He refused to follow the Hessian line into the Army and left the Darmstadt home at the age of fourteen to join the British Royal Navy. His passage smoothed by his status as a prince and his family connections, he became a proficient and skilful officer, surging his way through promotions – though not without his critics in England, who objected strongly to the advance of this German princeling. When he married the Hessian Princess Victoria, she came to join him in

London. The marriage received Queen Victoria's blessing: the young Prince Louis had become a favourite with her. Not so with her son-in-law, the reigning Grand Duke Louis IV of Hesse, who still looked upon the Battenbergs as the product of an unauthorized marriage.*

Prince Louis and Princess Victoria took a house in England, in Sussex, and, though they had very little money, set about producing their family. They had four children: Alice (Prince Philip's mother), born in 1885; Louise (who became Queen of Sweden by her marriage to King Gustaf VI Adolf of Sweden), born in 1889; George (Prince Louis's heir), born in 1892; and Louis (the future Earl Mountbatten of Burma), born in 1900.

Victoria was removed to Windsor Castle for her confinement for the birth of Alice and the infant became a particular favourite of her great-grandmother, Queen Victoria. She was a retiring child, in part because of her profound congenital deafness – a disability that eventually became a key factor in her rather enigmatic personality, both pushing her towards self-achievement and forcing her into her own private world. She was also pretty, described as one of the most beautiful young princesses in Europe, and was selected as a bridesmaid at the wedding of the futue King George V to Princess May in 1893. On that occasion Queen Victoria recorded her thoughts on the child: 'Very sweet . . . in white satin, with a little pink and red rose on the shoulder and some small bows of the same on the shoes.'

Alice was barely seventeen when Prince Andrew of Greece saw her; he was a dashing young Army officer of almost twenty, tall and blond, his Danish traits evident in his walk and manner. Like his brothers, he was a cheerful man who enjoyed pranks and practical jokes, as Prince Philip recalled in later years: 'When a few of them got together, it was like being with the Marx Brothers.'[5]

Andrew had spent six years in the Greek Military Academy in Athens and in 1902, after receiving his commission, he was posted to Darmstadt on attachment to the Hessian 23rd Dragoon Guards. At the same time, Princess Alice was visiting her father's family and, though their meeting was brief, they continued to correspond.

They did not see each other again until the Coronation of Edward VII of England on 9 August 1902; from then on romance blossomed, accord-

---

* That did not stop the Grand Duke entering a morganatic marriage of his own. On the night that Louis of Battenberg married Victoria, the Grand Duke, whose wife Alice had died of diphtheria six years earlier, secretly married his mistress, a Polish divorcee named Alexandrine de Kolemine. On hearing the devastating news that her son-in-law had married a divorced woman, Queen Victoria announced that the Hessian Court had been 'contaminated'.[4] She instructed the Prince of Wales to see that the marriage was annulled immediately, which he did, and extracted a promise from the Grand Duke that he would never see the charming Alexandrine again.

ing to some; others said bluntly that they were being pushed into marriage by Queen Alexandra. Communication was hampered by Alice's deafness, which meant she had to lip-read, and this was further complicated because he preferred to speak in Greek. It was a hurdle that she had long since learned to overcome, however, and she eventually taught herself to lip-read in Greek and several other languages.

Their courtship continued by letter for another year, with one more visit from Andrew before they announced their engagement. Since Alice was Queen Victoria's great-granddaughter, consent was required from King Edward under the British Royal Marriages Act 1772 and he gave it, with some prodding from Queen Alexandra who was anxious for her brother's son to be brought into the fold. The King, however, was not entirely satisfied with the choice of husband for Queen Victoria's great-granddaughter. 'He has no prospects,' the King would observe with acidity whenever Andrew's name was mentioned.[6]

Apart from his military career, Prince Andrew had little indeed to offer. As the second youngest son of the House of the Hellenes there was no royal future to speak of; and it was certainly no secret among the European ruling houses that the King of Greece was not wealthy – 'a poor man with a large family', they would say. Even the Battenbergs were now wealthier after some valuable inheritances received by both Prince Louis and Princess Victoria.

Some of the Danish and Russian relations helped out with contributions to get Andrew and Alice started in their married life. By now, Nicholas II was Tsar of Russia: he was rumoured to have given £100,000 to the impoverished couple.* But Edward, in his written permission, stipulated that they should be married in the Protestant Church, which caused some anguish back in Athens where politicians were naturally put out by such a demand. The solution was to have three wedding ceremonies – one civil, one in a Protestant church and the third according to Greek Orthodox rites.

The marriage on 9 October 1903 of Andrew of Greece and Alice of Battenberg was a typical royal party, attracting a vast representation from the European monarchies for a week-long round of ceremonies and galas in the little Grand Duchy of Hesse-Darmstadt. They were led by the bride's uncle and aunt, the Russian Tsar and Tsarina; the bridegroom's aunt, Queen Alexandra of England; a clutch of grand dukes and duchesses, some from the Romanov family, others from the Hesse line; Kaiser Wilhelm II, the bridegroom's brother-in-law, sent his own brother, Henry, Prince of Prussia, to represent him; there were archdukes from Austria and princes from Serbia, Italy and Hungary; and

---

* The Tsar was Prince Andrew's cousin and Princess Alice's uncle, having married her mother's sister, Princess Alexandra Feodorovna, another of the Hessian princesses.

there was the three-year-old brother of the bride, Louis, the future Earl Mountbatten.

During the ceremony, the bridegroom's brothers, Christopher and Nicholas – who himself had married Grand Duchess Helen, daughter of Grand Duke Vladimir of Russia – held two golden crowns over the heads of the couple as they took their vows. Alice, unable to hear the words of the officiating Archbishop, called out 'Yes' when she should have said 'No' and was prodded in the side by Christopher to correct herself; then the church was filled with the sound of the great Russian Imperial Choir, which Tsar Nicholas had imported specially from St Petersburg.

As the couple left in their carriage, the whole gaggle of European Royalty surrounded them with confetti and good wishes and high jinks. The Tsar threw a white satin slipper for good luck and it hit the bride firmly on the head. She stood up and lambasted him verbally about being a stupid donkey, leaving the Emperor of All the Russias in the middle of the road in tears of laughter.

The Grand Duchess of Württemberg, a dumpy, short-sighted woman who had tied her tiara to her head with elastic, was jostled so that it was perched precariously over her left ear; her spectacles, which had not been secured, were lost from the bridge of her nose and smashed into a thousand pieces on the road. In her anger, she hit an infant prince with her handbag and he ran off howling because he was not the perpetrator of the push.

After such a send-off, the newly-weds embarked on their married life and a frugal start in a wing of the great Palace of Athens. Their marriage was to prove something of a catalyst that, for a few years, bonded the ruling families of Europe even more closely. But how long could it last?

Prince Andrew pursued his career in the Army while his wife began learning languages and lip-reading. She also spent many hours each week at the School of Greek Embroidery, an art which she determined to make her own. Alice might well have been apprehensive. As her niece ex-Queen Alexandra of Yugoslavia later recalled: 'Deaf and vulnerable, she could not always follow the heated discussions that constantly raged. . . .'[7] Despite her difficulties, she seemed determined not to become a cottonwool princess and began carving her own life, becoming dedicated to her people and especially to the poor. Soon, also, their wing of the royal palace was to hear the sound of children, with the birth of Margarita in 1905, Theodora in 1906, Cecile in 1911 and Sophie in 1914. For their holidays, Princess Alice would take her daughters to England to stay at the Battenbergs' Hampshire estate of Broadlands.

Unrest inside Greece had been bubbling away and the Greek Royal Family faced attacks from within the country itself as a wave of Republicanism gained ground. In 1909 the King's sons, Constantine, Nicholas, Christopher and Andrew were forced to resign from the Army and their brother George from the Navy because of Republican demonstrations, linked with mounting discontent over their family ties with Germany.

The swing of domestic politics moved in their favour, however. With the Bulgarians and neighbouring Serbia and Montenegro preparing to go to war against the Greeks' arch-enemies, the Turks, the royal Princes were restored to their commissions after two idle and frustrating years. On the evening of 17 October 1912, the King read from the palace balcony the proclamation of war against Turkey, while Andrew held a candle to shed light on his papers.

Crown Prince Constantine was installed as head of the military – an ill-prepared and motley Army, yet determined to regain Greek territory lost to the Turks. Andrew and Christopher were beside their brother in the push against the enemy. During three weeks of fighting they slept rough, cooking animals donated by peasant farmers over open fires and eating them with their bare hands.

Constantine and Andrew headed the Greek troops as they took Salonika, where they established a base; Princess Alice came with them, leading a nursing unit for the wounded while her children remained at the Palace of Athens with their English nanny. The family basked in glory as the war began to turn in the Greeks' favour and for the moment the Republicans were put to flight. It heralded a promising start to the new year, 1913, which should have been the old King's happiest.

Fifty years had now passed since William of Denmark became George I of the Hellenes and he planned to abdicate in favour of Constantine in November 1913, the anniversary of his accession. Fate had other plans. One of his first acts of celebration that year was to ride into Salonika as monarch at the request of his politicians, who were anxious to thwart Bulgaria's claim over the port. He planned to remain there for some days, although his sons had now returned to Army headquarters. On the afternoon of 18 March, he was out walking the streets of the city with only an ADC for company. Suddenly a man lunged at him with a gun and shot him through the head. He was sixty-eight years old.

In Greece, there was a romantic legend that Constantinople, the ancient capital of the Byzantine Empire, would be reclaimed by the country when a Constantine and Sophie sat on the throne – a story doubtless originating from the fact that the last Byzantine Emperor, before the city was taken by the Ottoman Turks in 1453, was Constantine and his wife Sophie. So the murder of the old King, while mourned by the nation, brought with it a brief period of hope. Now the Greeks had their Constantine and Sophie. The Royal Family was given unprecedented accolade. In other parts of Europe, however, Constantine's accession was viewed with dismay and even fear because of his family ties to his brother-in-law, Kaiser Wilhelm of Germany.

The second Balkan War broke out in June 1913 over Bulgaria's claim to Salonika and Prince Andrew gave his oath of allegiance to his brother, as King still head of the military. The war was shortlived, ending in September, and the brothers delivered a crushing defeat upon the Bulgars. Within months, a more dreadful trouble had flared up.

On 28 June 1914, two days after the birth of Prince Philip's sister Sophie, Archduke Franz Ferdinand, heir to Franz-Josef and the Habsburg Empire, and his wife were assassinated by a gunman while visiting Sarajevo in neighbouring Bosnia. The assassin was a Serb, thought to be a member of the Serbian secret society known as the Black Hand which was campaigning against Austro-Hungarian oppression of its nationals in occupied territory. In London, King George V did not see the implication of the murder; he was more concerned for his contemporaries and merely commented, 'The poor old emperor.'

Austria–Hungary, which had long sought an excuse to deal with the Serbs, threatened an invasion of Serbia. Kaiser Wilhelm said Germany would support Austria. Tsar Nicholas announced that Russia could not remain indifferent if Serbia were invaded and ordered the mobilization of 1,200,000 troops.

The Austro-Hungarian forces invaded Serbia on 28 July. Kaiser Wilhelm warned the Tsar: 'Stay out of it,' but Nicholas refused, and on 1 August Wilhelm declared war on Russia, followed two days later by a similar move against France. Britain said she would stand by the 1839 Treaty of London guaranteeing neutrality to Belgium and protecting French coasts, and King George declared war on his cousin the Kaiser on 4 August. Then the Habsburgs of Austria–Hungary declared war on Russia, Serbia declared war on Germany and the Turks began mobilizing troops against Greece.

The cauldron of Balkan treachery had spilled over into terrible conflict; and in the royal houses of Europe, brothers and sisters-in-law, uncles, nephews and cousins found themselves pitted against one another.

The effect on the Greek house was catastrophic; through its interwoven relationships, it was split and divided. If Constantine showed sympathy to his brother-in-law the German Kaiser, he would be outcast by his Russian and English cousins, and vice versa. In the few days before war broke out, the Kaiser was on holiday in Norway with the Greek family's relatives at Fredensborg, while Crown Prince George of Greece and his uncle Prince Christopher were visiting England, and were actually staying with Queen Alexandra at Marlborough House. Only four months earlier the Kaiser had entertained King George and Queen Mary at a family occasion in Berlin; Queen Mary thought the visit had done 'some lasting good'.

In the international community, Constantine and his brothers were tarred with the Kaiser's brush. Wasn't Constantine married to the Kaiser's sister? Hadn't he received several military decorations from

17

Germany, and didn't he hold the honorary rank of Field Marshal in the German Army, dating from his association with the Hessian troops? He was viewed in many quarters as weak and pro-German. As the war progressed this view did not alter and the Allies surrounded the Greek Royals with spies.

Prince Andrew, widely thought to be in concert with a pro-German general, was despatched to England in the spring of 1916 to assure King George that Constantine had chosen a middle road and that he wished to remain strictly neutral; his brother Nicholas was sent to Russia to give similar assurances to the Tsar. In London, Andrew found himself an unwelcome visitor. The newspapers were already headlining 'TINO'S TREACHERY' and 'TINO BETRAYS ALLIES'. Some newspapers had accused him of plotting to set up refuelling facilities for German U-boats on the island of Corfu.

Prince Andrew lunched with King George and Queen Mary at Buckingham Palace, but after a pleasant meal the King became brusque: Andrew should tell his brother that he would be running 'grave risks' if he did not side with the Allies. King George's mother, Queen Alexandra, meanwhile, was bombarding her son with incoherent letters about Tino, urging that George should help the 'poor boy'. King George wrote, 'I am not prepared now on account of the strong feelings which certainly exist about him to do anything; in fact no one would listen to me if I did.' Alexandra was not easily put off and persisted, until the King said, 'I simply cannot make Mother dear hear, much less understand, anything at all about Greece.'[8]

Constantine's alleged neutrality angered the Allies and finally an Anglo-French force invaded Piraeus, the port of Athens, and began advancing towards the capital. The pro-Allies Prime Minister of Greece, Eleuthérios Venizélos, had set up a new government in Salonika and now threw the city open for an Allied landing of his country. French warships, meanwhile, were shelling Athens and to end further bloodshed Constantine agreed to abdicate in June 1917. His brothers were drummed out of the Royal Greek Army and ordered to leave the country.

Princess Alice was serving in the charity shop she ran in Athens when the ships' guns began firing; she drove as fast as she could in her little car to the palace, where she discovered that a shell had landed outside the King's study window and bullets had shattered the nursery window where her daughters played. That night King Constantine was dethroned and his second son, Alexander, aged twenty-four, was installed as King. Venizélos had chosen him in preference to the heir, Crown Prince George, who was also thought to be a supporter of the Kaiser. Alexander broke down and cried as he took the oath of allegiance before the Archbishop of Athens and then immediately upset some of his supporters by announcing his morganatic marriage to a commoner, a girl named

Aspasia Manos, whom his father had banned him from seeing. Then, as Venizélos's mouthpiece, he announced that he would be joining the Allies in the war against Germany.

The palace was surrounded by crowds, spurred on by rumours and conjecture; thousands in the mob were violently against the Royals, while others were still fervently behind their hero Constantine and his brothers; for hours the family dared not venture out of the palace. Finally, in the dead of night, they managed to elude the crowds by escaping through a rear exit and at the Athens harbour the royal yacht was waiting to take them to exile in Switzerland.

At the same time, other relatives were suffering various degrees of discomfort. In London whispers circulated against King George, who, it was said, was not doing much to win the war because he was really pro-German and supported King Constantine. George paled when he heard the rumours[9] and immediately ordered a survey of his family names. At a meeting of the Privy Council on 17 July 1917,[10] King George agreed to relinquish all his German titles and to establish a British royal house, free of German influence. No one, it seems, was quite sure of the British monarch's true family name, so the College of Heralds was consulted. They arrived at a solution: the Royal Family's surname should be anglicized to Windsor. Kaiser Wilhelm seemed to be under no illusion about their correct title: back in Germany, he responded by ordering a performance of 'The Merry Wives of Saxe-Coburg-Gotha'. King George also ordered that all members of his family who had foreign titles should replace them with English names. His brother-in-law the Duke of Teck became the Marquess of Cambridge and Prince Alexander of Teck became the Earl of Athlone. The increasingly insular British public opinion against the Kaiser also forced the King to change the rules of royal matrimony under which the heir to the throne had invariably married a spouse from foreign Royalty. On that day of 17 July, he wrote in his diary, 'I also informed the council that May and I had decided some time ago that our children would be allowed to marry into British families. It was quite an historic occasion.'[11]

The King's face-saving scheme, however, did not save Princess Alice's father, Prince Louis of Battenberg, from considerable personal distress. He had reached the supreme rank of First Sea Lord to the Admiralty – not without some very bitter opponents objecting to the charmed life of the German princeling – but at the height of the war he succumbed to a vitriolic campaign against him and resigned. The last straw came when the German ships *Goeben* and *Breslau* got through; there were rumours – as Earl Mountbatten himself recounted many years later – that Prince Louis was in fact a spy passing information to his Greek and German relations, disregarding totally the fact that, as First Sea Lord, he had signed the order setting the British Royal Navy against the country of his birth. He sat out the rest of the war, shattered and disappointed, with the new title of Marquess of Milford Haven and his family name anglicized to Mountbatten. His career was over and the Battenberg name never recovered from the stigma.

Chapter Three
Escape in an Orange Box

Prince Philip's paternal grandmother, the widowed Queen Olga of Greece, spent the First World War in Russia and temporarily lost contact with her children. Throughout Europe, Royalty sought scant and irregular news from any source about their relations on the opposing sides. Queen Alexandra used to get her letters to Europe smuggled from Britain via a devious maritime route of neutral ships. As one of their number said, 'Mere wars do not separate us.' But, of course, they would.

At the outbreak of war, Olga was visiting her family home near Pavlosk and, because of the turmoil within her family and Greece itself, she stayed on to help establish and run a military hospital in the huge grand-ducal palace. As a Russian by birth, a Greek by adoption and mother-in-law of a German princess, she was in a political no man's land and settled for sitting out the war in her homeland, unaware that even greater danger faced her from Lenin and his revolutionaries. For two years or more, she worked for the war-wounded. She witnessed the last shambolic stages of the reign of her cousin Tsar Nicholas, who spent almost his entire time at the warfront, leaving the running of his government and country to the Tsarina Alexandra and the 'mad monk' Rasputin. She saw the strange power the bearded, unkempt peasant holy man exercised over the Tsarina after he had allegedly cured her son Alexei of haemophilia.

Queen Olga, like her relations in England, had long worried about Nicholas's autocratic traits and his wife's mystic obsessions. Now catastrophe struck them. In 1916 came the news that Rasputin had been murdered; in 1917 Russian moderates forced the Tsar to abdicate – but too late to stop Lenin's Revolution; the Tsar and his wife and children were imprisoned at Ekaterinburg (now Sverdlovsk), where they were murdered in July 1918. In the Revolution of October 1917 the Bolsheviks seized power. Tsarism had gone for ever.

21

As a Russian Grand Duchess herself, Olga faced the same fate under the new Russian regime. Like many of the aristocracy, her immediate thoughts were of saving what remained of her wealth, and herself afterwards. The first might even have been a means to the second. She had some expensive jewels hidden away and wanted to get them out of the country; by then it was no easy task. Escaping nobility with their riches sewn into their clothes, or hidden in their trunks, were being arrested daily.* Pofessional gangs, usually Poles or Finns, were offering their services to help get valuables out of Russia. Homes and palaces were ransacked by the revolutionaries and some of the less indoctrinated were themselves stealing trinkets and smuggling them across the Russian frontiers for sale at giveaway prices. Ten years later, in Paris, Prince Christopher of Greece was shown the Romanov's Bride's Crown by Pierre Cartier.[1] Consisting of a circle of magnificent diamonds held by six claws, it had been used for every wedding in the Imperial Russian Family since Catherine the Great; bride after bride had worn it. Queen Olga herself had worn it on her marriage to King George of Greece. The value was anyone's guess. Cartier had found it by chance: he saw it in the window of an antique shop, where its arrival could not be explained, other than that it had been sold by a Bolshevik. That was in 1928, and Cartier said he was going to keep it intact until the Russian house was restored; he would have a long wait ahead of him.

Queen Olga had a priceless set of emeralds, along with many other items. Shortly before she attempted her own escape, a lady-in-waiting made a wooden box for the jewels and arranged for them to be collected by a Greek student, who called at the house carrying a package of books and left with a similar package containing the box. He took them straight to the Danish Legation and they were forwarded to Olga's relations in Copenhagen.

She herself crossed the frontier some months after the end of the First World War aboard a train carrying German prisoners-of-war. She arrived in Switzerland to rejoin her family a shadow of her former self, having lived for the past months, like the rest of Russia, on a starvation diet of stale bread soaked in oil. Behind her echoed the dying cries of her relatives. Seventeen of them were murdered by the Bolsheviks.

Olga's own family in the House of the Hellenes had not suffered too greatly in exile, although all of them later complained about how desperate their situation was: that they had no money and had to rely on the generosity of relatives to send them donations and help pay the rent on

---

* As we will see in the last chapter of this book, the success of these dangerous escapades of smuggling out the jewels was to have a major impact on the financial standing on Britain's Mountbatten-Windsor family – which acquired a goodly collection – in the second half of the twentieth century.

their in fact quite pleasant accommodation. They sat out the rest of the war in the protected haven of neutral Switzerland, still waited upon by the servants they had brought with them from Athens. Princess Alice's mother, Victoria, sold some of her dwindling securities (she had lost many of her own jewels, which had been left in Russia, and her husband had seen all his heavy Russian investments vanish) and from the sale of Burmah Oil stock she was able to assist. She wrote from London, 'Alice, poor girl, will probably need it for immediate use but it will be an unexpected windfall & I am only sorry I can't see her face when she gets my letter.'[2]

The family's collective plight was aided by the marriage in February 1920 of Prince Christopher to Mrs Nancy Leeds, the American widow of a tin-mine tycoon with access to a very substantial fortune. Their brother Prince George also fared quite well financially. He married Marie Bonaparte, granddaughter of Napoleon I's brother Lucien. She in turn had inherited considerable wealth from her mother's family, the Blancs, who had established the first casino in Monte Carlo and owned several houses in Europe, as well as a pleasant mansion in Paris, which, as we will see, was to be the anchor of Prince Philip's early life.

The young King Alexander, the ally of Britain whom they had left behind in their great Palace of Athens, would doubtless have changed places with any one of them. According to Prince Christopher, he had become 'one of the most pathetic figures in Europe . . . a lonely, unhappy young man, a king in name only.'[3] His orders went unheeded, he was surrounded by spies and if he showed the slightest favour to any member of his staff or household, that person would disappear.

His misery ended in tragic fashion. In October 1920, while out in the grounds of the Tatoi house, a pet monkey owned by a vineyard keeper jumped out of a cottage window and began attacking his dog. As Alexander tried to separate them, the monkey bit his ankle. He hobbled back to the house and two days later collapsed from blood-poisoning.

After days of agonizing pain and delirium, Alexander slipped into a coma and died in the arms of his wife on 25 October 1920, never to see the child she was expecting. Their daughter, Alexandra, who was to become one of Prince Philip's closest childhood cousins and friends (and later married King Peter of Yugoslavia), was born three months later.

Greece had lost its puppet king and turmoil once again hit the higher echelons of politics. Alexander's wife was still referred to as Madame Mano. She had no official rank, since she was a commoner when they married and the Greeks had refused to recognize her as their Queen. Now he was dead, they showed her no sympathy and insisted that she leave the royal palace at once. Ex-Queen Sophie, Alexander's mother, was brought back temporarily as Regent. Prime Minister Venizélos was so confident that the Greek Royals had lost their popularity that he offered to hold a referendum. He was defeated. The people of Greece voted to restore their deposed King Constantine; the brothers were free to return.

Prince Andrew and Christopher went as the advance party, and were met at Athens harbour by a huge crowd who hoisted them shoulder-high and carried them cheering through the streets. Alice described the scene proudly in letters to London:

> They were accorded an enthusiastic reception and were dragged from their car and borne on the shoulders of the populace, frenzied with joy the whole way from Phaleron Bay to Athens and he [Andrew] was forced to make a speech from the balcony of the palace to the vast crowd gathered below.[4]

The brothers of the House of the Hellenes were back in their domain with their growing family of royal children. One more was soon to arrive.

It was seven years since the birth of Princess Alice's last child, Princess Sophie. Now she was pregnant again at the age of thirty-six and, since conception came during the family's exile in Switzerland when their future was, to say the least, uncertain, it seems unlikely that this latest addition was a planned event.

Prince Andrew and his wife took their young family to Corfu on their return to Greece. The holiday villa of Mon Repos had been left to Andrew by his father and had remained unused for almost four years. One recorded description of the house terms it a 'royal slum'.[5] Like the Palace of Athens, the house certainly had its defects. There was no electricity or hot water, the plumbing was ancient and the interior showed many visible signs of its years of neglect. The property was sited at the end of a curling hillside road; there were three rooms downstairs, bedrooms on the first floor and two more in the attic. The modest Civil income which had been restored to the family was supplemented by bequests from the late King George I but, according to their English housekeeper Mrs Agnes Blower in an interview she gave in 1962, Prince Andrew and Princess Alice were 'as poor as church mice'.[6]

They arrived there in early 1921 and were joined by Agnes and her handyman husband. An English nanny, Miss Roose – known in the family as Roosie – was loaned to them. Grey-haired and ageing, Roosie had once nursed Princess Alice herself and, as often happens with nannies, she had stayed with the Battenberg family, eventually reaching the employ of Philip's uncle, Prince Nicholas. She, too, came to Mon Repos, where, in British style, she began acquiring stocks of baby foods and woollens for the winter cold, ordered especially through her London contacts.

Once his family had been settled, Prince Andrew, now thirty-nine, returned to Athens to new political unrest and found himself recalled into military service; he became a corps commander. His visits to Corfu were few and far between. As Philip's cousin ex-Queen Alexandra of Yugoslavia wrote, 'Instead of a proud father, it was four little sisters . . . who gazed down at the infant prince in his cradle.'[7]

The child, whose name was registered as Philippos, arrived in this world in ignoble circumstances at 10 a.m. on Friday, 10 June 1921. Prince Andrew was still away when Alice went into labour and the only doctor on the island was summoned for the delivery. He decided that the birth should not be in Princess Alice's bedroom but downstairs on the dining-room table. Perhaps her age, her state of tension at the time and the need to be close to the sparse plumbing facilities caused the doctor to make such a decision; Agnes Blower reckoned the dining-room table was used because it was the only item of furniture in the house that was suitable as a maternity bed. Whatever the reason, the boy who was to father a new dynasty in the British monarchy let out his first yell as he emerged on to that dining table – a healthy, fair-haired child whose lusty cry signalled his arrival as sixth in line to the Greek throne.

Agnes recalled the blissful months ahead:

He was the sweetest prettiest baby; what a joy he was to us all. I can see him now, kicking his legs in the sunshine and for eighteen months in Corfu I watched him grow up. It was a lovely outdoor life, although he didn't have many toys, hardly any. They were very poor.[8]

Mrs Blower claimed some credit for Philip's early 'bonny baby' look. She persuaded his mother to allow her to bring Scots Porage Oats for breakfast and she made tapioca puddings for lunch. Years later, as she spent her last days in a Peterborough old-folks' home, Agnes reflected: 'He's turned out quite well, surprisingly well, my little royal treasure, Philip. He had such a hard time of it . . . now I have to smile when I see him with our own Queen – that I used to give a ticking off for sucking his thumb.'

In the week of Philip's birth, the Greeks had embarked on new campaigns against the Turks in a continuing round of fighting which had already lasted over a year and had in fact never really been settled since the two Balkan Wars and the First World War. Greece had occupied Anatolia and ambitiously set its sights on Constantinople – to fulfil the legend of Constantine and Sophie – and on the vast plains of Asia Minor. Prince

Andrew became an integral part of the campaign and, at the time, must have been as enthusiastic as any of the generals in the new regime. He was promoted to the rank of Lieutenant General in command of the Second Army Corps of Greece. In July he put forward a plan to his brother the King which was adopted, against the advice of General Papoulas, the Commander in Chief in Anatolia, who pointed out that the manœuvre would entail a fifteen-day march across a waterless desert.

The campaign went ahead. At the end of it, 40,000 soldiers, weakened by their march, died in the fighting with the Kemalists. The Greeks would hold Prince Andrew responsible.

Princess Alice, meanwhile, was called home to England on the news that her father, Prince Louis of Battenberg, Marquess of Milford Haven, had died suddenly. With nanny Roosie for company, she set off for the funeral. Though in saddened circumstances, it was the first major family reunion since the exile. It was also Philip's first trip to England and, at the unaware age of three months, he was pampered by the London contingent, resplendent in their mourning. Philip's aunts and uncles and cousins and his newly widowed grandmother, Victoria, were all shown the new boy. Alice's brother George, who had married Nada de Torby, daughter of the Grand Duke Michael of Russia, cradled him in his arms. As successor to the title Marquess of Milford Haven, George was to become one of the greatest guiding forces of this infant's life, though that prospect had yet to confront him; the events that would precipitate his virtual adoption of Philip were being played out in the Greek campaigns.

Lord Louis Mountbatten was also there to be reunited with his sister. His courtesy title of 'Lord' had come to him when his father was created Marquess, and he would remain Lord Louis until he was ennobled as Earl Mountbatten of Burma in 1946. In that autumn of 1921, he was an impressionable, fast-talking young man who had acquired some of the British public-school way of speaking – things were wonderful or beastly or swinish. Like his brother George, he had dedicated himself to the Navy and their joint careers had blossomed both through their own considerable efforts and the sympathy felt in the naval hierarchy over the forced resignation of their father from the Admiralty.

Dickie, as he was known to everyone, had much to tell his sister, especially the impression he had created with his cousin David (Edward), Prince of Wales, who had chosen him the previous year to accompany him to Australia on the first of his Commonwealth tours. Dickie was his cousin's shadow: too close. On board ship, the young Mountbatten was castigated for his behaviour and, among other things, branded a creep.

Now they were due to set sail again, on 16 November, for the ill-starred visit to India, where the Prince of Wales was to complain that his cousin contributed nothing more than an heroic display on the polo field. 'He has become my best friend,' said Dickie, 'and I his.'

He would also have mentioned breathlessly to Alice that he had fallen in love with a young girl he had just met named Edwina Ashley, whose grandfather, Ernest Cassel, coincidentally, had also recently passed on, leaving her the bulk of his £7.5 million fortune and a magnificent London mansion called Brook House. Money like that, in 1921, was wealth indeed. Mountbatten was landing a pretty fish, dripping with gold. And the two of them were soon to become central figures in the life of young Philip.

Princess Alice returned to Corfu heavy in heart, having lain her father to rest and regretting that she had not seen as much of him during these past years as she would have liked. But she was full of gossip for Andrew when he came home in October 1921, when he also took the time to register his son's birth. Their reunion was brief. Andrew, worried about his position, talked constantly and gloomily of the internecine treachery and intrigue within both government and military circles, on which he blamed the heavy losses the Greeks had suffered. He was extremely depressed as the war dragged on, and in his own account of the troubles claimed that he twice asked to be relieved of his post but the request was refused.

The following spring Princess Alice received news from England. Her brother, Lord Louis, had proposed to Edwina Ashley after a long-distance courtship by letter. King George V had given his blessing and a wedding had been arranged to take place in July. Alice's four daughters were required as bridesmaids and the Prince of Wales himself had agreed to be best man. The Mountbatten nuptials were to be the social event of the year; and indeed they were.

Fifteen hundred invitations were sent and the European Royals were there *en masse* in suitable magnificence. By 5 a.m. on the morning of 18 July, thousands were gathering outside St Margaret's, Westminster. The discontent of post-war Britain was temporarily set aside and the newspapers were full of the occasion. Prince Philip's four sisters, dressed in blue and white, performed their task with childish elegance while their brother remained in the care of the nursery staff at Kensington Palace. For a few hours, the Greek relations, of late used to a more mundane life, enjoyed the glorious celebration and show of wealth typical of the English aristocracy, recorded as ever in yards of newspaper column-inches to set the British people dreaming for a day or two of a life so dazzlingly different from their own drab existence.

Yet, as the Mountbattens set off on their five-month honeymoon, to be fêted in America by movie stars and other rich and famous hosts anxious to rub shoulders with Royalty, there was widespread criticism over their German bias. Before going on to America, the couple was to visit Darmstadt and the family castles of the Battenbergs and Hesses. The *Daily Mail* quickly rapped their knuckles: 'That the Mountbattens should choose to stay in Germany for part of their honeymoon is surely a *faux pas*. True, his lordship is wholly of German parentage and his wife is half-German . . . but Prince Louis had severed all connections with the Fatherland.'9

Such criticism was a mere fly in the ointment compared with the troubles facing Mountbatten's sister. The Greek contingent had to dash home immediately after the wedding. The news was bad. Greek forces had suffered heavy defeat by the Turks and had taken flight. At the end of August, Turkish troops captured the Greek Commander in Chief, General Tricoupis, and four days later Greece asked for an armistice as the Turkish Army advanced on Smyrna. Prince Andrew, as a corps commander, was in the firing line as his Army sustained appalling casualties. Civilians were massacred and more than a million Greeks were forced to flee ahead of Turkish forces. On 14 September 1,000 Greeks died as the Turks burned Smyrna.10

The political turmoil in Athens reached new heights, with insurrection in the Army and a takeover by a rebel military junta led by the Greek brothers' arch-enemy, Venizélos. On 26 September King Constantine was once again forced to abdicate, this time in favour of his eldest son, George, and five of his ministers and an Army general were arrested. Prince Andrew was thrown out of the Army. He rejoined Princess Alice and the children in Corfu, where he spent two days composing a long report on the reasons why the action had failed; it was a vain attempt to get himself off the hook.

A few days later, a messenger from Athens brought news of his summons to the capital on 5 October 1922; he was told he was required to give evidence at the trial of the King's old ministers. It was a trap, and he fell into the net. On arrival in the capital, Andrew was arrested. The charge was treason: that he had abandoned his position when in contact with the enemy and had disobeyed orders. Much of the blame for the Greek fiasco was being laid at the Prince's feet. He was thrown into a cell and deprived of all contact with his family. Only one of his brothers was allowed to see him. Food parcels sent in by his relatives were kept by his gaolers while Andrew was fed stale bread and water. Messages were smuggled in, however, on rolled cigarette papers.

His interrogators were former colleagues from the military academy, among them General Pangalos, who asked, 'How many children do you have?'

'Five,' Andrew replied.

'What a pity,' said the General. 'The poor little things will soon be orphans.'

In Corfu, Princess Alice feared she would never see her husband alive and in her anguish began a personal campaign to save him. She contacted her mother and brothers, and sent a personal letter to her cousin King George V, pleading for his help; she wrote to the Prime Minister of France, to King Alfonso of Spain and even to the Pope.

Fearing the worst, Andrew's relatives in Athens went almost daily to the British Legation to plead for help, and in London Lord Louis Mountbatten went to see the King. Queen Alexandra bombarded her son with letters pleading for British help for her nephew, who had now all but given up hope of seeing the outside of his Athens gaol cell again – except perhaps to march before his executioners.

Lord Curzon, the British Foreign Secretary, was summoned by King George and the result was an immediate British rescue mission to save Andrew. Underlings at the Foreign Office, half-hearted anyway about Greek Royalty, may well have questioned the ability of the British to free the Prince if his own nephew, who was King of Greece, could not do so. The explanation came later: King George II of Greece was powerless, practically a prisoner in his own palace, King in name only, with his own future hanging precariously on the whim of Venizélos.

Curzon arranged for a retired British naval attaché to Athens, Commander Gerald Talbot, to seek the immediate release of Prince Andrew. Colourful reports that he arrived in Athens as a secret agent in disguise are not borne out by public records of the event, which merely state that he went to Athens as the King's personal representative to plead for Prince Andrew's life. At the same time, HMS *Calypso*, a six-inch-gunned cruiser, sailed to the edge of Phaleron Bay, where it laid anchor while Talbot began his delicate negotiations. Despite the apparent threat of retaliatory action – which, according to documents now on file at the British Public Record Office, Kew, never seemed a possibility[11] – rumours abounded that the British were planning to sweep in and rescue the Prince from his cell. Commander Talbot said nothing to rule out that possibility, but the Greek revolutionaries stood firm.

Andrew was brought before the military tribunal and found guilty. The addendum to the court's ruling, revealed when British documents on the affair became available for viewing, is ruthlessly critical of Prince Andrew. It reads: 'Consideration being given to extenuating circumstances of lack of experience in commanding a large unit, he has been degraded and condemned to perpetual banishment.' When the documents were released in 1972, Prince Philip felt his father had been unjustly attacked and would have preferred these criticisms to have been withheld from publication, because, as he put it, 'people might think they were true'.

The Greeks, however, were in no doubt of their feelings at the time. They had spared Prince Andrew's life only because of the British intervention. Yet deportation and cancellation of Andrew's Greek citizenship by 'perpetual banishment' was a message in itself. The five ministers and the Army general who also stood trial were not so lucky; they were taken before a firing squad and shot on 28 November 1922.

At daybreak on 3 December, the tribunal chairman General Pangalos went personally to Andrew's cell with Princess Alice, who was waiting to meet her husband upon his release. They went to the British Legation to seek temporary shelter before being taken aboard HMS *Calypso* to safety. The ship sailed on to Corfu to collect their daughters and Prince Philip, now eighteen months old, and what few personal possessions they could carry.

With no facilities on board for children, sailors of the British Royal Navy made a crib for the infant out of an orange box, little realizing that they were providing a cot for a boy who would marry their future Queen. And thus Philip made his exit from Greece, banished with his father, his family rendered stateless and homeless. Stateless they would remain – although they were allowed by Denmark to resume honorary citizenship and retain royal title. In Philip's case, his nationality would become resolved only twenty-five years later when, along with hundreds of refugees from the Second World War, he paid his £10 fee to be granted British citizenship prior to his marriage.

In the years he spent reflecting his situation, Prince Andrew began writing a book about the Greek fiasco and his own experiences, which he entitled *Towards Disaster*. It was a sombre attempt at justification, and would perhaps have been better left unwritten. Published in Britain in 1930, his wife having made the translation, he bitterly condemned his trial as a biased search for scapegoats in which he was allowed to call only three witnesses for his defence. 'It suffices to read the accusations of the revolutionary prosecutor to be convinced of the prejudice of those who tried me,' he wrote.[12]

He tried hard to justify the Greek campaigns, and perhaps when he wrote his words they were less open to ridicule than they are today:

> For the first time after many centuries, since the time of the Byzantine rulers, a Greek king and a Greek army trod the immense plains of Asia Minor. Full of eagerness, faith and self-sacrifice, the Greek soldier threw himself into the age-old struggle of his race. . . . Is it in vain, this last sacrifice of Asia Minor? No! For the seed sown by Greek soldiers will one day burst forth into a great and flourishing tree.

Such ambitions for his country and his family's fight to place their King upon those plains – an adventure that cost so many Greek lives and ultimately put 1.5 million people to flight as refugees – have still not been achieved as the twentieth century enters its last decade. Only the Turks could be pleased, and the campaigns which led to Andrew's banishment remained an open sore for many years.

Back in England, King George and the Mountbatten family were duly relieved that the Greek Prince had been saved. The King showed his appreciation to Commander Talbot by giving him a knighthood.

Chapter Four
No Place to Call Home

As the *Calypso* sailed away, so began a nomadic early life for Prince Philip. He would have no permanent home until he married. It might well be here, too, that one should look for the moulding characteristics of the man. This banishment, viewed as staggering by his aunts and uncles in London, could well have been the starting-point for insecurities which would manifest themselves throughout his childhood and youth in a defiant need to prove himself in whatever task he was set and with an apparent devil-may-care attitude which would lead him into perilous waters.

That Christmas of 1922, a large family reunion was arranged by Philip's maternal grandmother, Victoria. Prince Andrew was filled with despair and reluctant to settle in England: there were still unhappy memories of his visit at the start of the war, when he was regarded as a German–Greek. In the new year, therefore, leaving the children in the care of Nannie Roose, Andrew and Alice sailed to America at the invitation of his brother Prince Christopher, now enjoying a more opulent lifestyle under the auspices of his wealthy wife.

While they were travelling, news came over the ship's radio that Andrew's brother ex-King Constantine had died in exile in Florence. He was to be buried there in a crypt at the Russian Church. The Italians gave him a fitting departure, with a gun-carriage leading the cortège through streets lined with troops of the Italian Army. His death went unmarked in Athens, with the exception of a few Royalist memorial services.

For Princess Alice the news was one more knock, one more link in the Greek tragedy in which she had become involved. Her nerves were at breaking-point; years of strain over her husband's seemingly continual precarious plight had taken their toll on her health. Her mother was especially worried and wrote of her concern.

The trip to New York, a holiday at Palm Beach and a cruise in Mrs

Leeds's yacht, all at her expense, did them the power of good. But if Christopher made any suggestion of their settling in the bright New World he had discovered for himself, they were quickly rejected and the Prince and Princess returned to Europe intent on finding a home.

Andrew's brother George came to the rescue with the offer of accommodation for the vagrant family at his Paris home in the rue Adolphe Ivan, near the Bois de Boulogne. He and Marie Bonaparte offered them the servants' quarters, which they turned into an apartment for them. Philip and his four sisters were brought to the house with Nanny Roose, and with the help of bequests from ex-King Constantine and the joint support of their two uncles George – Prince George in Paris and the Marquess of Milford Haven in England – they settled into a solvent, if impoverished, life.

Later, as the apartment became too crowded for Andrew's boisterous young family, George provided them with their own home, a small house in the rue de Mont Valérian at St-Cloud. Prince Christopher, or more correctly Mrs Leeds, chipped in by paying Philip's fees for his attendance at an upper-class kindergarten, The Elms at St-Cloud, which was full of the offspring of other European Royalty and the children of American diplomatic and business millionaires. The latter were the new order, new money. The former were a diminishing band; the monarchs, the princes, the grand dukes and archdukes were losing their power, their thrones, their land and even their lives in ever-increasing numbers. There were still quite a few left, however, and some wealthy princes would soon be casting their eyes over Philip's charming cousins and sisters. If nothing else, the Greek family had provided a welcome influx of young princesses for marriage into the remaining important houses.

While they were all in exile, for instance, Crown Prince Carol of Romania came looking for a wife on the instructions of his father, King Ferdinand. Carol had got himself into deep trouble, having secretly married a commoner named Zizi Lambrino, who was as flighty as her name. Ferdinand was furious. He banished them from Court and they fled to Rome. The condition for Carol's return was that he should renounce his marriage, have it annulled and find a more suitable bride. This he eventually agreed to do. The British Court of King George looked on with interest; Romania was another vital link in the volatile Balkan chain. In Switzerland, Carol found Princess Helen, the very beautiful daughter of ex-King Constantine. They were married the following year, though the union brought nothing but heartbreak and misery for Helen; Carol's roving eye for pretty girls had by no means been diminished.

Another of the Greek princesses found more lasting happiness. In 1923 Philip's cousin Olga, elder daughter of Prince Nicholas, became engaged to Prince Paul of Yugoslavia and their marriage in October became an important event in the royal calendar. King George V was sufficiently anxious to be represented in order to reinforce British ties that he sent his second son, Bertie, the Duke of York, with his own new bride. (He had married Lady Elizabeth Bowes-Lyon in April that year.) The trip had a dual role for Bertie; as well as attending Olga's wedding, he also stood as godfather at the christening of Peter, the first son of King Alexander of Yugoslavia.*

The reception for Princess Olga's wedding was held in the groom's home capital of Belgrade; Athens was no safe place for monarchy. The King they had left behind in Athens, George II, was about to be evicted and Greece declared a republic. With such rumblings in this politically sensitive arena, the British looked upon the Yugoslavs as important allies with a modicum of stability. One more wedding – with Prince Paul becoming second cousin by marriage to King George V – could do no harm at all in strengthening the dynastic ties that were supposed to bind them all together. The whole clan of Balkan Royalty turned up in a rather obvious show of strength; in comparison with the rest, the Greeks were rather pathetic figures.

In spite of it all, the wheel kept turning. Bertie was not to know it then, but he was to become even more entwined with the Greeks when his brother the Duke of Kent married Olga's younger sister Marina a decade later, and, of course, the youngest of the Greek family, Philip, was destined to become his own son-in-law.

Back in Paris, Andrew was struggling with his memoirs and playing with his children. It was a frustrating time for a man whose life had been so full of incident. For the last ten or more years, one problem after another had weighed upon him and his brothers; now he was free of them, but he was not a happy man. The bitterness over the way his country had treated him continued to play on his mind and only his interest in his son and daughters brought him lighter relief.

Princess Alice turned to religion and charity work and opened a small shop, which she called Hellas, in St-Cloud, selling Greek-style embroidery. What little money she made was not to be lavished on her own family; her increasing dedication to helping others less fortunate led her to use the money to aid other Greek refugees in Paris. The thought of one of their own serving in a humble little charity shop apparently enraged some members of her family, particularly the English side.

As with her husband, the strain was showing on Alice, but in other ways. Her health continued to suffer and her mother made regular visits to Paris, where she noted with concern her daughter's deteriorating condition, eventually recommending that she seek medical care for

---

* Two and a half decades later Peter also married a Greek princess – Alexandra, daughter of the ill-fated King Alexander of Greece and his morganatic bride, Aspasia Mano.

nervous exhaustion and a chest complaint. For the next twelve years Princess Alice would be separated from her family for long periods while she received treatment at hospitals, sanatoria and high-class nursing homes in Switzerland and Germany, paid for entirely by contributions from the family. She was, as one close associate recalled, at times severely unstable.

Despite this constant worry over his mother and their irregular family life, the early years in France and England appear to have been happy and eventful for the boy Philip. There were always plenty of relatives around to take Andrew's children into temporary care, including a contingent of the Greeks who had moved closer in March 1924 when the Greek Parliament voted to turn the country into a republic. As a contemporary newspaper report noted:

> This can have come as no surprise to the unfortunate Monarch, George II, for the hostility to his dynasty is so great that the Monarch was forced to flee last year and go into exile to Rumania, homeland of his wife Queen Elizabeth. Given the present temper of the people, republicans are confident that the House of the Hellenes will disappear for ever . . . the last chapter in the bizarre history of the modern Greek monarchy.

The unseated Greek Royals made the best of their itinerant life. Philip's cousin Alexandra gives us colourful descriptions of summer holidays by the Baltic Sea at a villa in Panka belonging to the Hesse family, where ex-Queen Sophie, the widow of King Constantine, went to stay with her sister. Everyone was very affectionate towards Philip, whom they looked upon as a virtual orphan despite the fact that both his parents were alive, and were all very caring towards him. The boy must have suffered in spite of these efforts. There was simply no heart to the family into which he was born, and he was surrounded by an atmosphere of miserable uncertainty.

The itinerancy brought new friendships, however, including one that was to last a lifetime. He was taken to a large holiday home near Marseilles owned by a family friend, Madame Anna Foufounis, widow of a wealthy Greek Royalist. She had three children – a son Jean, who was Philip's age, and two daughters, Ria and Hélène, who in later years became better known as the London singer and cabaret entertainer Hélène Cordet. She would figure in Philip's life for many years to come. Her recollections of those childhood days show that Philip spent a great deal of time virtually lodging with her family, so much so that she became jealous of him:

> The little blue-eyed boy with the most fascinating blond-white hair seemed to have everything I lacked. In my mind, he became a great danger . . . my mother could switch her affections from me

to him. . . . I had the incredible idea that I was the least loved in our family.[1]

This lavishing of affection was confirmed by Madame Foufounis: 'He was with us so often people used to ask, "Are you his guardian or governess?" I was neither, yet much more. I loved my Philip as my own.'[2]

These affections, coming as they did from so many different quarters, must have made some kind of mark on a child who was barely five but, according to the reminiscences of his English relatives, no ominous effect was apparent other than his extreme high spirits which required regular correction. Discipline seems to have been missing from his life in Paris and his Uncle George Milford Haven for one felt that he needed a firm hand.

With Princess Alice unwell again, Philip and the four girls went to England for the summer of 1926. Princess Victoria was in charge of the arrangements and, while parking the girls with friends in the Midlands, arranged for Philip to stay with his Uncle Dickie. She wrote, 'Philip goes to Adsdean where they can keep him until autumn if desired. Only for Goodwood week his room will be needed for guests.'[3] Adsdean, situated twelve miles from Portsmouth, was the country home of Lord Louis and Edwina (and remained so until Edwina inherited Broadlands in 1939), and Philip loved to go there. Their London home, Brook House, was even more of an adventure in all its magnificence – a startling contrast to the depressingly dire financial straits that prevailed throughout Britain in the late twenties and thirties. The original Park Lane mansion was better than any palace of Dickie's crowned relatives. Edwina's grandfather, when he bought it, had imported 800 tons of marble from the quarries once used by Michelangelo in Italy for the interior renovations. Even the kitchen was lined with it. There were twelve vast reception rooms; the dining room, elaborately panelled in oak, could accommodate 100 guests at a single sitting.

Increasingly, these English surroundings were to become the scene of Philip's upbringing, and after the age of five he saw little of his parents. Instead, he would alternate between his grandmother, Victoria, at her grace-and-favour home in Kensington Palace, his Uncle George and Aunt Nada at Lynden Manor on the upper reaches of the Thames, and Uncle Dickie and Aunt Edwina at Brook House or Adsdean. Another surrogate mother was Lady Anastasia Zia Wernher, Nada's sister, who was married to Harold Wernher, Chairman of Electrolux.*

The Wernhers, in fact, outlasted them all in terms of long-term

* Quite coincidentally, the Duke of Windsor was befriended in the Bahamas in 1940 by Wernher's then boss, the Swedish millionaire founder of Electrolux, Axel Wenner-Gren. But this connection is one the Royals prefer to forget. Wenner-Gren, a friend of Mussolini and Goering, was blacklisted by the Americans as a suspected enemy consort during the war and was described by Churchill as a 'very dangerous man'.

friendship and provided many secluded weekends of relaxation at their Luton Hoo mansion for Prince Philip after his marriage to Princess Elizabeth. Prince Andrew virtually relinquished direct supervision of the boy in favour of his mother-in-law and two brothers-in-law. Victoria remained the organizer of his visits: 'I hope it won't be too much trouble having Philip for so long,' she wrote to one of her child-minders.[4]

Philip continued to return to Paris for his schooling at St-Cloud for the next couple of years, though the English members of the family were quietly moving towards providing a permanent home for him as his parents slowly drifted apart. Prince Andrew, handsome and imposing in his forties, saw no prospects for himself in any career. As so many others of his kind were to discover, unemployed Royalty have as much chance of getting a job as snow-clearers on the equator. While two of his brothers had married into money, the third, Nicholas – father of Olga and Marina – found added income by selling his paintings, at which he had become adept during the exile years in Switzerland. Andrew's self-pitying depressions were interspersed with his enjoyment of what social life he managed to afford either in Paris or Monte Carlo, where his son recalled that he always seemed to have a bottle of something on ice.[5] Monte Carlo became the magnet for Andrew, and he began to spend much of his time there, eking out an existence on his meagre funds. There was neither room nor money in his life for his children – and especially not the means to provide an expensive education for his son; nevertheless, he continued a fatherly interest from afar as he moved into the indolent existence of a minor playboy.

Princess Alice, meantime, had become ever more obsessed with her religious and charity work, which was interrupted only by her medical treatment. Their daughters, now edging towards young adulthood, were becoming independent and aligning themselves towards the German side of the family rather than the English. The Hesses at Darmstadt were seeing a lot of them; the children were regular visitors to the German palaces and holiday villas. Philip was the misfit because of his age, though his cousin Alexandra did not think he suffered through it. She wrote:

> In Paris in those days there were so many cousins and uncles, so many arrivals and departures of the Hesse family and the Mountbattens that I am sure my cousin Philip was never for a moment aware that his father was under sentence of banishment.[6]

That Philip and the family ignored this aspect of their recent history is borne out by a letter he wrote to his teacher's dog in his final term at St-Cloud, in 1929, in which he still signed himself Philip of Greece. Other recollections from these years record memorable events in Philip's life, such as having to save up to buy a raincoat, and saving the cash he received as Christmas presents from uncles towards buying a bicycle. Hard times indeed, for Royalty, though Prince Andrew still managed to keep on a nanny and a valet through most of these years in France. But 1929 was something of a turning-point. Andrew's separation from his wife was becoming more permanent and he moved to Monte Carlo, where he had a mistress. The relations on both sides of the English Channel were now looking to provide Philip with his education.

The English faction won the first round of the polite custody battle and at the beginning of the autumn term he was enrolled at Cheam Preparatory School, chosen and paid for by the Marquess of Milford Haven. His own son, David, the Earl of Medina, who was two years older than Philip, was already a pupil there and would be an instant friend for a younger cousin seeking companionship in the fairly rigid, though progressive, regime of one of Britain's oldest and most famous preparatory schools. And, as the terms came and went, it was chiefly George who appeared as Philip's father-figure, turning up with Aunt Nada at speech days and sports days. With these somewhat Titan figures looming large in the background, Philip seems to have found a confidence that could well have been missing had he been left in Paris; prodded and encouraged, he proceeded with pace to find himself a niche, especially on the sports field where he excelled. His academic progress, however, was less impressive.

His headmaster at Cheam, the Reverend H. M. S. Taylor, recalled:

> He got into the usual schoolboy scrapes. I had to cane him more than once; when he was 12 my wife and I said he would make a good king, thinking then of him as King of Greece not as a husband for Princess Elizabeth. He has two vital qualities, leadership and personality.[7]

Philip clearly remembered Taylor's heavy hand; when he visited the school with Princess Elizabeth in 1947, he introduced his old head to her as 'the man who used to cane me'.

His base during his time at Cheam was Kensington Palace, which is where Philip said he 'kept things'.

> I liked my grandmother very much and she was very helpful. She was very good with children. Like my own mother she took the practical approach . . . treated them in the right way . . . the right combination of the rational and the emotional.[8]

At half-terms and holidays, it was back to the Milford Havens', or to Uncle Dickie's or to the Wernhers', or over the Channel to relatives in Europe.

The summer of 1929 was spent in Romania at the palace of his cousin Princess Helen and her son Michael. Helen's husband, Carol, was not present. In 1925 he had left the country for Switzerland with an attractive, red-haired Jewess named Madame Lupescu – the Romanian equivalent of Wallis Simpson – leaving Helen and the boy Michael behind. The Romanians took this to mean he had deserted them and insisted that either he return immediately or renounce his right to the throne. When he turned up in England for Queen Alexandra's funeral with Madame Lupescu still in tow, they realized he was not planning an early response to their demands. The outcast couple continued to wander the Continent. Then Carol's father, King Ferdinand, died in 1927 and Helen's young son Michael was proclaimed King, though only eight years old. And King he was still when Philip arrived for the summer holidays and some dramatic pony races in the grounds of the summer villa, which Philip invariably won.

Five months after that visit, Carol, with the backing of the military party, returned dramatically to reclaim his throne. He placed himself at the head of the Army and announced that he was now King. Though blameless in the whole affair, Princess Helen sent word to her estranged husband that she was prepared to consider a reconciliation for the sake of the country. King Carol II callously rejected her offer; he arrived at her house in Bucharest one morning and told her simply: 'I no longer wish to see your face at my Court. You may not call yourself Queen but you may have the title Your Majesty.'⁹ Helen refused to accept the situation and left the country a short time later to join other dispossessed relatives in Florence. Carol would not allow Michael to travel with her and for many years she was barred from re-entering her adopted country. She took a small house in Florence and seldom saw her son in his youth. King Carol, meanwhile, continued to rule, flagrantly flaunting his mistress, Madame Lupescu, until he abdicated in 1940 ahead of the German invasion.

For Prince Philip, these developments ended his visits to Romania; next it would be Germany, where his involvements were soon to take on a new kind of significance – not just for himself but for the whole of his family.

PART TWO

Chapter Five

German Connections

Concern over Prince Philip's immediate German connections, quietly kept in the background in 1947, had its beginnings in the early thirties when the Greek house continued to provide brides for European princes. As the new decade turned, there occurred a series of startling family developments that were seriously to affect Prince Philip's short-term future as a discreet battle for custody of him emerged between the families in Britain and Germany.

His four sisters – two of whom were in their mid-twenties and were more like aunts – were married within nine months of each other. It was the youngest, Princess Sophie, known in the family as Tiny, who set the pace. Barely sixteen and apparently fed up with a home life made difficult by the strange and separate lifestyles of her parents, in November 1930 she rushed into marriage with her cousin Prince Christopher of Hesse, aged twenty-one, whom she had first met on holidays with her aunts. He was of the Hesse-Kassel line.*

The second youngest, Cecile, aged nineteen, also went to a Hesse-Darmstadt, the most important one of all. She married George Donatus, heir to the title of Grand Duke of Hesse and the Rhine. Of all the marriages, this one pleased Philip's grandmother Victoria the most, since it brought a Greek princess back to the heart of the Hessian dynasty presently ruled over by her brother Ernst. Two months later, in March

---

* Christopher's father, Frederick of Hesse, married Kaiser Wilhelm II's youngest sister, Margaret, in 1893. His aunt was ex-Queen Sophie of Greece and Queen Victoria was his great-grandmother; thus he was also a cousin to Prince Philip of Greece as well as becoming his brother-in-law. He became a fanatical Nazi, but as historian A. J. P. Taylor has said, 'German royal houses ran easily to eccentrics and lunatics. Ceaseless inbreeding . . . produced mad princes as a normal event. The mad King of Bavaria, the mad Duke of Brunswick, the mad Elector of Hesse, the imbecile Emperor – these phrases are commonplace of German history; and of the utterly petty princes hardly one was sane.'[1]

1931, the eldest of the four sisters, Margarita, aged twenty-five, married her mother's second cousin, Godfrey, Prince of Hohenlohe-Langenburg, and in August Princess Theodora (nicknamed 'Dolla'), twenty-four, married her distant cousin Berthold, Prince and Margrave of Baden. It was this last marriage that was to be the cause of Prince Philip's eventual arrival for schooling in Germany.

As a prelude to this event, there were family visits and holidays spent in the vast, treasure-filled German castles of his sisters' spouses. Philip may well have heard the name of Hitler, who was much discussed and admired among some in the House of Hesse, which welcomed the advent of National Socialism and Hitler's arrival as Chancellor. Grandmother Victoria wrote from Darmstadt in the spring of 1933 that the *coup d'état* was 'very popular here. There was an enormous torchlight procession last night which passed without any disturbances . . . when all the town was out on the streets.'[2] It all sounded rather pleasant, according to Victoria's missive. She had no way of knowing, of course, that within a few years she would be watching cousin set once more against cousin and, like her daughter Alice, regretting that Philip's four sisters had ever married back into Germany.

As the Greek Princesses settled into their new life, away from the sphere of the Paris Greeks and the English factions, there was a move, led by Theodora, to retrieve Philip from the care of the Mountbatten family. They wanted to have him educated and brought up with them in Germany. These thoughts may well have been influenced by two developments. First, as the brothers George Milford Haven and Lord Louis Mountbatten advanced in their naval careers and had increasing social commitments – especially around the Mediterranean, where they had both been stationed – it must have been apparent to the sisters that Philip was being handed around the family and had no single, stable home. What was going on? How could Philip possibly be receiving the right sort of upbringing in the midst of all that was happening on the glittering periphery of the British Court? Goodness knows what modern professors of child psychology would have made of it. A catalyst to their thoughts about their brother may have come when George Milford Haven left the Navy in the early thirties and went into the investment business, which took him on long trips to America.

Second, it could not have escaped the notice of the Greek Princesses and their new German husbands that the lifestyle of some of the English relatives with whom Philip was spending most of his time was being openly criticized and was subject to wild and wonderful speculation. Secrets which were then strictly for family consumption must have reached their ears; and in addition, certain members of the family were in and out of the gossip pages with alarming regularity; the adventures of Dickie and Edwina, in particular, were charted like those of the movie stars with whom Mountbatten was fascinated. In early 1930, for example, he was to be found back in Hollywood, arriving like a king in a special coach on the rail crossing from the east to the west coast. While he was devoted to his naval career, he also enjoyed the flamboyance that his association with the world of showbiz brought into his life – not to mention these heady years when he was starring in international polo events in various parts of the world.

Edwina, meanwhile, was going her own way, and an item in one of the glossy magazines of the day summed up her activities in a nutshell: 'Lady Mountbatten is expected back from America soon. Her many friends must often regret the wanderlust which takes her away so often and so far, leaving her short intervals to spend in London.'[3] This was coded newspaper jargon for telling readers that the Mountbatten marriage appeared to be in severe trouble. Lord Beaverbrook – for whom Edwina had worked at the *Daily Express* during the General Strike – had already saved her from a notorious divorce scandal which threatened to name her as the co-respondent. In a telegram to New York lawyers, Beaverbrook said 'utmost importance that suit should be stopped . . . our money resources are sufficient or if money is of no use we will offer immense social influence.'[4] Edwina was rumoured to have paid out a large sum to keep her name out of it, though she did not escape damaging publicity with stories in America under such headlines as 'A ROYAL SPANKING FOR GAY LADY MOUNTBATTEN'. She was notorious for her many affairs and Mountbatten's close friend Noël Coward even used her as the model for the character of Amanada Prynne in his play *Private Lives*.

In later years, Mountbatten admitted quite openly that he and his wife had promiscuously hopped in and out of other people's beds; and perhaps at the time his relatives might also have heard the rumours that seem to have been promoted as fact since his death, that he was a practising homosexual.[5] Some have gone so far as to suggest that he was part of a homosexual network 'that operated in prewar London circles . . . those in the know claim that it revolved about Edward, Prince of Wales, his brother George, Duke of Kent, Queen Elizabeth's brother David Bowes-Lyon and their cousin Lord Louis Mountbatten.'[6]

In the world of travel and madly gay party-time existence in which she indulged for several years, Edwina was often accompanied by her sister-in-law Nada, wife of George Milford Haven. Nada also enjoyed something of a 'reputation'. One description of her tells us that she 'shared with Thelma [Furness] and Gloria [Vanderbilt] membership in a high-powered group of society lesbians who were the cause of constant hothouse gossip in the Mayfair salons.'[7] A later reference mentions her presence at a society party in the south of France at which Wallis Simpson was 'embarrassed to find an uncomfortable situation . . . a maid strolled into Gloria's room for no apparent reason and found Gloria and Nada in negligées enjoying a passionate French kiss.'[8] Nada was just as devil-may-care as Edwina, who revelled in everything that could be attained by her wealth and privilege.

Edwina's style of living before the war (when she switched to the role of heroine) has been described as decadent, self-indulgent, meaningless – a life in which the rules of the game were 'generously flexible'.[9] Her closeness to Nada also gave rise to a whisper or two; it was hotly rumoured in café society that they had a lesbian relationship and speculation was only heightened in 1932 when the two of them set off on a wild and dangerous escapade, travelling east to Arabia, Jerusalem and Damascus, then driving across rough desert terrain to Baghdad.

What inspired a jaunt which took the two women so predominant in Philip's early upbringing – his joint substitute mothers, almost – into a single-minded madcap fling for adventure, virtually unheard of among the genteel women of the thirties?

One explanation may well have been to get away from the awful gossip ablaze in London, which finally came to a head in May 1932 when the *Sunday People* caused a furore with its now famous salacious story headlined 'SOCIETY SHAKEN BY TERRIBLE SCANDAL'. The article went on to say that a 'woman highly connected and immensely rich has become involved with a coloured man.' The allegation was that they had been caught in 'compromising circumstances'. The male party was not named but in London's gossipy, village-like café society there were already murmurings about Edwina's association with two coloured entertainers, Leslie Hutchinson, the highly acclaimed nightclub singer and pianist who regularly appeared at parties given at Brook House, and Paul Robeson. The newspaper article went on to say that the lady in question had been 'given the hint to clear out of London for a couple of years to let the affair blow over and the hint comes from a quarter that cannot be ignored' (the King).[10]

Buckingham Palace took legal advice and for the first time since 1891, when the future Edward VII was called to give evidence in a common slander case over cheating at baccarat,* members of the charmed circle were to become involved in a seedy court action. The Palace insisted that Edwina should sue. Perhaps they were not aware of the background. Paul Robeson was on the verge of separating from his wife and on 31 May a reporter from the *Daily Herald* called on Mrs Robeson to ask her to confirm whether she was naming Lady Mountbatten as co-respondent in a divorce action. The talk of the town continued and the society set scavenged upon every morsel; best of all was the gossip that Edwina had to sell her mansion in Park Lane to 'pay off' Mrs Robeson. (She had indeed sold Brook House for redevelopment, but that was coincidental.) Robeson's wife laughed at suggestions that she had received money, but at least these rumoured attempts at a cover-up were kept in the

* See footnote to p. 56.

background when the case itself was embarrassingly flushed out at the court action in July. Edwina won by denying she even knew Paul Robeson. The newspaper was ordered to pay £25,000 damages – though as would become apparent in later years, Paul Robeson himself was extremely hurt by Edwina's denial of his friendship.[11]

As the resulting publicity directed even greater attention to the Mountbatten marriage, Buckingham Palace took the opportunity of lecturing Mountbatten over the activities of his wife and himself; Queen Mary insisted that Edwina's presence before them was an embarrassment. Though she was not 'banished' to foreign parts, Edwina did suffer the humiliation of being virtually excluded from the Court of King George for the remainder of his reign, to which she responded unconcernedly with the words, 'I don't give a rap!'

The scandal concerning the Mountbattens was simply one of a string of romantic entanglements that were the talk of Palace circles at the time and which the Germans were watching closely. Dickie's cousin, the Prince of Wales, as we know, had been the subject of continual innuendo over his affairs with married women, while being rather backward in discovering a suitable bride to sit beside him when he became King. Now that awful woman, in the eyes of his family, Mrs Wallis Simpson seemed to be capturing his attentions.

As David neared forty with no sign of a betrothal, Mountbatten drew up for his cousin a list of eligible princesses in Europe to pick from, so that he would have a Queen in readiness. One of them was Philip's first cousin Marina, second daughter of Prince Nicholas, whose elder daughter Olga had married Paul of Yugoslavia.

Princess Marina was brought to England in 1933 as a possible bride for the Prince of Wales; had that piece of planning worked out, she would have become Queen, ended the aspirations of Mrs Simpson, perhaps produced an immediate heir and so deprived her cousin Philip of his future role in life. The Prince of Wales steadfastly rejected her, however; his thoughts were by now devoured totally by Wallis. Queen Mary's hopes for Marina's admission to the family received a temporary setback when the Greek Princess turned up at Buckingham Palace with red fingernails. 'I'm afraid the King doesn't like painted nails,' said the Queen in her familiar icy tones. 'Can you do something about it?'[12] There was a hint of further acrimony when Marina described Elizabeth, Duchess of York, as 'that common little Scottish girl'.[13]

Marina, who was to become one of Philip's closest friends and allies after his own marriage, was also unconventional in her attitude to the behaviour of Royalty. She had studied art in Paris, where she, like Philip, had spent most of her recent life and where she had travelled about unaccompanied on buses or the Métro. She was known for her kindness and sympathy, though as her father Nicholas constantly remarked, she could certainly stand up for herself. And so, after the Prince of Wales's stubborn refusal of her as a bride, she became earmarked for his brother Prince George, to rescue him from 'an errant love'.[14]

George, Duke of Kent, was the favourite son whose bisexual social calendar caused his mother many sleepless nights. As far back as 1926 he had got himself into various scrapes, including an embarrassing romance with the diminutive black American singer Florence Mills, who came to London in a C. B. Cochran review. He had a relaxed attitude to his sexual relationships and Noël Coward boasted that he first seduced the Prince in 1923.[15] In the early thirties, his mother and father were wishing he would marry, but at the time he was deeply involved with an American girl who introduced him to drugs. At one stage, the Prince of Wales kept him a virtual prisoner at his own apartments to try to wean him from his addiction to cocaine. His brother also got him off the hook when a young man in Paris to whom George had written some rather explicit love letters began to threaten blackmail.[16] Edward sent one of his aides to retrieve the letters on payment of a suitable sum. As one of the Buckingham Palace staff of the day later wrote, 'George had more brains than his brothers . . . but he was a scamp. He was always in trouble with girls . . . Scotland Yard chased so many out of the country that the palace stopped counting.'[17] To describe him as a 'scamp' must have been one of the politest ways possible of indicating the Prince's extraordinary behaviour as a front-line member of the Royal Family. His rampant sexual activity with dubious members of both sexes was nothing short of outrageous, though by all accounts he was a pleasant enough chap and exceedingly good company.

Any woman of royal birth who could bring Prince George, then aged thirty-two, to heel was to be favoured. And Princess Marina was that person. 'She has not a cent,' King George told Ramsay MacDonald,[18] but clearly she had endeared herself to him with her grace, poise and beauty and, according to her mother, the King was 'the perfect angel to Marina when she arrived in England as a shy bride.'[19] Their wedding, in 1934, was a hurried one. By the end of the summer they were engaged and they married in November. It was staged with great style and panache, the finest England had seen since the Mountbatten nuptials; the public, for a moment, ignored the dire economic depression and were enchanted by this seemingly loving couple; it all served as a brief reminder of some of the great royal occasions of the past when the ruling houses would come together to watch their dynasties bound ever closer by matrimony. King George was surprised by public reaction to the wedding; dubious and miserable in what were the last days of his reign, he had not realized how popular the monarchy had become.

With the exception of the wedding of Princess Elizabeth to Prince

Philip, it was probably the last such great occasion and one, incidentally, from which Philip's mother Alice and Lord and Lady Mountbatten were absent. It was another feather in the cap of the Greeks; they had managed a good toehold in the heart of the British Royal Family.

At a State reception given by King George at Buckingham Palace two days before Marina's wedding, Wallis Simpson and her husband Ernest appeared, invited by the Prince of Wales – even though Queen Mary had ordered that they should be struck from the guest-list. 'He smuggled them into the palace,' King George later told one of his confidants.[20] According to Prince Paul, Wallis wore 'the most striking gown in the room', outdoing the Greeks and the Duchess of York. The Prince of Wales was introducing her to members of his family. Philip's Uncle Christopher recalled that David laid a hand on his arm in his impulsive way.

'Christo, come with me. I want you to meet Mrs Simpson.'
'Who is she?'
'An American. She's wonderful.'[21]
If only they had known . . .

One other echo: Bertie and Elizabeth, the Duke and Duchess of York, were quietly getting on with their own lives, free of scandal, whiter than white and not anticipating a life too onerous. The King had recently bestowed upon them a pleasant little country home, the Royal Lodge in Windsor Great Park, where the first governess for their two little Princesses, Elizabeth and Margaret Rose, arrived – it was Marion Crawford, who would spend her next seventeen years in total devotion to the royal children and then fall from favour when she wrote a book about her experiences.

The Queen's early childhood makes an interesting comparison with that of her future husband. Her mother had a definite idea of the training she wanted for her daughters, long before the Abdication put Elizabeth in direct line of succession. She wanted them to spend as much time as possible in the open air, achieve perfect deportment, good manners and all the prime graces of femininity, plus all the book learning that was possible within their capacity.[22] Above all, the Duchess of York sought for her two daughters a loving, stable home life, untroubled by external pressures of which, at the start of this fateful decade, there were many.

Philip's sisters seem to have had the same kind of ambitions for him as they conferred in Germany on the subject of his education and upbringing. Given their knowledge of facts which came into the public domain only many years later, it would be quite understandable if they felt they should remove their young brother from these unsettling influences at once.

It was a major turning-point in the moulding of Prince Philip, who, we are told by his cousin Alexandra, was blissfully unaware that 'once again a family tug-of-war raged over his head.'[23]

Chapter Six
Hitler's Hand

Prince Philip's second eldest sister, Theodora, with her husband, Berthold, Margrave of Baden, was the main instigator of getting her brother to Germany. Berthold's father, Max von Baden, was the last Imperial Chancellor and at his side as the old German Empire faded into oblivion in the autumn of 1918 was his Private Secretary Kurt Hahn, a young man who, in other circumstances, might have risen to high rank in government and who, it has been said, made Prince Philip the man he is today.

Since that statement could be double-edged, the development of Hahn's educational ideas is worth more than a cursory glance. He returned to his native Germany in 1914 as war broke out after studying at Oxford, where he was a brilliant Rhodes Scholar, and initially became an Intelligence officer. As an expert on British affairs, he moved closer to the nerve-centre of German politics and to Max von Baden himself; he became a close adviser in Germany's war with Britain and her allies.

At the end of the war, Hahn made a vital contribution to the Versailles peace settlement by the advice he gave to the German Foreign Minister, Brockdorff-Rantzau. Indeed, it was well known that the minister's explosive speech denying Germany's war guilt was largely the work of Kurt Hahn. Ironically, it was to rebound upon him; as a Jew he became a victim of the hysterical campaign for revenge and rearmament which began in 1933 and which used that self-same speech as a starting-point in the German preliminaries to the Second World War.

After the Von Baden government resigned and the Kaiser abdicated and went into exile in The Netherlands at the end of the First World War, Max retired to his castle at Salem while Hahn decided to become a teacher, devising a totally new system of education aimed at the children of outstanding families. He outlined his plan to Max von Baden, who liked the sound of it and offered to finance him and allow the

51

school to be established in the rambling old Schloss, once a Cistercian monastery, on the shores of Lake Constance.

The Hahn system, which was to shape not just Prince Philip but also his son Prince Charles, was based upon seven principles:

To give children the opportunity for self-discovery.
To make them meet triumph and defeat.
To provide the opportunity of self-effacement for a common cause.
To allow periods of silence.
To train the imagination.
To make games important but not predominant.
To free sons of the wealthy and powerful from the enervating sense of privilege.

In many respects, it all sounded very similar to the nationalistic ideals of Germany itself, without the nasty bits.

Hahn's new school opened for business on 21 April 1920, with eight boarders and twenty day pupils, including Max von Baden's own son Berthold. Thirteen years later, when Berthold was impressing upon his wife the advantages of putting Philip into the system, it had grown to be one of the foremost schools in Europe, and certainly the most progressive, with 400 pupils. Unfortunately, Kurt Hahn did not see eye to eye with Hitler and even before Philip arrived at Salem the Nazi patriotic view was being forced upon the school; eventually it would lead to Hahn's arrest and departure.

One afternoon a man was kicked to death not far from Schloss Salem by Nazi stormtroopers. Hitler personally congratulated these murderous thugs for ridding Germany of another undesirable Communist. Hahn was horrified and called his full complement of pupils to assembly, telling them that they themselves must choose between the philosophies of the school and Nazism. In effect, as Sir Robert Birtley, headmaster at Eton, later put it, Hahn gave his boys the alternative of 'terminating their allegiance either to Hitler or to Salem.'[1] This pronouncement quickly attracted the attention of Hitler's secret police. Evidently there were boys, or parents, associated with the school whose allegiance clearly lay with Hitler and a few days later, in March 1933, a bunch of heavy-handed stormtroopers marched into the Schloss and arrested Hahn on the trumped-up charge of being a Communist and of 'the decadent corruption of German youth'. The fact that he was a Jew who had mocked Hitler had more to do with his incarceration. No Jew could be allowed to educate Germans, especially Germans of such high-born influential families.

Hahn was locked away in a Nazi prison and seemed destined to join the waves of other Jews who were being driven out of Germany, prior to the advent of concentration camps and mass extermination. However, educationalists throughout Europe mounted a campaign to have him freed and the support of the British Prime Minister Ramsay MacDonald was enlisted. Hahn was subsequently released and allowed to leave Germany. He chose Britain, where he had been educated, as the country in which he would seek shelter. Already plans were forming in his mind to start a new school, eventually to be called Gordonstoun – where, coincidentally, he was to be viewed with suspicion by the British during the Second World War and accused of spying, just like the Battenbergs in the First World War.

He was on his way to British shores as the young Philip was heading for Germany. Philip's brother-in-law, Berthold, had taken over as headmaster at Salem. The school had declined in numbers after the arrest of Hahn. Many boys, mostly those of foreign parents, had been withdrawn and by the time Philip arrived in September 1933, Berthold had given way to Ministry of Education pressures and introduced a rigid, pro-Nazi regime. Though a liberal, he had little choice; he either accepted the Nazi doctrine or closed down completely.

More than that, the Margrave of Baden had to take instructions from the overseers of the Hitler Youth, whose young leader had extreme powers of authority that enabled him to enforce his orders. As Philip himself later recalled, there was much heel-clicking, and shouts of '*Heil Hitler!*' were compulsory for German nationals. As a foreigner he was exempt from the more extreme indoctrination, though he still had to endure 'a lot of ghastly footslogging'. We are told he enjoyed the regime of the school itself, or what was left of the Hahn principles, but hated the atmosphere.

The school day was rather more rigorous than what he had been used to at Cheam. It began with a cold shower and a short run, followed by five minutes of Christian meditation. There were more exercises before breakfast, then on into the morning curriculum, which by now had certain Nazi add-ons including for German boys compulsory membership of the Hitler Youth. Some older boys and certain members of staff also joined the SA (stormtroopers).

Philip has recalled an incident in which he came close to serious trouble. One of the senior boys responsible for juniors, including Philip, struck out against the Nazi ways: 'it so displeased the thugs that they caught him and shaved his head. I lent him my Cheam 2nd XI cricket cap and hope he has still got it.'[2]

In the short time he was at the school, Philip became a rebellious embarrassment to his German kin. Alignment to the Nazis, perhaps reluctantly on the part of the Margrave of Baden, was more enthusiastically followed by another of Philip's brothers-in-law in the House of Hesse, whose family was wholeheartedly behind the Hitler takeover. Hitler's rise to power had, in fact, put the German Royals in a quandary. They were hardly at one with the vulgar little upstart who was rousing the rabble all over their beloved countryside, yet they would not be sorry to see changes in the decadent, inflation-ravaged society of the Weimar Republic. Ex-Kaiser Wilhelm himself thought that Hitler might even restore the monarchy at some point and his sons and nephews joined the Stahlhelm, an organization dedicated to upholding law and order, which was later absorbed into the Nazi Party. None of them seemed to appreciate that the Nazis were not the old-fashioned right-wing conservatives but a new revolutionary force.

Not the least sympathetic of the Royals was Uncle Charlie, as he was usually known, the Duke of Coburg, Queen Mary's brother-in-law by marriage and the former Duke of Albany. He had been sent to Germany from Britain by Queen Victoria to take the vacant title of the Duchy – once the home of Victoria's Albert – when he was only fourteen, and he was a fully fledged Nazi. With his connections, he became Hitler's personal emissary to the Court of Windsor in the mid-thirties, carrying messages between the Führer and Edward VIII. But he was just one of a number of embarrassments.

Prince Christopher of Hesse had become an ardent, devoted Nazi by the end of 1933. Slightly less fanatical but still enthusiastic was his brother Philip of Hesse, who was married to Princess Mafalda, the King of Italy's second daughter.* Philip was a close friend of Hermann Goering, who had long had dealings with the Hesse family. When Goering returned to Germany at the end of 1927 following four years of exile after the 1923 Putsch, he earned his living as a consultant to the German airline Lufthansa and other companies. Among his contacts in the prominent circles of business and government was Prince Philip of Hesse, who helped him on his way.[4] These favours were remembered when, in 1932, the Nazis became the largest party in the Reichstag, of which Goering became President. He appointed Philip's brother Christopher head of the Luftwaffe Research Office, which was to provide Goering with his power-base as it set about establishing an extraordinary Intelligence system of wire-tapping and monitoring the telephone conversations of embassies and their diplomatic staffs.

Philip of Hesse was even closer to the hub of activity during the Nazification of Germany and beyond. From a starting-point of Obergruppenführer in the brownshirts, he moved into the position of close confidant of Goering and on into Hitler's inner circle. As son-in-law of the King of Italy and cousin to those in Britain whose friendship Hitler

---

* Their wedding in 1927 was a very grand affair at Racconigi, the King of Italy's estate near Turin. It was another gathering of the clans and the Greeks were well represented. Prince Christopher of Greece remembered, 'We first met Mussolini at the wedding and were struck by his stupendous personality . . . a magnificent supper was staged for the hundreds of guests. . . . we climbed into the Fiat touring cars but there was no seat for Mussolini. Both Prince Paul of Yugoslavia and myself offered him ours but he refused and squashed in between us.'[3]

sought, Philip of Hesse became a rather vital cog in the wheel. Shrewdly, Hitler tried to maintain old royal alliances with the ruling German houses, and though the Kaiser was still in exile at Doorn in The Netherlands, his vast German properties had never been confiscated and his great array of remaining relatives were offered the Führer's protection.

Albert Speer recalled how Hitler treated Philip of Hesse with deference and respect:

> Philip was useful to him and especially in the early days of the Third Reich had arranged contacts with heads of Italian Fascism. In addition, he helped Hitler purchase valuable art works. The Prince had been able to arrange their export from Italy through his connections with the Italian royal house.[5]

Philip of Hesse was earmarked specifically as a contact with both the Italian and British Royal Families – notably with Edward, first as Prince of Wales, then as King and later as Duke of Windsor, and with his brother the Duke of Kent. It was through the German cousins – and the Duke of Coburg – that Hitler sought to curry favour with the British Royals. He even got into the act of trying to find a bride for the Prince of Wales by asking the Kaiser's daughter Princess Victoria Louise to 'arrange a match' between Edward and her daughter Princess Frederika, thus forging a new tie with Germany. The Princess was said to be 'astounded' by Hitler's proposal[6] and Frederika instead married Prince Philip's first cousin Paul of Greece, later King Paul of the Hellenes.

But, as we know, half the aristocracy of England, many major bankers and businessmen and not a few politicians were all showing friendship towards the Nazis. Not least the Prince of Wales.

Though Wales's tenderness for all things German has been well documented elsewhere, one of the lesser-known sources that provides useful royal insight to this vital period is to be found in the Austrian State Archives. The papers of Count Albert Mensdorff, a former Austrian Ambassador to London and great friend and cousin of King George V, contain the following entry for the year 1933, when Prince Philip was entering Salem:

> I was summoned to see the Prince of Wales. I am still under his charm. It is remarkable how he expressed his sympathies for the Nazis in Germany: 'Of course, it is the only thing to do; we will have to come to it as we are in great danger from the communists. I hope and believe we will never fight another war but if we do, we must be on the winning side and that will be Germany, not the French'. . . . it is interesting and significant that he shows so much sympathy for Germany and the Nazis.[7]

With half his relatives showing dangerous inclinations towards Nazism, it might well be expected that at the impressionable age of twelve some might have rubbed off on young Philip. Apparently not. According to General Sir Leslie Hollis, former Commandant General of the Royal Marines, who came to know Prince Philip well in that capacity, the young Prince liked Salem as a school but hated the Nazi overtones and what was going on in Germany.

His dislike was intense for one so young. Characteristically, it found expression not in youthful political speechmaking but in a flagrant irreverence. All the heel-clicking and saluting struck him as ridiculous. . . . Philip would have none of it and his constant refusal to take the Nazi ways could lead in the end to serious trouble, not only for himself but for members of his family.[8]

Philip found the arm-stretched salute hilarious and refused to participate, even though it was now compulsory for everyone. Finally, in the autumn of 1934, the Margrave and Theodora decided to return him to the custody of George, Marquess of Milford Haven, in England. 'We thought it better for him,' said Theodora, adding honestly, 'and for us.' From that, we are able to deduce that Philip rather innocently saved himself from a German upbringing, which would perhaps have led to marriage to a German princess and presumably to a career in the German Navy and eventual oblivion along with the rest of his German relatives; another stroke of good luck!

Kurt Hahn took little time to re-establish himself in Britain. He found the ideal location, Gordonstoun House, a few miles from the town of Elgin in Morayshire – a large country mansion where the Gordon Cumming family once entertained Royalty.* The property had everything that Hahn wanted – open countryside, cliffs and caves, farms and fishing, sailing and outdoor sports opportunities. It was still a controversial school; there were echoes of Nazism and of Oswald Mosley's Fascist dream of creating a nation fathered by 'supermen', pure-bred British males untarnished by interbreeding with other races. Hahn's ideals were not as extreme, but the similarities were evident and comparisons not entirely out of order. They were enough for critics to accuse him of attempting to bring German influences into British education; others were more forthright in the view that the school

* Gordonstoun was once the home of Sir William Gordon Cumming, at the time a lieutenant colonel in the Scots Guards, who was at the centre of the Tranby Croft gambling scandal at which – to Queen Victoria's horror – Edward VII when Prince of Wales was called to give evidence. Gordon Cumming was accused of cheating while the Prince was dealing. He brought a case for slander, lost and was kicked out of the Army and London society.

represented nothing more than a snobbish training course for the sons of the élite and, in its fledgling pre-war years and in the austere post-war years, there were numerous opponents to Hahn's methods as the ramblings of a crank.

George Milford Haven arranged for Philip to go to Gordonstoun as a boarder and paid the school fees, since there was no one else who would do it when his nephew returned from Germany at the age of thirteen.

What sort of boy was he, this gangling youth who had been without parental influence for so long? Had his continental wanderings and uneven journey through life so far affected his character? Cutting through the sycophancy of handed-down assessments by people who were unlikely to report differently even if they wanted to, a pattern emerges of his putting up a blustering confidence in all that he attempted. He was lean and strong and getting tall for his age; he had a raucous laugh which could be heard everywhere – a characteristic he seems to have carried through his life – and Kurt Hahn tells us he was able to derive great fun from the smallest incident.

> When Philip first came to Gordonstoun, his most remarkable trait was his undefeatable spirit. He felt the emotions of both joy and sadness deeply and the way he looked and the way he moved indicated the way he felt. For the most part he enjoyed life; his laughter could be heard everywhere and created merriness around him. . . . In work he showed lively intelligence but also a determination not to exert himself more than was necessary to avoid trouble. . . . when he was in the middle school he got into a fair number of scrapes through recklessness and wildness. He was often naughty, never nasty.[9]

He also excelled in community work and, once he had made a task his own, he showed meticulous attention to detail and a pride of workmanship in which he was never content with the mediocre.

Sports and every kind of outdoor activity were his forte. At Gordonstoun, as at Salem, the regime was rigorous, with the same icy shower to start the day, the same pre-breakfast run, the same morning break for athletics. The diet for these growing, energy-using boys was interesting and enlightened for the age: the Gordonstoun boys sat down to a two-course breakfast, a three-course lunch and a two-course supper. Meat was seldom served more than four times a week and never at night; milk, plenty of vegetables, fresh fruit and wholemeal bread were the staple ingredients of the menu. To succeed, the boys needed a self-discipline that was unrivalled in 'normal' British schools. Each morning, Philip sprinted down the long lawn from the school building and around the lake, aiming to run the half mile in 2 minutes 30 seconds. In the athletics break, he would set himself new daily targets for the high jump, and though cricket, rugby and hockey had been 'dethroned', to use Hahn's own description, he became useful in each of those sports, eventually becoming team captain in both cricket and hockey as the 'born leadership' qualities that his headmaster had observed began to surface. He was playing right into the system, as Hahn later explained:

> Once a boy has started training he will be gripped by magic, a very simple magic, the magic of the puzzle, for you cannot help going through with a game of patience that has begun to 'come out', and will struggle on against odds until one day he is winning through in spite of some disability. There is always some disability but in the end he will triumph.[10]

It was heady stuff for boys barely in their teens; few of them could have understood the underlying aims of the Hahn philosophy, which put less emphasis on the rigid academic and traditional sports-orientated system of the British public schools and went straight towards the character-building techniques which Philip obviously thought successful enough to bolster up his own sons.

Chapter Seven
Return to Athens

The changing heart of the Greek nation brought euphoria back to the House of the Hellenes and the promise of new beginnings for the entire family. On 25 November 1935 Prince Philip's cousin King George II of Greece was restored to the throne by referendum and returned to Athens following an eleven-year exile. That had pleasant implications for Philip and the rest: they were now part of a working monarchy again. In the meantime, the King-in-waiting had lived quietly at Brown's Hotel in London, receiving occasional visits from his mistress, Mrs Dorothy Jones, who, according to Sir Robert Bruce Lockhart, had become the Greeks' own Mrs Simpson.[1] This rather personal matter had been generously overlooked by King George V, who had kept his cousin in touch with worldly matters by regular dining engagements at Buckingham Palace. However, it did mean that the Greek King had to return to his throne without a Queen, having divorced his wife, Princess Elizabeth of Romania, earlier that year.

Back in the old country, Prime Minister Venizélos, the monarchy's most ardent critic who had brought Philip's father to within an inch of the firing squad, had himself been ousted by General Kondylis in 1935 and died three months later. The new regime invited the Greek Royal Family to come home with the words, 'The presence of the King as supreme arbiter will bring an end to internal dissensions. A new era starts from today.'[2] They were words of hope and promise; unfortunately, they would not be entirely fulfilled. The Greek family's future remained as precarious as ever amid the ever-shifting politics of Greece, as was perhaps demonstrated by the 'friendly but not exuberant' welcome from their people.

However, on King George's instruction, the Greek Royals turned out in force for a carefully orchestrated return in triumphal style, with exaggerated monarchist pomp and theatre, to which they added the supreme drama: they brought with them the disinterred bodies of ex-Queen Olga, her son ex-King Constantine and ex-Queen Sophie, who had all died in exile and whose remains had until now lain in a crypt in Florence. At the Italian end of the proceedings, Mussolini provided a fitting departure for the demised Greeks with a colourful send-off for their coffins as they were taken aboard the Greek warship *Averoff* at Brindisi; it was the same ship on which Constantine had returned to Athens from exile fifteen years earlier.

In Athens itself, all was prepared with supreme military precision as the Greek family began to arrive. Among them was the fourteen-year-old Prince Philip, tall, blond and lanky, but handsome for one so youthful. It was quite a family reunion as all the Greek Princes and Princesses turned out for the emotional, if somewhat macabre, ceremony of re-burying their dead and receiving the welcome home of their people.

Philip's mother was not present; she was still being cared for in a nursing home. Prince Andrew, however, was able to come, though he had no intention of staying.

The entire Hôtel Grande Bretagne had been reserved for the Royals, since the palace was no longer suitable for their accommodation. At the banquet on the night before the procession through Athens, Philip wore a dinner suit and was full of stories of his adventures in Scotland. But, for the first time, the thought occurred to him that one day this might be his life, here in Greece. He was old enough to appreciate his ancestry and fired questions and more questions about his surroundings, about his family history, about Greece itself. One question after another. At last he was able to see for himself some kind of heritage, something physical and tangible that he could see with his own eyes instead of having to rest upon the descriptions of others. Never in his life had he been able to view the home of his forebears with all its current participants present.

This sudden insight into his family background came at a time when, after a year at Gordonstoun, he was actually experiencing a more settled life. Still, the thought of returning here in later life suddenly became a prospect that weighed heavily on his mind. He had moved closer down the line of succession – he was now third in line – and it was feasible that he could actually become King of Greece. Kurt Hahn felt that this possibility had a profound effect on Philip:

> At the time, the Crown Prince had not married and Philip was not far from the succession. There is no doubt that for a short time he was tempted by both the hazards and the comforts likely to come to a Prince of Greece in residence in Athens. The lure of early and undeserved importance was definitely felt.[3]

Come the cold November day of the procession, with winds whistling off the sea, the three coffins were laid on gun-carriages surrounded and drawn by contingents of blue-jacketed soldiers and escorted by single-file lines of Evzones in their pleated white skirts and maroon coats. The streets were lined with crowds come to witness this spectacle as the procession, headed by the King, his uncles and cousins, went slowly to the Cathedral where the remains lay in state for six days; the brothers Christopher, Andrew and Nicholas and their nephew Paul stood guard-of-honour at each corner of the dais. The men wore either uniform or black morning suits; the women wore black coats with veils over their faces.

Philip disgraced himself. Dressed in morning suit with top hat, he felt ill during the parade. He was unable to break rank with the rest and dash to the nearest convenient spot for his impending sickness, and the feeling only got worse as they entered the car that was to carry them with funereal slowness to the service. Philip could hold back no longer and grabbed his topper, into which he emptied the contents of his stomach, heaving from a disagreeable lobster consumed the night before. At the end of the journey he felt better but had the embarrassment of holding a top hat containing a strong-smelling fluid; he disposed of it by handing it unconcernedly to an ADC as he passed.

The year turned and 1936 would herald some significant developments drastically affecting the future life and status of Prince Philip. King George V was as prophetic as anyone could be when he said to Prime Minister Stanley Baldwin shortly before his death in January 1936, 'After I am dead the boy will ruin himself within twelve months.'[4] David would take slightly less than the time predicted by his father, thus placing his young niece Elizabeth in the direct line of ascendancy. And by the year's end, Philip may well have become earmarked in the minds of some of his relatives for a very special role in life.

First, there were more discussions about his immediate future. These arose on another trip to Athens, a few months after the restoration of the monarchy, when the King's younger brother Paul married Frederika of Hanover, the girl once selected by Hitler as a possible bride for the Prince of Wales. Had that arrangement taken place, she would now be Queen of England.*

While they were all together for the festivities, Philip's father, Prince Andrew, took his son aside for a chat about his future prospects. It had been suggested to Andrew in Court circles that he should encourage Philip to follow the family tradition of a commission in the Greek services by first enrolling in the Greek Nautical College, then going on to join the Royal Hellenic Navy. It is interesting at this point to consider that,

* Her brother Prince George of Hanover, incidentally, became Prince Philip's brother-in-law as the second husband of his youngest sister, Sophie, nine years later.

had he done so, the course of history might have changed; but then, in royal circles life is full of ifs and buts. The suggestion was not seriously pursued, either by Prince Andrew for his own bitter reasons or by his son, who was quite happy in England and at Gordonstoun where he had recently become captain of hockey and cricket and had stood out in athletics. School reports showed that he had been putting a lot of effort into his academic work as well. He was described as sound rather than exceptional and showed a preference for geography and mathematics. He was also good at languages, perhaps naturally as a result of his continental journeys, and excelled in German and French. His 'home' life was more enjoyable, too. Holidays and half-term breaks were often spent in the company of his cousin David Milford Haven, and at the country house in Lynden the two of them had a pair of two-stroke motor bikes, went canoeing on the river, duelled at roller-skate hockey and disappeared on some exciting night-time excursions when George and Nada were out. Once they rode their bicycles to Dover and hitch-hiked back on a Thames barge, sleeping on grain sacks. Life was better, more settled.

There was no reason to adopt Greek traditions or seek entry into the service of a country which had variously threatened to shoot his father, banished his immediate family and exiled their King on three occasions. It was an uncertain environment, to say the least.

Other developments seriously affecting his future were beginning to materialize. Even before King George V had been buried, the Nazi Duke of Coburg, who was staying with the Countess of Athlone at Kensington Palace, visited the new King Edward VIII and presented him with Adolf Hitler's compliments. The Führer had commissioned him to seek an audience with Edward at the earliest moment to establish a relationship between Buckingham Palace and Berlin. Coburg was soon able to report back that the new monarch was very kindly disposed to an Anglo-German alliance:

> it was for him a very urgent necessity and a guiding principle for British foreign policy. The King asked me to visit him frequently in order that confidential matters might be more speedily clarified. . . . I promised – subject to the Führer's approval – to fly to London at any time he wished.[5]

And then there was Mrs Simpson. The romantic and political pressures that would before long see Edward forced out of Buckingham Palace were already well advanced.

It was an odd coincidence that the crisis over the new King's association with Wallis Simpson should blow up in a big way in Greece. Edward and his lady sailed to Corfu aboard their chartered yacht, the *Nahlin*, and were mobbed by reporters and cameramen from the world's press, anxious to tell their readers the secret that had to be kept from the British public: that the King and Mrs Simpson were rather close friends. The royal-watchers had been given more than a glimpse of the pair lounging on the yacht's decks when they boarded it in Yugoslavia after a journey by rail to visit Prince Paul and Princess Olga. Paul and Olga had recently become an important couple in the Balkans, as virtual rulers of their country. Paul had been appointed Prince Regent following the assassination of King Alexander, shot by Croatian terrorists in October 1934. Alexander's son and heir Peter, a second cousin of Philip, was too young to take the crown, so his cousin Paul became Regent.

When the royal yacht reached Greece, King George II came to greet them, bringing his mistress Mrs Jones on board – a pair of kings and two non-queens enjoying a luncheon interlude. In Greece the political atmosphere was again tense. Only two weeks earlier, Prince Andrew's former friend General John Metaxas had seized power and begun soothing relationships with the Fascist regimes in Italy and Germany. The Greek King was an important pawn; even more important was the arrival of the British King, who was whisked into Athens for a two-hour meeting with Metaxas,[6] and then 'the good ship Swastika', as Malcolm Muggeridge dubbed the *Nahlin*, proceeded on its voyage.

The three cousins, Paul, George and Edward, certainly had one thing in common: they were all being courted by Hitler.

What were Edward's impressions of George, one king of another? Something of them emerged later when he wrote:

> I asked him how he was getting along and he answered almost bitterly he wasn't getting along at all. He had returned to Greece to find loyalties divided. . . . 'I am king in name only; I might just as well be back at Brown's Hotel.' As I took leave of him, he gripped my hand and said 'I hope you have better luck.'[7]

It was a touch of classic irony. They were both heading for a miserable time.

Back in London the pace was quickening. Joachim von Ribbentrop, German Ambassador to Britain, had been pointed towards the right circle by some of his royal connections in Germany. It was no coincidence either that Prince Louis of Hesse, brother-in-law of Philip's sister Cecile, was appointed honorary cultural attaché to the German Embassy in London, under Ribbentrop, as a further link between the Third Reich and the British Royals. As we now know, Ribbentrop targeted all the courtiers and hangers-on he could sucker to and especially those around Wallis Simpson. He virtually admitted in his memoirs that one of the reasons he was promoted to the London job was because of his close relationship with Wallis and there is perhaps no better assessment of the developing Abdication Crisis than that of a little-known paper by Orme Sargent, a future permanent undersecretary, who wrote:

Ribbentrop explained that Mr Baldwin's real motive was purely a political one, namely to defeat those Germanophile forces which had been working through Mrs Simpson and the King with the object of reversing the present British policy and bringing about Anglo-German entente. Ribbentrop held this view strongly, more particularly as he based his whole strategy on the role that Mrs Simpson was expected to play in Anglo-German affairs.

Hitler, through Ribbentrop and various members of the Hesse family, kept close watch on the London situation. But events were moving along so rapidly that by the time Prince Louis of Hesse had been officially installed at the Embassy, Britain had a new King, much to Hitler's annoyance. As the Orme paper noted: 'The Führer was very distressed at the turn that affairs had taken . . . since he looked upon the King [Edward] as a man after his own heart who understood the Führerprinzip and was ready to introduce it into this country.'9 Hitler thought that the new King, George VI, would be ready to follow Foreign Office policy. Conversely, the two Queens, Mary and Elizabeth, were ready to believe that Mrs Simpson had been plotting with Ribbentrop to get Hitler's support for an Edward VIII *coup*, supported by Mosley, as the Abdication Crisis neared its conclusion.10 Anything was possible, and the fears of Their Majesties certainly could not be ruled out; in fact, they were only heightened the following year when the Duke and Duchess of Windsor were fêted by Hitler on their visit to Germany.

The British Royals were in Hitler's bad books. When Prince Louis of Hesse arrived to take up his appointment, the Führer in his anger banned him from attending a special family party that the Mountbattens had arranged at Brook House* at which King George VI and Queen Elizabeth were to welcome their German cousin. Outside in Park Lane, crowds gathered to see the new King and Queen and the other notable guests. Only Prince Louis himself was missing. Hitler was in high dudgeon with the family for their treatment of Edward and the 'very

---

* Although they had sold the original mansion, the deal was that the new development would provide them with a penthouse suite overlooking Park Lane and the name Brook House was transferred to it. It was one of the first penthouses in London, fitted with every imaginable gadget and what Mountbatten boasted was the fastest lift in London. Although only an 'apartment', it was still substantial with thirty rooms of breathtaking beauty. The five main reception rooms had collapsible walls which could fold back to make a huge ballroom; there was a theatre capable of seating approximately 150; a long gallery hung with four Van Dycks, for which an incredible double image was achieved by mirrors on the opposite walls; and, of course, Mountbatten's bedroom was done out like a ship's captain's cabin, complete with portholes.

clever' Mrs Simpson, and no member of his London staff was going to be allowed to socialize.

Though Mountbatten had remained one of Edward VIII's staunchest supporters during the Crisis, Prince Philip could not be drawn by his schoolfriends on his views of the Abdication. He refused to discuss it outside his own family circle[11] but we are told that he sympathized with the King's action which 'must undoubtedly have reawoken painful echoes of his father's fall from grace'.[12] Neither Mountbatten nor Edwina had any sympathy with the Nazis – 'I'd hate to be German,' Mountbatten wrote to his cousin Prince Louis[13] – and that feeling occasionally caused family differences. Edwina's own father, Lord Mount Temple, with the co-operation of the Duke of Coburg, had formed the Anglo-German Fellowship and became its President in 1935. He was credited with some very indiscreet remarks about Germany 'fighting fair' and his views became staunchly pro-Nazi and anti-Semitic, although he began to retract before his death in 1939.

One other important event: Prince Philip, along with his family, attended the Coronation of King George VI. Princess Elizabeth was there, too, aged just eleven, and sixteen-year-old boys do not pay much attention to such young girls. Neither remembered especially noticing the other. He was probably more interested by the masses of colourful uniforms in the great procession of assorted Armies of the great British Empire, brought from around the world as a show of strength for Hitler's benefit – though Hitler knew what everyone in the British government knew: George VI's Armies, Navy and Air Force were ill-equipped and ill-prepared for war.

It was a significant day for Prince Philip. The nation celebrated with street parties, house parties, banquets and balls. And at the great Coronation Ball, Philip's sister Cecile was unquestionably a star in a magnificent gown of classical Greek design. Her death, and that of another of those closest to Philip, within the next few months would affect him deeply.

During the summer of 1937 Mountbatten and Edwina were together briefly, visiting the Hesse family in Germany. It was a change to see them at each other's side; it was a brief respite from her travels before her final pre-war fling.

Prince Philip also spent a short time at Darmstadt with his father that summer. There was some good news. Prince Louis of Hesse had become engaged to the Honourable Margaret Geddes, daughter of Lord and Lady Geddes, and they were to be married in England on 23 October. Hitler, it appears, did not object to this new link with the British aristocracy and preparations were already in hand for another gathering of the clans from both sides of the Channel.

Fourteen days before the wedding, however, Louis's father Ernst, Grand Duke of Hesse,* collapsed and died. He had been ill for some months. George Donatus, husband of Philip's sister Cecile, succeeded to the title and the vast Hesse estates in Germany. A family conference was called and it was agreed that Prince Louis's wedding should go ahead as arranged, though it was postponed for a month.

On a cold but otherwise clear day, 16 November, Cecile and George, the new Grand Duke and Duchess of Hesse, set off from Frankfurt to fly to England for the wedding. With them aboard the Sabena Airlines aircraft were Ernst's widow, Onor, and Cecile's two sons, Louis and Alexander. Only their youngest child, daughter Johanna, was left behind. Cecile was expecting their fourth child.

They were to make one stop at Ostend and were due to arrive at Croydon, London, late that afternoon. At Ostend, however, a thick mist had blown up and the afternoon light was beginning to fade into a murky night. As it came in to land, the plane hit a tall brick chimney and crashed. There were no survivors. Philip's closest sister and almost her entire family was wiped out, along with six other passengers and the crew. The bridal pair, with Dickie and Edwina, were told the news as they waited at Croydon to greet the Hessian ducal party.

Another family conference was called and Philip's grandmother Victoria, now seventy-four, decreed that the wedding should go ahead in spite of this further tragedy, though it should be staged quietly and without the traditional post-wedding celebrations. Two days later, relatives in black mourning arrived for the sombre marriage of the young couple,† Mountbatten stepping in as best man in place of the groom's dead brother. Prince Philip, who was naturally deeply upset by the deaths of his sister, brother-in-law and young nephews, chose not to attend the wedding. He had learned of his sister's death from Kurt Hahn, who called him into his study at Gordonstoun to deliver the bad news. Philip, said Hahn, was deeply affected but 'did not break down when he heard this terrible news. His sorrow was that of a man.'[14]

Fate had not done with Philip's family yet. First, his mother, Princess Alice, who had been recovering with her daughters in Germany and had achieved good health and, at last, some stability, suddenly relapsed with pneumonia. She was admitted to a hospital in Cologne and her condition grew so serious that her children gathered about her. The Princess never gave up, however, and recovered.

Then in December Philip's Uncle George Milford Haven had a fall

---

* Prince Philip's great-uncle.

† Prince Louis, by virtue of George Donatus's death should have become Grand Duke. In fact he never took up the title and, since he had no children, it went eventually to another line in the family.

and broke a leg. Doctors were at a loss when the broken bone refused to heal and towards the end of 1937 he was diagnosed as having cancer of the bone. For many weeks he lay in severe pain, growing weaker as the days passed; towards the end his mind wandered and he was unable to recognize his family. Philip visited him regularly and was kept in touch with the news by letters from his grandmother, Victoria. 'Such a lot of worries on top of each other,' she wrote to him in the winter of 1937.[15] George, she would say, was like a father to the boy; Philip was desperately concerned. In April 1938 he was informed that George had died.

The death of his uncle affected him deeply. Now he had lost his main guiding force and benefactor. The consequences were enormous, since that responsibility now passed to his Uncle Dickie, who would become perhaps the greatest influence of his adult life and the arranger-in-chief of his future role and destiny. Philip himself never failed to recognize publicly the contribution of his Uncle George to his upbringing and in later years was often resentful of assertions that he had been brought up entirely by the Mountbattens. He once said, 'I don't think anybody thinks I had a father. Most people think that Dickie's my father anyway.'[16]

His real father, Andrew, did not become any more involved in Philip's life now than he had been when George was alive; he viewed his son's progress from afar, mostly from Monte Carlo, where he lived at the Villa Alexandra, a house owned by the Hôtel Metropole. His was a sad life with few highlights, and apart from occasional visits his influence over his son appears to have been negligible. He had formed a relationship with Madame Andrée de la Bigne, a tall, attractive Frenchwoman of moderate wealth who once went under the stage-name of Mademoiselle Lafayette. She owned a small yacht, moored at Monte Carlo, on which they lived together from time to time, though she discreetly kept her distance when Philip came to visit, leaving son to join father in the daily jaunt for a livener in the bar of the Hôtel de Paris.

That year, too, Philip's mother moved further away from her son's upbringing by returning to Athens, where she took a small house in Kolonaki Square with a female friend and companion and surrounded herself with photographs of her family. Alice, who had become devoted to the Greek Orthodox Church some years earlier, had decided to give all her energies, her very existence, to helping the sick and needy. She actually asked Philip to come and live with her but that was never a prospect he could consider.

During the summer of 1938, when Philip required some relief from the recent spate of bad news, he was offered holiday accommodation in Venice with his Aunt Aspasia, widow of King Alexander of Greece. She had lived abroad since her husband's death from the monkey bite. Prince

Andrew took a passing interest by issuing instructions to Aspasia to 'keep him out of girl trouble . . . he has exams to pass.' That might have proved difficult; Aspasia and her daughter Alexandra introduced him to a fast-moving social whirl along the canals of Venice. There were parties at Lord and Lady Melchett's, or with the Count and Countess Volpi (Mussolini's Foreign Minister), or the super-rich Count and Countess Castelboros. Wine flowed, there were plenty of young girls and Philip enjoyed himself, 'dancing about the terrace like a young faun' and 'swinging from the pergola.'[17] His cousin's version of that holiday gives us a colourful picture of him at seventeen: 'like a huge, hungry dog, a friendly collie who never had a basket of his own . . . yet there were undertones of complete heartlessness; though never sorry for himself, to be fed and looked after meant so much to him.'[18] At the end of the summer he returned to Gordonstoun to begin the last stage of his education before going to naval college.

Philip's base and anchor remained for the time being his grandmother's bleak apartment in Kensington Palace rather than with the Mountbattens at Brook House. He still spent weekends at Dickie and Edwina's country home at Adsdean, and David Milford Haven, the new Marquess, remained his closest friend. The prospect of finding Dickie or Edwina actually at home was never great; Mountbatten, though still a relatively junior naval captain, managed to find time to continue his travels and at the time of his brother George's death, for instance, he was touring Jamaica as captain of an English team in an international polo tournament. Edwina's excursions had not been curtailed much either; the previous year she and Nada went off on a long expedition to East Africa, exploring the wilds of Kenya, Rhodesia and other historic centres, disappearing for days on end into the bush with only a guide for company and backpacks of camping gear. When they returned, Edwina was carrying a tiny lion cub as she emerged from the plane at Croydon and for weeks afterwards it roamed free at Adsdean, much to the consternation of the servants. There were also trips to America, and to Harlem during a time which her friends called her 'black period'; then in 1938 she was off again, restless as ever, on an adventure to the Far East with two other women friends. In Sumatra she bought a car to drive the length of the new 800-mile Burma Road.

And so at this point of Philip's life, the Mountbattens could hardly be considered an ever-present influence. In fact, in a letter to Edwina, Mountbatten himself seemed strangely surprised by the young man's charm and wit after he had stayed at Adsdean for a weekend with David Milford Haven. Mountbatten wrote that his nephew had 'had his meals with us and really is killingly funny. I like him very much.'[19] Though their time together may have been sparse, it is hard to believe that no thought had crossed Mountbatten's mind, arch-plotter that he was, that

Prince Philip would make an admirable husband for the future Queen Elizabeth.

And the first meeting between the two, when such thoughts began to gell, was just around the corner.

Chapter Eight
Families at War

War came closer as Prince Philip ended his last term at Gordonstoun. Events in Europe weighed heavily on his family. The older members began talking about the last time brother had been pitted against brother, cousin against cousin. In 1935 King George V had raged, 'I will not have another war. I will not . . . I will go into Trafalgar Square and wave a red flag myself sooner than allow this country to be brought in!'[1] But George was gone and there was no one to wave the red flag. Just like last time, things were running out of control. Cousins had joined the menacing fray, and over the water Hitler would soon be asking the old King's exiled son the Duke of Windsor to 'hold himself in readiness' for a return, backed up by a tantalizing offer of 50 million Swiss francs deposited for his benefit and use in a Swiss bank account. Wallis's eyes lit up.[2] What was David up to? they were asking themselves in London as news filtered through of his associations with a motley bunch of Nazi-linked cronies and of his plans to visit Berlin.

King George VI was working away into the night, paying meticulous attention to his ever-mounting workload. He didn't much care for his government's agreement to allow Hitler to take over Austria on 11 March 1938. Everyone was still talking to each other; Prime Minister Neville Chamberlain was still trying for peace and to keep the warmongers cool, but Hitler's ambitions grew more outrageous as the days passed.

What did Philip make of it all? At seventeen, perhaps he was more preoccupied by his own immediate future as he walked away from the moulding influence of Dr Kurt Hahn for the last time in the spring of 1939 with a school report that was honestly reflective of his character:

> Prince Philip is universally trusted, liked and respected. He has the greatest sense of service of all the boys in the school . . . a born leader but will need the exacting demands of a great service to do justice to himself. Prince Philip will make his mark in any

profession where he will have to prove himself in a full trial of strength.

Hahn added another telling comment, which we now know would prove entirely accurate: that his pupil's performance had been at times 'marred by his impatience and intolerance'.

To this accolade other tributes to the schoolboy were later added in the first official potted biography of Prince Philip issued by the British Information Service in 1947:

> He was well-known to the townspeople of Elgin and made friends with many of the local boys whom he met on the cricket field and on fishing and sailing expeditions; he kept up many of these friendships and during the war would renew old contacts when on leave in the north. His love of the sea showed itself early . . . he and his schoolmates built a cutter and took part in several sailing trips to the Shetlands, the Hebrides and Norway. He was so expert a sailor that he was allowed – a privilege granted to few – to be in charge of an open boat under sail in the Moray Firth without an adult on board.[3]

Praise indeed! But, of course, the words were vetted by Philip himself.

Now he was heading for the Senior Service – of that there had never really been much doubt. The smell of the salt water had been with him throughout his days at Gordonstoun, where the rigorous ways that Hahn insisted were part of character-building had developed his yearning for the sea. He was also egged on by Mountbatten and his sisters towards a career in keeping with family tradition: entry to the Royal Naval College at Dartmouth, which had produced Mountbatten himself, as well as Uncle George and the three last kings, George V, Edward VIII and George VI, and which latterly had given his best friend, David Milford Haven, a start. Hahn seemed relatively pleased with his pupil academically, though he was not brilliant: there were weaknesses that had to be overcome before the entrance examination for Dartmouth. At Mountbatten's behest, Philip moved to Cheltenham as a live-in pupil of his exam coach, a retired naval officer. When the final results came in, he had passed his entry to Dartmouth adequately though not spectacularly, coming sixteenth out of thirty-four students; however, he was a late entrant – others had already been through preparatory schooling for Dartmouth.

In May 1939 he arrived at Dartmouth, where for the first time he was able to wear the uniform of a naval cadet, which for the next few years would become his most frequent attire since he did not possess any large wardrobe of clothes.

The regime at Gordonstoun may well have equipped Philip for the college rather better than life had prepared some of his predecessors. The Duke of Windsor, though then a quiet, shy boy from a sheltered background, remembered with some bitterness the bullying he received there, which showed that tutors and senior boys alike were singularly unimpressed by his royal rank: 'We were quickly reminded of our lowly station . . . and persecutions they devised were all the worse for the years of practice they had had. . . . they told us we were a lazy, idle bunch of warts. I had not dared to complain.'[4] Mountbatten's own reflections concerned the 'swinish' things some of the boys got up to: 'some people in the other dormitories have begun to do some filthy things, I have heard.'[5] But Mountbatten, too, was a smallish boy then, 7 stones and 5 foot 5 inches. Prince Philip, tall and strong with Gordonstoun muscle, was more able to take care of himself and he soon settled to a self-imposed discipline of hard work and studies.

The fateful meeting with his future wife is alleged to have come on a rainy summer's day in July 1939, two months after his arrival at the college. King George VI, Queen Elizabeth, Lord Louis Mountbatten – now the King's personal aide-de-camp – and the Princesses Elizabeth and Margaret sailed towards Dartmouth aboard the gold and white royal yacht *Victoria and Albert* for an official visit to the Royal Naval College. Much has been made of the visit; it is supposed to have provided that special moment when eyes met and love set in. Certainly in the biography of King George VI by Sir John Wheeler-Bennett, which was approved by the Queen personally, early lines of reference to Prince Philip pronounce: 'This was the man with whom Princess Elizabeth had been in love from their first meeting.'[6]

Elizabeth was now thirteen and a shy girl who still liked ginger crackers and lemonade. Was it on this day that she fell in love with her Greek Prince? Dartmouth was not in fact their first meeting: as we have seen, they had been together at the Coronation of her father two years earlier, at the wedding of Philip's cousin Marina in 1934 and at various parties and film shows held at Brook House for the two Mountbatten daughters. Neither Queen Elizabeth II nor Prince Philip, it has been said, had any recollection of those earlier meetings, so we must assume that the 'first' time was there at Dartmouth, with the hand of Mountbatten playing a very definite role.

For while Lord Louis took the King and Queen on a tour of the college, Prince Philip was called to attend the two young Princesses. The College Commandant, Rear Admiral Freddy Dalrymple-Hamilton, had received a telephone call from Mountbatten prior to the royal visit suggesting that Philip might be the captain's doggie (messenger) that weekend; Philip would thus be required to stay very close to the royal visitors and give help where needed. Additionally, when the King and

Queen arrived, the Rear Admiral pointed out that two of his boys were down with mumps and perhaps it might not be wise for the Princesses to accompany Their Majesties on the tour. Mountbatten was ever-ready with a suggestion: 'Perhaps we could get Philip out of church to amuse the girls.'

Governess Marion Crawford, who was with the Princesses, recalled his entrance: 'a fair-haired boy, rather like a Viking, with a sharp face and piercing blue eyes' who came over and said, 'How do you do?' It was an accurate observation on Crawfie's part; she would not have known then that the Greek Prince had no Greek blood in his veins but was from Danish and Aryan stock. Outside, he began showing off, with demonstrations of tennis (he leapt over the net with inches to spare) and at croquet; Elizabeth, we are told by the nanny, was suitably impressed and spoke the immortal and much-quoted line: 'How good he is, Crawfie. How high he can jump.' Next day, his uncle procured an invitation for Philip to take tea with the Royal Family on board their yacht. There he merrily put down several plates of shrimps, a banana split and some trifles, while the two sheltered Princesses looked on with amazement. Crawfie said that to the girls a boy of any kind was 'like a creature out of another world. Lillibet sat pink-faced enjoying it all. To Margaret, anyone who could eat so many shrimps was a hero.'[7]

Well, that was the governess's version of the first real meeting; others have made less of it. Philip's cousin Alexandra said he resented having to squire two young girls around, although this alleged reluctance did not appear to dampen his enthusiasm in saying farewell to the royal party. As the yacht sailed away, he was the leader of a number of cadets in small craft who stayed close to the ship, until his alone was the last little boat left trailing in their wake and brought an angry response from the King: 'Damned young fool. Signal him to go back.' Philip was showing off again, one supposes, because even if his future bride had fallen for him, it seems unlikely that he had any reciprocal feelings for such a young girl after two brief meetings – unless, of course, he had been advised by his uncle to show them some attention. Elizabeth, we have been told purringly by Marion Crawford, 'watched him fondly through binoculars.' And so these gushing accounts of the first meeting have continued.

But does it matter when or where they met? If the young Princess fell in love with him on that day, so be it, but it would not necessarily follow that her father would, seven and a half years later, give his consent to their marriage. Uncle Dickie would have rather more groundwork to put in to achieve the alliance of the branches of the family which he was now so obviously plotting. Within a year of that encounter at Dartmouth, however, some of Philip's closest relatives would be saying that he was to be the consort of the future Queen – and the heiress was only just fourteen.

As we have seen, such thoughts were far from the King that July. Back at Buckingham Palace, he listened intently as Neville Chamberlain told him that both he and the Cabinet were of the view that what hope there might be of preventing war perhaps lay in demonstrating to Hitler that Britain was serious and would resist any further acts of German expansion. In this, the King agreed. After Chamberlain had left, the King thought of using his German connections, and specifically his cousin Prince Philip of Hesse, as a possible means of getting that message across to Hitler. The King wrote a short note to Chamberlain: 'I have met Philip of Hesse . . . he seemed to be sensible. . . . do you think it would be possible to get him over here and use him as a messenger to convey to Hitler that we really are in earnest?'[8] Chamberlain replied that he had heard from three different sources that Hitler was well aware of Britain's resolution and he did not think any useful purpose would be served in contacting Philip of Hesse.

In any event, Philip of Hesse had already become something of a messenger boy for Hitler himself, for which he was rewarded with an honorary generalship in the SA. The Führer used him as his personal courier of sensitive tidings to would-be political allies like Mussolini and to other members of German and associated Royal Families – including the Duke of Windsor. A transcript of one tape-recorded telephone conversation between the Hessian Prince and Hitler demonstrates the subservient manner with which the royal aide now responded. Philip was in Rome, having just delivered a letter to Mussolini explaining Germany's actions in Austria, and Hitler was rattling off further instructions over the telephone: 'Tell the Duce . . . I will be ready to go with him through thick and thin – through anything.' Philip sounded nervously attentive: 'Yes, sir, I have told him that . . . Yes, sir . . . Yes, my Führer . . . Yes, my Führer . . .' was all he could say as Hitler pounded away before slamming the phone down without so much as a passing word for Philip himself.[9]

In another telephone conversation, this time with Goering, the topic was still Austria and concerned the exodus of Communists and Jews. It was reported that 25,000 Viennese Jews had fled across the border into Poland in the first twenty-four hours of German occupation. 'We could leave the border open,' Philip suggested to Goering. 'We could get rid of the entire scum like that.' Goering thought it a good idea, then pulled up sharp with an afterthought: 'But not those with any foreign currency . . . the Jews can go but their money they will have to leave behind. It's stolen anyway. . . .'[10]

Coincidentally, these telephone calls were being monitored by Goering's technicians – as were all telephone calls to the Chancellory from foreign locations – in the department now headed by Prince Christopher of Hesse, rigidly devoted to his career in the Nazi regime. His dedication was rewarded with promotion to the rank of Ministerialdirektor in

Goering's Prussian Ministry, but his most significant role in the rise of the Third Reich came as head of the Forschungsamt Agency which operated from Berlin. Literally translated, it means Research Office and it was one of the most secret of Goering's Intelligence-gathering operations. Access to the information it provided was restricted to Goering himself and Hitler. Under Hesse, the Research Office developed into what was recognized as one of Hitler's most ruthlessly successful Intelligence agencies. It was best known for its prodigious output of reports on literally hundreds of thousands of separate files logged in its ten years of operation from April 1935[11] and largely based on its phone-tapping operations. Intercepted telephone calls provided Goering with a constant stream of material which he used to secure his power-base in Hitler's hierarchy; as a result of them, many so-called enemies of the Third Reich were arrested or murdered. Next, the department provided important general Intelligence from its readings of foreign signals, notably from the US Legation at Berne. The measure of its success can be seen from its move to prestigious premises in Berlin's Charlottenburg district. Its employees were specially selected Nazi devotees in whom Goering and Hesse placed implicit trust; even so they had to swear an oath of secrecy and sign a declaration recognizing that in the event of violation they would be shot. Christopher of Hesse's deep commitment to the agency can be discovered from a recorded note in the agency documents in which he wrote in 1938: 'The work of the FA will have both point and profit only if its secrecy is safeguarded by every possible means. Inadequate security will result in the enemy taking precautions and our sources will dry up.'[12] When the Duke and Duchess of Windsor visited Berlin in 1937, Goering ordered him to tap their phones, as happened with most visiting politicians, important businessmen and so-called guests of the Third Reich.

Christopher of Hesse was listed as an officer in the Luftwaffe after 1939, when his agency came under the auspices of the Air Force. It has been claimed that Christopher was a Luftwaffe pilot and Lord Lambton went so far as to suggest that he was among those who conducted bombing raids on London (in one of which Buckingham Palace was hit), though he makes this as an aside; evidence is lacking.

Another of Prince Philip's brothers-in-law, Prince Gottfried of Hohenlohe-Langenburg (husband of his eldest sister Margarita) had joined the German Army as a corps commander on the Austrian push. Theodora's Berthold, Margrave of Baden, was in the foreground of the German moves towards France before being invalided out through bad wounds received from a machine-gun attack. Prince Louis of Hesse, meanwhile, was posted to the Eastern Front and eventually managed to escape the main thrust of the war. Other relatives, like Princess Frederika – the wife of Philip's cousin Paul – were similarly affected by divided allegiances. She had four brothers in the German armies but

Greece was now her country and she continued to support her husband's family; still the Greeks didn't much care for her.

Meanwhile, Prince Philip's cousin Olga, wife of the Yugoslav Regent Prince Paul, was also trapped as Hitler breathed down their necks urging an alliance. First they were given an accolade in London by being invited to stay at Buckingham Palace at the end of 1938 while Paul was lectured on the reasons for maintaining Yugoslavia as an Allied protectorate. Their State visit was given front-page headlines and everyone was convinced that Yugoslavia would remain an ally. They had hardly had time to unpack on their return to Belgrade when Hitler invited them for a State visit to Germany. For seven nights in a row, Olga sat alongside the Führer at dinner.[13] They were fêted by the Third Reich, with the VIP treatment of crowd-lined streets and an SS guard-of-honour as they joined the Führer at Berchtesgaden. The Germans made sure that their welcome was far more celebrated than the reception they had received in London. Hitler told Goering, who had special responsibility for Yugoslavia, to give them an air display – more as a threat, probably – so some of the Luftwaffe's best equipment thundered a few feet above Berlin. Paul and Olga were scared to death of Hitler; but, at his wits' end over his loyalties to the British Crown and relatives in London, gradually the Regent was edging closer towards throwing in his lot with the Germans.

The same thing happened to King Carol II of Romania, who was also given a State visit to both countries. Britain was especially worried that Romania's oil would fall into German hands, and King Carol told George VI he had no intention of allowing that to happen.[14] However, Carol would not be allowed to stay too long on his throne; as Sir Reginald Hoare, the British Minister in Bucharest, reported: 'The young Prince Michael is becoming difficult. . . . I wonder whether it would be possible for someone to convey to King Carol that children require careful handling.'[15] George VI did indeed have words with Carol about the difficult Michael; it was to no avail. When the time came, and the Germans were knocking on the door, it was Carol who was forced to abdicate and Michael became King again.

The ties were all coming apart. Those 'binding' royal relationships were not strong enough to hold things together, undermined by too much treachery and double-talk. A prime example came when Prince Philip's uncle, King Gustaf V of Sweden, offered to act as a go-between as the war began. He was disdainfully rejected by King George's government. Winston Churchill commented: 'The intrusion of the ignominious King of Sweden as a peace-maker after his desertion of Finland and Norway . . . and while he is absolutely in German grip . . . is singularly distasteful.'[16] King George responded to Gustav that 'no useful purpose would be served' by such a suggestion.[17]

The Queen of Sweden, Louise – Mountbatten's sister – did keep the royal adversaries in touch with each other, though. She acted as a neutral posting box, receiving letters from both sides and forwarding them until the end of 1940, when she was forced to give up the service.

Prince Philip in England remained in touch with his father, whom he would see for the last time in 1940, and with his mother back in Athens, but lost all contact with his three surviving sisters, as did his grandmother Victoria and Uncle Dickie.

In the months before the outbreak of war, Cadet Philip of Greece had been working hard to achieve his ambitions at Dartmouth. He was one of the most intensely studious of the college inmates, as his classmates remember well. He was seen as 'a bit of a bully . . . that Germanic arrogance of command. . . . he was saved from priggishness by his sense of humour and he could laugh at himself.'[18] He was voted Best All-round Cadet of his term and won the King's Dirk; later he was awarded the prestigious Eardley-Howard-Crockett Prize for Best Cadet and eventually he passed his final examinations with distinction. A year later, after service at sea, he gained his Sub-lieutenant rank with four first-class examination marks and one second class.

On 1 January 1940, less than a year after entering Dartmouth, Philip was given naval orders, becoming the third of the Mountbatten clan to enter the Royal Navy. His Uncle Dickie had already hit the headlines, first by gaining the captaincy of HMS *Kelly* and then by ferrying the Duke and Duchess of Windsor back and forth across the Channel on 12 September 1939 for the Duke to discover if there was a role for him in England. There wasn't, and he was sent back to France. No one was keen on having Wallis anywhere near sensitive military establishments.

Prince Philip's closest friend and cousin, David Milford Haven, was the third member of his immediate family in the Navy; he was already at sea in the destroyer HMS *Kandahar*. For Philip, however, a problem had had to be overcome before he could gain a naval posting. He was still, by rights, a Greek prince and a subject of Greece, and since the naturalization procedures had been abandoned at the outbreak of war, he had been unable to carry out plans for his formal application for British citizenship. Mountbatten lobbied the Royal Navy to admit him; wasn't he after all a direct descendant of Queen Victoria? It was a question which received the consideration of the Foreign Office, the Home Office and Buckingham Palace itself before Mountbatten succeeded in getting his nephew accepted, though apparently not without some heart-searching. Once Philip had been accepted, Mountbatten selected his posting, which, in accordance with Admiralty instructions, was to be a vessel out of the main war arena so as not to give rise to any embarrassing circumstances that might involve the foreign Prince of neutral nationality. Mountbatten telegraphed his old friend Vice-Admiral Harold Baillie-Grohman, asking if he would take his nephew aboard his ship, HMS *Ramillies*. He agreed.

The battleship was an ageing old tub on escort duty with vessels bringing troops and supplies from Australia and New Zealand to the war zones of Europe. For Philip, it was a fairly unattractive first posting and he was not pleased with it, though he appreciated that it was probably the best his uncle could do, given the current climate.

Before leaving Dartmouth he joined the Mountbattens for a short break, during which he went with Uncle Dickie and the King and Queen to see the London stage production of *Funny Side Up*. He was also at a party given by the Queen at the Royal Lodge at Windsor, where he met Princess Elizabeth again. Other guests at the large gathering, which was the last royal party before the war, included Mountbatten, Nada Milford Haven, Harold and Zia Wernher, Princess Marina and Prince George of Kent. 'Hitler', said the young Princess Margaret, 'is spoiling everything.'[19] Then Philip was off to Ceylon where he was to rendezvous with his ship, which he soon discovered to be uncomfortable, noisy and hot; the most popular sleeping quarters for midshipmen like Philip were the gunroom; beds were a couple of armchairs and a sofa and facilities were spartan. But the *Ramillies* did provide him with his first visit to Australia. He was the ship's dogsbody, running errands and making cocoa for the Captain – a 'thin, leggy youth,' went one description, 'but always a quiet dignity for one so young. Australians were rarely dignified, so this characteristic was particularly noticed when he came ashore in Sydney'.[20]

His initial welcome by his shipmates had not been soothed by an order from the Admiralty that he should be addressed as 'Prince Philip'; he soon insisted on being called Philip, or Philip of Greece, and dropped the 'Prince' prefix whenever he could. This apparently impressed shipmates on his next post, to the cruiser HMS *Kent*,* whose men had been trapped by the outbreak of war and had been serving without leave for two years. The prospect of wet-nursing some young prince, not even a British one, who was joining them as midshipman did not go down too well with men whose patience was beginning to wear a trifle thin. Philip tried to change their minds. He dashed about the ship, doing his best to please, and we have learned from accounts of life on board the *Kent* that he soon endeared himself to his tired comrades, even down to rolling hand-made cigarettes for them.

Noticeable character traits were already emerging. The 'dignity' he displayed could just as easily be replaced by a warm informality and a definite respect for his elders, yet even then he had the ability to cut through layers of rhetoric with a biting, sometimes sarcastic comment, such as his observation while on *Kent* that he had to keep his eyes peeled for enemy aircraft, 'knowing the seeming incapability of lookouts of ever seeing anything.'[21]

---

* Philip joined the *Kent* on 12 April 1940, having been moved to it because *Ramillies* had moved too close to war.

A short term of duty at the shore station of Colombo gave Philip the opportunity to explore the Ceylonese countryside and he wrote impressively about the Buddha's tooth festival at which he encountered eighty elephants and a colourful array of dancers. In October 1940 he was posted again, this time to HMS *Shropshire* – which, as he put it, was 'the third ship in eight months to receive this singular honour'.[22] That soon became four: in January 1941 he went aboard HMS *Valiant* and into the real war. The *Valiant* was part of the vital Mediterranean fleet and a fully fledged battleship with eight fifteen-inch guns and fourteen six-inch guns.

This move, which brought Philip into direct confrontation, was precipitated by developments in his home country, where King George II and General Metaxas had, until now, attempted to maintain a neutral stance. On 28 October Italian troops had crossed the border after George's government had refused to accede to a three-hour ultimatum from Mussolini demanding the right of passage for Italian troops across Greece. Ten divisions of Mussolini's armies moved in from the already conquered Albanian territories and Italian bombers attacked Athens; the Greeks fought back and pushed the Italians back into Albania. Now, at last, Greece sided with the Allies and King George VI sent messages of support to the Greek Royal Family. Prince Philip himself could no longer be considered a 'neutral' foreigner in the British Navy – though as far as he was concerned, he had been on the British side from the outset, even if his superiors might have been nervous about him. There were still those at the Admiralty who remembered Philip's grandfather, Prince Louis of Battenberg, and how he was drummed out for being German.

Were there anxious thoughts for Philip back home? Was the young Princess Elizabeth worried about the handsome blue-eyed Prince she had met again at Dartmouth? When the threat of invasion seemed a distinct possibility, the King decided that Windsor Castle was the safest place to accommodate his two daughters, though official announcements proclaimed that they had been sent to a 'house somewhere in the country'. There they remained until towards the end of the war, along with the Crown Jewels – wrapped unceremoniously in old newspapers and stacked in cardboard boxes in the Castle vaults – and with anti-aircraft gunners peering over the battlements at the German bombers heading towards the cities of the Midlands. What flickers of an emerging romance could there have been in that young girl's mind?

Well, there are a few pointers towards what others were thinking. We know, for instance, that Princess Elizabeth was 'rather disappointed' to discover that her father had not sent Prince Philip a Christmas card for the first year he was away. But he rectified the situation on 13 January. Next, we turn to the mischievous writings of Sir Henry 'Chips' Channon, who was to Royalty and politics what Hedda Hopper was to Hollywood. He was in the thick of it in Greece at the beginning of 1941. He found the situation there 'complicated' and wrote:

There is the isolated King [George II] who sees no one; there are the Crown Prince [Paul] and Princess [Frederika] who, madly in love, remain aloof from the world with their babies and their passion. There is Princess Andrew who is eccentric to say the least and lives in semi-retirement and there is Prince Andrew who philanders on the Riviera whilst his son Prince Philip serves in our Navy.[23]

By coincidence, Prince Philip himself was in Greece at the time of Channon's arrival. He had been granted a short leave to visit his mother and cousins and he met Channon at a cocktail party in Athens. His ears must have been burning. Channon had been discussing him earlier that day: 'Philip of Greece is extraordinarily handsome,' Channon wrote in his diary. 'I recalled my afternoon's conversation with Princess Nicholas.* He is to be our Prince Consort (by eventually marrying Princess Elizabeth) and that is why he is serving in our Navy. He is charming but I deplore such a marriage; he and Princess Elizabeth are too inter-related.'[24]

The date was 21 January 1941, six and a half years before his engagement to Elizabeth. Philip has since dismissed Channon's prophetic note as 'inevitable . . . precisely the sort of language that they used. . . . people only had to say something like that for Chips Channon to go one step further and say it's already decided.'[25]

Channon, however, was not alone in his predictions of an eventual betrothal. At least two other sources quote Philip himself as the teller of the tale. Vice-Admiral Baillie-Grohman recalls a conversation soon after Philip joined the *Ramillies*. The Captain had asked him if he intended to make his career in the Navy and if he planned to apply for naturalization.

'Yes,' Philip replied emphatically. 'My Uncle Dickie has plans for me; he thinks I should marry Princess Elizabeth.'

'Are you fond of her?' the Captain asked.

'Oh yes,' came the reply. 'I write to her every week.'[26]

Baillie-Grohman, surprised by this admission, advised his young midshipman not to mention his prospects to anyone else on board.

The second note of intentions was recorded in 1941 when his cousin Princess Alexandra discovered Philip writing a letter to Princess Elizabeth. Alexandra rebuked him and said, 'But she [Elizabeth] is only a baby.'

Philip replied, 'But perhaps I am going to marry her.'[27]

* Philip's aunt and Marina, Duchess of Kent's mother.

In any other courtship, such incidents might be regarded with singular lack of interest; but Philip was now clearly aware of his uncle's ambitions.

Even if Mountbatten and Philip had designs on the British throne at that point, it was fairly unimportant compared with contemporary events, which were to send those of Philip's relatives who remained in royal positions scattering for shelter. For most of them the end of their dynastical heritage was near and, once again, the chain-reaction was sparked off by events in Yugoslavia.

In early March 1941, Prince Paul of Yugoslavia was summoned back to Germany by Hitler and 'invited' to join the German–Italian axis; the alternative was immediate invasion by German troops. Paul gave in and returned to announce a pact with Germany. In London, King George VI was consulted as Hugh Dalton's Special Operations Executive planned its first major initiative of the war: to oust the Yugoslav government and arrest Paul and Olga – at whose wedding, it will be recalled, the King and Queen, then Duke and Duchess of York, had been guests. The plan was given approval, and on the night of 27 March British SOE agents directed a successful *coup d'état*.[28] Paul and Olga were taken into custody and whisked out of the country immediately to Greece; from Athens they were moved on to internment in Africa. Prince Philip's cousin, the young King Peter, not yet seventeen, was crowned monarch of Yugoslavia and a new government was formed under Air Force General Simouić. Churchill declared that Yugoslavia had 'found its soul' at last. Jubilation in London was short-lived, however. The following day, Hitler announced that as far as he was concerned Yugoslavia no longer existed. He launched an immediate invasion and a massive air attack, virtually flattening Belgrade. King Peter and his government fled the capital and, with German troops advancing by the minute, escaped by flying boat sent by King George. They went first to the Middle East and then on into exile in London, never to return to their country. After the war, the monarchy of Yugoslavia was abolished by Tito.

Ten days later – and just three months after Prince Philip's visit – Greece suffered the knock-on effect. The Germans forced the British garrisons from Greek territory after days of heroic exploits by the Allied troops. Hitler's Army marched into Athens on the morning of 27 April 1941 to raise the Swastika over the Acropolis. King George II gathered up the remnants of his family and fled to Crete, some in flying boats, others aboard HMS *Decoy*. Before long, with Crete under attack, the *Decoy* again came to the rescue and took them all off to Egypt, then on to London. For the moment, the Greek monarchy too was in abeyance.

Philip, coming up to his twentieth birthday, found himself at the hub of battle. On 28 March 1941 the Navy intercepted part of the Italian fleet at the Battle of Cape Matapan and his ship, HMS *Valiant*, joined Mountbatten's old ship, HMS *Warspite*, in the attack, with Philip manning the searchlights to illuminate the opposing vessels as his comrades fired their salvoes. The elusive Italian fleet was sent scuttling and never again sailed out of safe waters, except to surrender. After the action, Commander in Chief, Mediterranean, Admiral Sir Andrew Cunningham, mentioned Philip in dispatches and Rear Admiral Sir Charles Morgan stated, 'Thanks to his [Philip's] alertness and appreciation of the situation we were able to sink within five minutes two eight-inch gun cruisers.' King George II of Greece also showed his appreciation to his cousin by awarding him the Greek War Cross for this action.

On 20 May, as the Germans began their all-out attack on Crete, the *Valiant* joined the British warships who fought off a seaborne invasion of the island, only to be out-manœuvred by the Germans, who made their first airborne invasion of the war, parachuting troops led by General Student while the Luftwaffe kept the British Mediterranean fleet busy under a cloud of bombs. Down below, Philip's log of events told the tale in a clinical, matter-of-fact way: ship after ship hit. The *Greyhound* sunk, the *Gloucester* listing badly and sunk some hours later, the *Juno* sunk, the *Naiad* and the *Carlisle* both hit . . . 'a signal came in asking for assistance so we steamed at 20 knots. . . . as we came within sight of the straits, we saw the *Naiad* and the *Carlisle* being attacked by bombers. . . . we went right to within ten miles of Crete and then the bombing started in earnest.' A huge bomb hit the *Valiant* on 22 May and, despite the horror of the blood and flesh of his shipmates all around him, Philip, we are told, was 'functioning at top efficiency'.

Three days later, in the continuing Battle of Crete, Philip was on watch in the upper parts of the *Valiant* when he caught sight of his uncle's ship, HMS *Kelly*, sailing towards its fate. The *Valiant*, battered and carrying wounded, sought anchor at Alexandria, there to be joined by the equally battered *Kandahar*, listing and limping into harbour with David Milford Haven aboard, safe and unhurt. One more member of the family was already in Alexandria. Princess Alexandra, *en route* from Greece with other escaping Royals, was sought out by Philip and David and they all went swimming. Later, when Alexandra went on to Cairo, Philip followed in a tiny car he had somehow acquired use of and tracked her to a local hotel from where they went swimming and exploring the town together. They talked and played; Philip was worried about his mother but was apparently philosophical about his sisters in their German castles. As one reads Alexandra's account of their meeting in this interlude of war, her affection for her cousin is obvious. Their destinies, however, lay in separate quarters and soon she herself would become a Queen, albeit without a country.

Soon Mountbatten arrived to join his two nephews in Alexandria. Under merciless heavy fire from dive-bombers, both the *Kelly* and the *Kashmir* had quickly sunk and 210 lives had been lost; 279 officers and men, including Mountbatten himself, had been picked up from the flotsam by the destroyer *Kipling*. Philip welcomed his oil-smeared, exhausted uncle, looking like a 'nigger-minstrel'. Noël Coward's version of events, as told in the film *In Which We Serve*, justifiably accorded acclaim for the men's heroism but inspired the onset of public attacks against Mountbatten, who was said to have been shown in true light as a 'vain and ruthless careerist'. Not least of Mountbatten's critics would be Lord Beaverbrook, who took it as a personal insult that a copy of his newspaper, the *Daily Express*, was to be seen in one scene of the film floating upwards in the gutter, its pre-war headline proclaiming 'NO WAR THIS YEAR OR NEXT YEAR'.

As they all scattered from the crossfire of the German onslaught, the blue early summer skies stained with black palls of smoke, the seas and land running with the red of blood, a solitary member of the clan remained in that torn and ravaged land. Philip's mother, Princess Alice, refused to leave. She fought on in her own way, assisting the sick and needy, giving shelter to the victims of the Nazis. Jews, Greeks, Protestants, Catholics all came to her for help; she used to give them her last morsels of food and starve herself. She put herself at grave personal risk, although her daughters in Germany managed to get food parcels and letters through. She was not to see her son for four years . . . and she would never set eyes on her husband again.

Chapter Nine
A Budding Romance

As Britain took the full force of the Blitz, the sight of King George and Queen Elizabeth touring the areas of desolation became encouragingly familiar. Their two daughters remained ensconced at Windsor with hardly an outing to relieve the monotony. Three Officers of the Guard attended them during the day, beginning with the household breakfast. The men who came and went on their specific rounds of duty had all been chosen for their youth and sense of humour in the presence of the Princesses. Members of the family, according to Helen Cathcart, 'noted with amusement'[1] that Princess Elizabeth began taking much greater care of her appearance.

Philip came back on the scene in the summer of 1941. He was ordered to England to complete his examinations before promotion to Sub-lieutenant. He left the *Valiant* at Alexandria and, along with four other midshipmen, took a lift on an old coal-powered troopship sailing from Port Said. The journey through the Mediterranean looked hazardous, so the skipper decided to try the long route through the Red Sea and Indian Ocean to the Cape of Good Hope. At Cape Town, Philip took shore leave and made contact with his Greek relatives who had now arrived in South Africa, where they would reside for the time being, sheltering from the war. Princess Alexandra was there along with Crown Prince Paul of Greece, his wife Frederika and others. Frederika had bought a small car which she lent to Philip for a tour of the Cape Province before he set sail again for England.

From Cape Town, his tired old ship steamed across the Atlantic to Halifax, Nova Scotia, to collect a detachment of Canadian troops bound for the fighting. *En route* they called at Puerto Rico, where the Chinese stokers jumped ship; for the remainder of the journey to Newport, Virginia, Philip was in the ship's ancient boiler room wearing just a pair of dirty shorts, shovelling coal into the hungry furnace. There, for days, he stood alongside his comrades, his bare body and blond hair black from the coal dust, sweating pints in unbearable temperatures for which he received a certificate as a 'trimmer', hung later on his study wall.

Throughout, Philip had kept up a regular correspondence with Princess Elizabeth, though, as Mountbatten had once chastized him, his letters were irregular and infrequent and he appeared to have nothing more than an affectionate consideration for the fourteen-year-old girl thousands of miles away. Elizabeth, on the other hand, could be excused for taking the whole matter more seriously. She sent regular letters and food parcels, and made sure the family remembered him at Christmas. His grandmother, Victoria, was one of the few waiting to welcome him when he arrived home and she had him brought straight to Kensington Palace, where she remained for the duration, bombs or no bombs.

On 18 October he went to see his 'Uncle Bertie and Aunt Elizabeth' at Windsor. Philip found the King out in the garden, pruning a rhododendron bush and wearing a rabbit-skin cap to keep out the cold; they chatted about the war. During the afternoon, the two Princesses were brought from the protective confines of the Castle to the Royal Lodge, where Philip joined them all for tea. Later, as they all sat around a log fire in the octagonal sitting room, Philip gave what the King later described as a 'highly entertaining account' of his adventures at sea.

Queen Mary later suggested to her friend Lady Airlie that this was the moment that true love set in on Elizabeth's part.[2] A further milestone in the romance occurred four weeks later when Princess Marina gave a party at Coppins in celebration of the seventh anniversary of her marriage to the Duke of Kent. And weren't there some very interested onlookers as Philip took Elizabeth in his arms for the first time to dance with her?

Princess Marina's own radiant happiness was soon to be ended: her husband was killed in an air crash in Scotland in August 1942, his Sunderland Flying Boat bound for Iceland inexplicably coming down on a mountainside half an hour after take-off from Invergordon. The misery of the funeral brought to the Royal Family some of the anguish being felt by so many of the King's subjects.

There were bitter echoes, though, from pre-war days when George, Duke of Kent, had been the favourite brother of King Edward VIII: now Marina received not a word of written sympathy from the Duke and Duchess of Windsor, exiled in the Bahamas and still causing the King and Winston Churchill as much trouble as ever. Further, Marina's sister Olga, languishing in Kenya with her disgraced Yugoslav Prince Paul, suddenly became the centre of a vitriolic political campaign. George VI, upon the death of his brother, sent a telegram to Olga suggesting that she might come to England immediately. Her hazardous journey through Uganda, the Cameroons, Nigeria, Portugal and finally Ireland, by car, rail, flying boat and sea, took a week. On the King's personal orders, she was to be given priority at every point of transit. Soon after her arrival in England became known, Captain Alec Cunningham Reid,

Conservative Member of Parliament for Marylebone, berated those who had assisted her with the words: 'We have deliberately brought this sinister woman over to the British Isles and have allowed her, to all intents and purposes, complete freedom. If you are a quisling and you happen to be royalty, it appears that you are automatically trusted and forgiven.'2 The nastiness continued, and as late as the autumn of 1942 the Captain was still trying to get Princess Olga interned or returned to her 'traitorous rat' of a husband.

Princess Marina's world had truly fallen apart and, without doubt, she later compensated for her loss by her attention to and guidance of her young cousin Philip, who made a point of visiting her at Coppins whenever he could. Regardless of the tragedy she had suffered and the continuing strange rumours surrounding the air crash that killed her husband – suggesting that perhaps it was not an accident, though no serious motives have ever been offered – she and Philip, by association with Olga, could not escape some tarnish in the resultant publicity.

Philip was promoted to Sub-lieutenant on 1 February 1942 and sent back to sea aboard HMS *Wallace*, in which he was to serve for the next two years. The ship was another ageing, unglamorous vessel but employed, none the less, on dangerous convoy work in the North Sea, dodging mines, bombs and torpedoes between Rosyth and Sheerness. Promotion to First Lieutenant came shortly after his twenty-first birthday, and October of that year saw him as second in command of his ship. Those men who served with him at the time recorded that he was deserving of promotion; words such as 'perfectionist' and 'disciplinarian' were applied to him. These were formative days for his future commitments. He was becoming known as a good officer with a sense of perfection in his job, the same definition Kurt Hahn had given of him. His language could be tough and colourful; and he led by example, even in minutiae. Once when a ship's cook served saddle of lamb without gravy, he went to the galley and made his own. When he ordered a paint job on his ship and the time available was too short, he painted the bridge himself.

His ideal of turning the *Wallace* into the best-run destroyer in the squadron brought him into contact with an immediate rival. Lieutenant Michael Parker, an Australian who had joined the Royal Navy a year before the war, had the same thoughts for his ship, HMS *Lauderdale*, which was on similar duty. The two young officers of like mind and spirit met and an instant friendship developed. Brief shore leaves at Scapa Flow or Rosyth were spent together; good times, slightly rowdy but with conduct no worse than that of any other serving officer seeking wartime relief, were enjoyed. Other leaves were spent with David Milford Haven, who, slightly older than Philip, was already edging his way into the gossip columns. They made up foursomes with attractive young things in the London black-out and went off dancing. There was an almost catastrophic end to one night on the town in March 1942 when David and Philip borrowed their Uncle Dickie's Vauxhall car for a tour of the nightclubs. On their way home at 4.30 a.m. the car crashed into a traffic island and they arrived back at the Mountbatten home in Chester Street – they had vacated the Brook House penthouse at the onset of war – where they slept on campbeds in the dining room, with their faces cut and bleeding.

Philip's face became well known at their favourite haunts and among his cousin's 'set' he was the talk of the girls, something of a heart-throb. They gushed about him; one tried to contact him through Kensington Palace and had to be told that he had gone away. He temporarily fell for a girl whose father sold cars – but then he would be reminded of the Princess back at Windsor, where he continued to visit at the invitation of the Queen when his leaves permitted.

He hardly ever saw his uncle and just as little of Aunt Edwina, whose wartime work in the St John Ambulance Brigade and other ventures had taken on heroic proportions. She had become the SJAB figure-head, organizer-in-chief, occasional ambulance driver and sometimes financier. Her tours of air-raid shelters, especially at night during the bombing, were legendary. She would arrive in the shelters, many of them stinking and without sanitation, packed with hundreds of men, women and children, looking immaculate in her uniform, not a hair out of place, not a smudge to her lipstick. It was a harsh programme she had set herself, with twelve- and fourteen-hour days becoming the norm; she seemed intent on compensating for those irresponsible, wasteful years before the war when her own pleasure-seeking excursions came above all else. Still, her involvements outside her marriage had not ceased; she continued her relationship with a lover whom she had met before the war to the degree that Mountbatten contemplated divorce. That possibility ended only when Edwina's extra-marital man found another towards the end of 1944 and married; sympathetically, Mountbatten wrote to her expressing his hope that she would recover from this unhappiness.

During the war Philip was reunited with his childhood friend Hélène Cordet. He kept in constant touch with her after she arrived in London before the war with her mother, Madame Foufounis, whose fortune had evaporated with alarming speed since the death of her husband. They were now poverty-stricken. Madame Foufounis took a small apartment in Princes Square, Bayswater, which initially had virtually no furniture, the beds consisting of mattresses strewn on the floor. Hélène had been studying at Oxford where she met a 23-year-old student, William Neal Kirby. They thought they were in love and married in 1938 at the Greek Orthodox Church in Bayswater. Philip's visits to Madame Foufounis were always welcome and when he learned that Hélène was to be married he volunteered to give her away. Madame Foufounis recalled, 'He ran the show. They hadn't got a best man so he did that as well. He even borrowed a car from his grandmother, the Dowager Marchioness of Milford Haven, to take us to the church.'4 The marriage didn't last, however, and when they met again during one of Philip's leaves he discovered that Hélène and Kirby had parted.

This is the point at which gossip about Philip began to circulate more widely. Unfortunately, Miss Cordet's own recollections of events were so blurred in her book *Born Bewildered* that they served only to fuel the speculation that lived on for forty years or more.

With her husband gone, Hélène was on her own. She makes vague references to her love for a French serviceman, but whether he was around in March 1943 – when she became pregnant – is not made entirely clear. Her first son, Max, was born at the Hayside Nursing Home in Maidenhead – a venue which itself gave rise to speculation, bearing in mind her lack of funds. The boy's father was named as William Kirby but this issue was clouded further when the Frenchman, Lieutenant Marcel Henri Boisot, later claimed to be the father. Various attempts have been made to show that Max was fathered by Prince Philip, with references such as 'she became pregnant . . . at a time when Prince Philip was in Britain and often in London.'5 Subsequent events did nothing to clarify the situation in the short-term. Hélène continued to see Philip during his leaves until July 1943 and later when he returned to England while awaiting a new posting. She was divorced by her first husband in November 1944; he cited the French serviceman Boisot as co-respondent. Hélène married Marcel in January 1945 and gave birth to a daughter, her second child, twenty-two days later. They had only two months together as man and wife before Marcel was sent back to France as the war ended, and in April he was posted to Cairo. In September he wrote asking for a divorce.

Wartime brought odd romantic encounters. Miss Cordet's was perhaps no more complicated than those of a thousand young women like her, whose tangled love lives became casualties of enforced separation. In Philip she had a benevolent, supportive friend, who was to provide yet more assistance when the war ended.

In July 1943 Philip's ship, HMS *Wallace*, was ordered to report for escort duty in the Mediterranean, to cover the landings of the Eighth Army while American and British airborne forces dropped from the skies for the Sicilian campaign. Again, he was in the thick of important action as the *Wallace* and other ships in the flotilla faced attempts by the Luftwaffe dive-bombers to stifle the Allied landings. There were plenty of heroics. One crewman recalled, 'On one occasion we were under attack from enemy aircraft for over two-and-a-half hours without any help being given, or expected, and Prince Philip coolly directed most of the operations from the bridge.'[6] When they sailed into Malta to refuel and re-arm, Philip received a surprise visitor. Mountbatten came into harbour with a captured Italian general and went aboard the *Wallace* for a drink with his nephew.

The task was virtually complete when the *Wallace* was ordered home for a refit in October. Philip was given several months' leave – a rather wholesome amount considering the seaborne operations were still in full flow. He remained on 'standby' waiting for his new ship to come into service – an event not scheduled until midsummer 1944. But that remains one of those little wartime mysteries. Christmas of 1943 saw him back at Windsor, where the two Princesses were to appear in the local pantomime – some relief for both, for, as Elizabeth complained, 'We have been incarcerated for weeks.' The family was more cheerful. News from the Mediterranean was brighter and, though talk of early victory was well premature, they were more confident. The King showed signs of his overwork. His voice in a broadcast was described as 'tired and lifeless'.[7]

'Guess who's coming to see us?' said Elizabeth excitedly to Marion Crawford when she heard that Philip would be joining them. Now she was seventeen and blooming; attractive, blue-eyed, with her new uniform of the ATS, which she had insisted upon joining, showing off her exquisite figure. What a change, even in the few months since they were last together. Philip, too, had matured: more than ever he was the tall, handsome Prince. There he sat in the front row with the King and Queen while Elizabeth, as the charming Principal Boy – in the part of Aladdin – gave a performance which we are told 'electrified' her suitor as he did her. Crawfie reckoned the Princess displayed a sparkle that night that none of them had noticed before. David Milford Haven joined the party later and the King allowed them to roll back the carpets and bring out the gramophone for dancing. David was as boisterous as ever. 'He and Philip went mad,' Princess Margaret wrote. 'We played charades . . . and then danced and danced . . .'[8] In the Princess's room that Christmas was placed a photograph of Philip and a reciprocal one of her joined him on his ship.

True romance was reserved for Philip's exiled cousins, King Peter of Yugoslavia and Princess Alexandra of Greece. Early in 1944 Peter announced that he and Alexandra wished to marry. Neither had the guiding hand of a father and since he had been in England Peter had received the British King's patronage – as godfather – through school and in other fatherly interests. Yet the King was many weeks in giving approval for the marriage; he considered them too young. In the end, however, he agreed and on 20 March 1944 Peter and Alexandra were married in a room at the Yugoslav Embassy in London. George VI stood as Peter's best man and George II of the Hellenes gave the bride away.

Other assorted refugee monarchy at the wedding included King Haakon of Norway, Queen Wilhelmina and Prince Bernhard of The Netherlands. The marriage seems to have spurred Prince Philip's own thoughts in that direction. His relationship with Elizabeth had progressed considerably from occasional meetings to a rather more serious attachment. At parties and family occasions it had become a matter of course that Philip should be invited. He had the time, having recently learned he was to become First Lieutenant on a new destroyer in the course of construction, HMS *Whelp*, and with Princess Elizabeth just a month away from her eighteenth birthday – when Royalty comes of age – his cousin King George of Greece joined the endeavours of Uncle Dickie by 'having a word' with her father.

Was Philip considering the possibility of an engagement before leaving for his next posting? If he wasn't, other members of the family had certainly given it some thought, including the King and Queen, as is revealed in a letter George VI wrote to his mother, Queen Mary, in June:

> We both think she is far too young for that now. She has never met any young men of her own age. . . . I like Philip, He is intelligent, has a good sense of humour and thinks about things in the right way. . . . We are going to tell George that P. had better not think any more about it at present.[9]

These developments came at a time when Philip had reactivated his quest for British citizenship. A key factor in securing both his ambitions would be officially to change his religion from Greek Orthodox to Church of England and in this he required the permission of his cousin George II of the Hellenes. Philip was, after all, still officially a Greek citizen and, more importantly, third in line to the Greek throne – should they ever regain it – after Crown Prince Paul and Prince Constantine. The route to British citizenship was now slightly easier, as Mountbatten had pointed out: Philip merely had to complete Form 'S', brought in during the war for aliens who fought for Britain. Mountbatten, even from his far vantage-point in South-east Asia, pulled out all the stops on his nephew's behalf – 'every ounce of pull' was one description of his efforts – and even wrote to George VI suggesting that he should 'take an interest' in Philip's case, providing influential backing for a swift resolution to the remaining obstacle in Philip's path. These hopes were dashed by George II of Greece's lack of haste in granting the required permissions.

The Greek King was by then in delicate and secret negotiations for a possible return to Greece when, in the second half of 1944, an evacuation of German troops from his country seemed imminent; it was hardly the time for one of their number to be seen publicly deserting the Greek cause. At the time, George of the Hellenes was positioned in Cairo and

Mountbatten arranged to visit him there. However, it seems that King George VI was especially anxious that Mountbatten should raise only the subject of Philip's citizenship and not his marriage prospects. He urged Mountbatten to back-pedal, saying that since his last talk he had 'come to the conclusion that we are going too fast', though he realized that 'you like to get things settled at once, once you have an idea in your mind.'[10] Even Philip himself occasionally bucked at his uncle's pushiness and wrote, 'Please I beg of you, not too much advice in an affair of the heart or I shall be forced to do the wooing by proxy.'[11]

So, on George VI's instructions, Mountbatten's meeting with George of Greece in Cairo in October 1944 was deliberately low-key; he let matters rest for the moment with the observation that the two young people were obviously devoted and a marriage was very likely to occur. The Greek King finally sent his approval for Philip's change of citizenship and religion towards the end of the year. But by the time it was received in London, Philip had already left for his new ship, so the question of his naturalization was once again put on ice.

With all this to-ing and fro-ing on Philip's behalf, it does appear from all available letters and documents on the subject that Mountbatten was in a desperate hurry to get the affair settled and his nephew engaged. Why was he devoting so much of his time to such a relatively unimportant issue when there was still a very active war going on, in which he was very deeply involved? Was he really trying to push through an engagement before the war ended? Some very obvious reasons for his haste became apparent only much later. As news filtered through from Germany, it became clear that knowledge of Philip's Hesse relationship might well prove an insurmountable embarrassment that could scuttle any possibility of a wedding.

In this, they were saved. When news finally came from Germany through letters to the Dowager Marchioness of Milford Haven, it was revealed that, although her home town of Darmstadt was in ruins, the only family casualty was Prince Christopher of Hesse, who was killed when his plane was shot down over the Apennines. Mountbatten said later that Christopher had finally turned against the Third Reich and, in consequence, a time-bomb was deliberately planted on his plane; as yet no one has discovered any evidence to support his theory and, as Lord Lambton has pointed out, 'would a valuable aircraft have been wasted on a Nazi traitor? A bullet would have been as effective and infinitely cheaper.'[12] Mountbatten, says Lambton, was eager to show Philip's brother-in-law in a slightly improved light, for obvious reasons. If Christopher had survived he would have been brought to trial at Nuremberg. This, in turn, would undoubtedly have killed off the Mountbattens' aspirations to marry the future Queen of England to their most eligible bachelor.

Prince Philip of Hesse remained a problem but extenuating circumstances could easily be proved. He did indeed fall foul of Hitler in 1943.

The Führer believed that Philip was secretly in touch with the King of Italy *after* he had transferred his allegiance to the Allies and he ordered that Philip's telephone should be tapped twenty-four hours a day, with all transcripts to be brought to Hitler himself. In August 1943, when the Prince requested permission to leave the headquarters of the German High Command, Hitler bluntly told him he would not be allowed to do so. Albert Speer recalled: 'He continued to treat him with the greatest outward courtesy and invited him to meals. But members of Hitler's entourage, who until then had been so fond of talking to a real prince, avoided him as if he had a contagious disease.'[13]

On 9 September 1943 Philip of Hesse was arrested by the Gestapo and spent a year in solitary confinement before being taken to Dachau concentration camp. His wife Mafalda – the Italian King's daughter – was arrested separately and taken, on Hitler's direct orders, to Buchenwald, where she died during American air-raids just over a year later. The Hessian Prince remained a captive in the camp until the end of the war when he was freed by the Americans and then, as we will discover, immediately re-arrested and accused of war crimes.

Most of the royal princes still in Hitler's service in 1943 were retired on his orders. But one remained in the Führer's fantasy world. In May 1943 he apparently still believed that the German occupation of the British Isles was a possibility and wrote: 'Only the King must go. In his place . . . the Duke of Windsor. With him we will make a permanent treaty of friendship.'[14]

There was one other death in the family in 1944. Prince Andrew, whom Philip had last seen in 1940, had survived the occupation of France and lived a quiet life in Monte Carlo, taking his daily constitutional at the Hôtel de Paris opposite the casino, though his health was failing through a heart condition. On the morning of 3 December 1944 Prince Andrew rose from his bed and put on his dressing gown, slipped his monocle into his right eye, sat in his armchair and passed away without further ado, meeting death, it was said, 'like a gentleman'. The principality of Monaco gave him a bit of a do, with a guard-of-honour from the French Army, and he was laid to rest in the Russian Orthodox Church at Nice. Few friends or relatives were on hand to mourn his departure. His belongings were bequeathed to his son, to be kept for him when he returned from the war: a couple of suits and an ivory-handled shaving brush. A Prince who had been the prisoner of his own bitter thoughts passed on without fanfare.

By then, Philip was aboard HMS *Whelp* and on active service with the 27th Flotilla based in Australia as part of Admiral Somerville's East Indies Fleet. This brought him under the overall command of his Uncle Dickie. One vignette from before he sailed away again: a girl reporter in Newcastle named Olga Franklin – later to achieve fame in London – heard news of 'some Greek prince' who travelled to work by bus and lived in a small hotel where he paid 6 guineas a week board. The Prince, she discovered, made occasional visits to the shipyard while awaiting the completion of HMS *Whelp* and Olga brought us this first piece of media exposure on Philip – the first press-cutting of millions:

> Few workers in a North-east shipyard are aware that the tall, ash-blond first lieutenant, RN, who travels by bus to work among them each day is a royal prince. Citizens have been equally unaware that this 23-year-old naval officer, Prince Philip of Greece, has been living quietly in a hotel while standing by on a British destroyer. Prince Philip, who has the looks of a typical Prince of a Hans Andersen fairy tale, will certainly have been noticed by many a girl worker at the shipyard. . . . This is the first time the Prince has been interviewed in this country . . . and I thanked him for the good-humoured and kindly way he accepted 'exposure'.[15]

If only Olga had known then the true extent of her obscure Prince's background and what devious negotiations were going on even then in the shadows of his life, she would have had the scoop of a lifetime! Philip's grandmother Victoria now believed that the 'marriage that had been an unspoken consideration of Prince Philip's relations for several years' was edging closer.[16]

The *Whelp* sailed from England on 5 August; the war had turned in the Allies' favour. The Red Army was surging forward, the Italians had come out of the Axis and Philip found himself backing the Allied landings in the south of France before sailing on to the Antipodes, where a quieter time was in prospect. The final months of the war would provide him with little action on his new ship. It was an anti-climax to have been hanging around in England for so many months and then to find himself well away from the finale that was being played out in the remaining danger zones of the world.

He was reunited with his old friend Michael Parker, who had followed him across the world aboard HMS *Wessex*, a destroyer which had been assigned to the same flotilla. Parker promised to show him some of the sights of his homeland. There were rumours already, whispers that Philip was earmarked for greater things in life, and much interest was shown whenever he came ashore. But that did not stop the two of them enjoying themselves in the social whirl of Sydney, Melbourne and other ports of call – the terrible twins, both now sporting seafaring beards and dressed in identical uniforms. Philip hired a small car and on more formal occasions the King's brother, the Duke of Gloucester, who was Governor-General of Australia at the time, lent him a grand shooting brake bearing the Royal Crown insignia. He and Parker chuckled as he drove through the city, receiving salutes from all and sundry. His final bachelor fling was taking place and perhaps he knew it, though Philip went to great lengths to scotch any rumours that passed his way. Friends were instructed that there should be no gossip linking his name with you-know-whom; probing questions were shunted back from whence they came with considerable dexterity and he would go to great lengths to avoid prying eyes, nosey reporters and roving camera lenses.

Once newspapermen followed Philip and Mike Parker to the races. They wrongly identified Parker as the Greek Prince and sought Philip's confirmation. Yes, that's Prince Philip, said Philip without the hint of a smile, and while the press horde followed his pal Philip went on with his day at the races.

On another occasion, Philip walked into a ritzy ball, staged in the less-than-ritzy surroundings of an aircraft hangar near Sydney. At the end of the evening he left with a well-known Australian débutante on his arm. Heads turned, rumours swept the hall and Philip, realizing instantly what was going on, decided upon action to extricate himself from an embarrassing situation. He drove the girl to the house of a friend, Judy Fallon, and got her husband to drive the deb home just in case there were any photographers waiting outside her home.[17]

The war was ending and Philip's ship was transferred to the final arena, where it was earmarked to escort Admiral Fraser's flagship, the *Duke of York*, which was sailing with the huge US fleet positioned off Okinawa. The devastating atomic flashes that hit Hiroshima on 6 August and Nagasaki on 9 August 1945 bought the conflict to its cataclysmic close. Mountbatten was dining at Windsor Castle on the night of the 6th and wrote in his diary the following day: 'Everybody was in good form as the atomic bomb has just fallen';[18] with hindsight his remark provides an alarming view of just how little anyone knew of the appalling repercussions to follow.

As Supreme Commander for South-east Asia, Mountbatten himself left Britain soon afterwards for the formalities of the Japanese surrender and made sure that his nephew was present on this historic occasion. For no other reason than his name and relationship to Mountbatten, Philip, just one of dozens of officers in the command, was brought specially from the *Whelp* to stand on the crowded deck of the USS *Missouri*, anchored in Tokyo Bay, and witness the final surrender of the Japanese to General MacArthur on 2 September. Ten days later, Mountbatten himself received the defeated Japanese generals, swordless and disconsolate – 'I have never seen six more villainous, depraved or brutal faces in my life',[19] he wrote – at Singapore Town Hall for the final surrender of 730,000 Japanese in South-east Asia.

Afterwards, Mountbatten appointed Philip to his personal staff to help in the vast task of settling the affairs of his far-eastern incumbency. His nephew was, in particular, involved in the enormous logistical problem of picking up and resettling hundreds of thousands of prisoners-of-war – a task which taught him many lessons, especially in gaining the confidence of his men and retaining their loyalty.

Philip's personal involvement ended with the new year of 1946 when the *Whelp* set sail for home. An entry in a visitors' book in Sydney for the night of his farewell party in Australia sums up as well as anything the beginning of the new life he was sailing towards on that January day: 'Whither the storm carries me, I go a willing guest.'[20]

PART THREE

PART THREE

Chapter Ten

An Intriguing Courtship

King George VI led the conga line as the Royals celebrated the Christmas of 1945 at Sandringham. Happier days had returned but he was tired, if not yet fatally sick. The King–Emperor, head of the Empire's 500 million inhabitants, had always taken a very personal involvement in the fate of his people – although some had responded unkindly with words like 'It's all right for them . . .' Now the King was back with his family, though his problems were far from over.

Philip was not present that first warless Christmas, of course, because he was still on duty with Mountbatten, but he was there in the thoughts of some and the comments of others. One member of the family was foolish enough to make fun of his upbringing in a 'crank school with theories of complete social equality where boys were taught to mix with all and sundry.'[1] What sort of background was that for a future son-in-law of the King?

'Useful,' was the sharp response of Queen Mary, in whom Elizabeth had found an ally.

The King was less sure. He was possessive and protective and the Queen, though less so, also felt that no harm would be done if her daughter had the opportunity to meet a few more young men of her own age. Some say that the King and Queen were already too late; that the Princess Elizabeth, now nineteen, was sufficiently strong-willed to make up her own mind, aided by a generous supply of arrows from the cupid Mountbatten.

Had not Victoria chosen Albert? And wasn't she deeply in love with him? Yes, of course. But Albert had also been chosen for Victoria. Almost from the day of his birth, his scheming relatives at the impecunious court of Saxe-Coburg had begun planning their eventual marriage. Plenty of comparisons between Philip and Albert could be made. Like Albert, Philip had arrived in England penniless; like Albert, he came from a broken home; like Albert, he had a plotting uncle, and others, intent on his marrying the future Queen; like Albert, the tangled blood of German Royalty ran in his veins. Other similarities could be drawn too, such as political indifference to another foreign consort. Had not Wellington opposed a British peerage for Albert? And did not Peel object to the size of his intended allowance? In Philip's case, it was still too early to be definite about anything. The King was certain only about his uncertainty, and for many more reasons than simply a possessive father's reluctance to let his daughter go, or holding her back to make sure she had made the right choice, especially as she had seen little of the outside world for so long.

For Elizabeth herself, the end of the war must have come as a relief, not just in terms of ending the awful fighting. She had spent six wartime birthdays at Windsor Castle. Within its walls she had been made Colonel in Chief of the Grenadier Guards; it was there that she came of royal age; and there that she signed her first State papers as a Councillor of State while her father was abroad. The secluded days were over at last in the spring of 1945 when she made her first visit to Royal Ascot; the crowds cheered and the King was even more conscious of the love and respect he and the Queen enjoyed from his people. The monarchy had been restored to the pedestal from which it had tottered during the pre-war days of Edward VIII; nothing must be allowed to damage it again.

Politics, protocol and the very sensitive feelings of the King's great British and Commonwealth public were to be considered in the marriage of the heir to the throne, and George knew better than most that difficulties could arise on Philip's side of the family – not to mention the King's own – that would have to be tactfully overcome. Mountbatten, too, was well aware of the problems and earnestly set about smoothing a path as soon as he returned from Burma, glistening with decorations to which the King added the Order of the Garter and an earldom. Mountbatten made little secret of his intentions to gain British nationality for his nephew and threw his full weight behind that single goal.

First, however, there was the reunion. Philip sailed back to England in January 1946 and, the first night he obtained leave, he made straight for Buckingham Palace where he was to be entertained to dinner by Princess Elizabeth, with her giggling, precocious sister Margaret acting as chaperon. Philip was full of spirit, full of talk about his adventures and marvelling at Uncle Dickie's command of the South-east Asian situation. Peels of laughter came from the three of them as the evening went on; but if at the end of it Philip and Elizabeth were eyeing each other with matrimony in mind and thinking that now nothing could stand in their way, they were to be proved very wrong.

Not least of the problems arose in Philip's home country, where King George II was still being refused entry – a shuddering fact of life which had also suddenly faced King Peter of Yugoslavia and was about to confront Philip's other cousin King, Michael of Romania. Similarly, the monarchy was being abolished in Bulgaria, Hungary, Albania and Italy, and there was no sign of its returning in Spain under Franco's Fascist regime. German 'Royalty', already in difficulties when Hitler came to power, was fractured and confused.

In Greece, virtual civil war had broken out between Royalists and Communists and the arrival of Anthony Eden as peacemaker demonstrated the seriousness with which the British viewed the situation. Republicans believed that the longer the King could be kept at bay, the better it would be for their cause; then he would never return. In March 1946 the Monarchists won the first election since 1936 and a temporary solution was arranged whereby Archbishop Damaskynos, who was seen to be entirely neutral in his Church position, would be declared Regent pending a plebiscite to obtain the nation's view on the return of their King.

Until this was done, any further moves that Philip wished to make, both in terms of his career with the Navy and his official courtship of Elizabeth, must once again be delayed, since both rested on his application for British citizenship. Mountbatten's approaches – which included conversations with the Prime Minister, the Home Office, the Foreign Office and the King himself – made no difference.[2] His argument that many foreign nationals – and German scientists in particular – were being granted British citizenship with ease brought the same response: until the Greek situation had been resolved, nothing more could be done for Philip. Britain could not be seen to be taking sides on the issue and to grant Philip naturalization could be taken as lack of interest in the restoration of the Greek monarchy, due for resolution by national vote on 1 September 1946.

During that summer, we are told by Robert Lacey, Elizabeth and Philip had taken matters into their own hands and had become unofficially engaged during his visit to Balmoral, where he stayed for a month with the rest of the Royal Family on their summer holiday. A long, romantic walk one day ended with a proposal – or, it had been suggested, a mutual acceptance and declaration of their love for each other – as they sat in the heather beside a small blue lake. Royal-watchers in the press moved their comments on from speculation about a royal engagement to a more hostile tone, imploring them to stop shilly-shallying and make the announcement.

The King had a 'serious talk' with Philip during that month's holiday at the suggestion of his then aide and confidant, Group Captain Peter Townsend. It has been said that Townsend suggested the inclusion of Philip in that summer's party at Balmoral as a vetting procedure; certainly Philip's relatives have spoken and written since of how he received the 'Balmoral treatment', which amounted to being put through his paces under various guises of deerstalking, sporting events, royal formalities and deep conversations, less formal parties and the usual royal game-playing such as charades (through which various reluctant politicians have, over the years, sat with endurance). Often, when Philip and Elizabeth were out riding, Townsend himself tagged along with Princess Margaret as chaperons.

Was he reporting back to the King? Who knows? Who cares, even? Except perhaps Prince Philip did. When he was told some years later that Townsend had suggested the 'going over', Philip exclaimed, 'What an infernal cheek . . . for a man already heading for divorce to set himself up as a marriage counsellor.'³ Philip, well used from his boyhood days to staying for long summers with whomever had offered him accommodation that year, overstayed his welcome at Balmoral. King George told Townsend, 'The boy must go south!' No engagement yet; quite the reverse.

The King authorized a statement from Buckingham Palace in early September categorically denying rumours of an imminent announcement. Sir Alan Lascelles, the King's Private Secretary, sardonic and saturnine, stated unconvincingly: 'Princess Elizabeth is not engaged to be married. Nothing is known of any impending engagement.'⁴

By then the situation in Greece was virtually resolved – George II had resumed the throne in 1946 – and, though it had been put forward as the reason in the past, therefore did not in itself totally explain George VI's reluctance to give the signal for a public courtship leading to engagement. He knew, however, what his daughter probably did not: that certain developments in Germany in the immediate wake of the war might yet blow up in all their faces and could be publicly damaging to the young couple's romantic aspirations. Cautious, careful handling of this situation was required, along with some co-operation from allied politicians. In fact, there were sufficient worrying matters to push the issue of Philip's possible engagement to his daughter well down the list of the King's priorities.

The plain fact of the matter was that, in September 1946, King George was still not at all sure whether he could allow the engagement to proceed. The whole matter must have weighed heavily on the tired King's mind in those difficult days; he was a man who treated every problem with great seriousness and study, and who thought through the consequences of his actions to the finest detail. We must surely consider that he was seriously concerned about the news emanating from Germany.

The final pieces of the story which demonstrate his concern did not emerge until 1987 when US Attorney John J. Loftus, an Intelligence expert and specialist in Nazi history who worked in the US Justice Department as a special investigator in the hunt for Nazi war criminals, came across previously classified documents relating to British dealings with the Nazis at the end of the war. His knowledge is such that he was called to give evidence at the Canadian Duschene Commission on 'hidden' Nazis and his findings confirm the author's own research, which had revealed a quite startling sequence of events at the end of the war. They demonstrate that in the eighteen months prior to Philip's engagement, the King's attention was distracted by developments in Germany to such a degree that he could be excused his extreme nervousness of Prince Philip – not because Philip himself had any Nazi affiliations but because of the whole German scene and its relationship both to the King himself and, more damagingly, to Philip. Under a Labour government and without Churchill to protect them, there was every possibility of difficulties arising that would jeopardize the future of the monarchy itself, let alone the marriage of the King's daughter.

On 29 April 1945 the American Army liberated Dachau and found Prince Philip of Hesse. Their list of potential Nazi war criminals was consulted; Philip was target number 53 and a high-priority capture.[5] Despite his suffering in the concentration camp and the death of his wife Mafalda in Buchenwald, he was immediately re-arrested by the Americans and confined in one of the Operation Ashcan compounds to join what the Americans had nicknamed the 'striped pants set'. Internees included scientists, doctors, diplomats, Wehrmacht officers, Intelligence experts and, like Philip of Hesse, those with particular connections.

This operation rounded up several thousand alleged German war criminals, many of whom were quietly set free without charge for various reasons, including co-operation with Allied Intelligence and scientific expertise. Attorney Loftus says that US Justice Department attorney Henry Wohrheide quietly delayed reviewing voluminous Nazi documents captured by the Allies while the internees were questioned. Furthermore, there was a tacit agreement between the British and Americans to help each other conceal Nazi affiliations among their own nationals and the US military had 'special instructions to spare the British royal family embarrassment.'[6]

It was through this agreement that the British authorities learned of boxes of documents, papers and letters relating to the British House of Windsor, stored in the Hesse family castles then in the possession of the Americans. At one castle in particular several boxes of sensitive papers were found in the attic rooms – a fact which was first confirmed to the *Sunday Times* by Prince Wolfgang of Hesse in 1979. The castle was that of Philip of Hesse's family, Schloss Friedrichschof at Kronberg, which had been commandeered by the Americans as a GI social and rest centre. The Hesse matriarch, Princess Margaret, lived in a villa nearby along with her sons and daughters-in-law. The officer who found the documents reported immediately to his superior, who informed Army Intelligence. One of the two Intelligence men who came to examine them later confirmed that some of the papers related to communications between

Hitler and the Duke of Windsor. The boxes also included intimate exchanges between the Hesses and the British Royals dating back to Queen Victoria.

Two or three weeks after the arrest of Prince Philip of Hesse, sometime in early May 1945, a British contingent arrived in an Army truck at the village of Kronberg. The truck brought two men on a special assignment: Anthony Blunt, an MI5 officer carrying covering papers from the OSS Art Looting Investigation Unit, and the then Royal Librarian from Windsor Castle, Owen Morshead, whose mission was so highly classified that even MI5 was prevented from an investigation thirty years later, according to Peter Wright in *Spycatcher*.[7]

Whatever the material was, it has never been seen since and is locked away in the Royal archives, the contents known only to King George VI and his successors. Most of the historical material was later returned to the Hessian archives in Germany. Blunt and Morshead were eventually knighted, though Blunt was stripped of his honour when his treachery was revealed. He retained his silence on what he brought back, even after he had been discovered and disgraced as a Russian agent. He also consistently denied that his knowledge of the contents of those files had anything to do with the fact that he was not publicly unmasked when his spying first became known, nor sacked as Surveyor of the Queen's Pictures until media pressure brought his case into the headlines some eight years after it became known that he had worked for the Russians.

On that spring day in 1945, Morshead and Blunt arrived at Kronberg carrying a letter from King George VI requesting the Hesse family's permission to remove sensitive documents to England – a matter on which only Prince Philip of Hesse, as titular head of the family, could give authority. Blunt obtained a signature from Princess Margaret, then aged seventy-two, for the removal of these documents, amounting to over 1,000 pages. The speculation that they included what became known as the 'Windsor File' on the Duke of Windsor's conversations with Hitler, and Prince Philip of Hesse's own early messenger-boy contact with Windsor and others, has now received corroboration in so many quarters that it is believable but not provable.

But that is not the point of relating the story in this context; it merely provides the starting-point for the next sequence of events, which, more definitely, could have led to the King's delaying his daughter's engagement.

The arrival of two British officers bearing a royal warrant and permission to search the castle intrigued American WAC Captain Kathleen Nash, who was nominally in charge of the GI rest centre. She told her boyfriend, Colonel Jack Durant, who was serving close by; he in turn brought in another Army friend, Major David Watson. Together they worked out that the castle might yet yield other treasures or documents that they could sell for a high price to either collectors or newspapers.

What they in fact discovered was beyond their wildest dreams.

As they made their search, a task which was made easy by Nash's control of the castle, they went down into the cellars and there came across an area of brickwork which looked newer than the rest. They tore away at it and revealed an entrance to another part of the cellar. It contained 1,238 bottles of fine vintage wines dating back to 1834; more importantly, it lead the plunderers to the Hesse strongbox – a huge chest lined with lead which had been buried beneath the flagstones.

They worked at it secretly, day and night, until the box was open. They stood aghast and laughing: before them lay millions of pounds in jewels, plus royal treasures of incalculable value; they pawed over their haul for an hour or more to let it sink in, looking like three escapees from a 1940s B-movie adventure – a scene doubtless mirrored on a smaller scale by other post-war looters.

The three American officers were so stunned by what they had found that they closed the lid and went away to consider their next move. They thought of taking a few small items and then decided to steal everything. They convinced themselves that it was legitimate wartime booty because it had belonged to ardent Nazis, some of whom were perhaps dead and the property might therefore never be returned. It was a standard excuse for all those caught looting and hundreds got away with it.

The theft was discovered in April 1946, when members of the Hesse family sought permission to go back into their castle to retrieve their jewels. Prince Christopher's widow, Princess Sophie, was about to remarry and she and the Hesse women were going to put on their finery for her wedding to Prince George William of Hanover. In the ruins, they were at least going to put on some kind of a 'royal' show. The day before the ceremony they went down into the cellars to open the strongbox.

The guests were assembling. Prince Philip of Greece had just arrived from England. It was the first time he had seen his sisters for seven years. They had wept and hugged him and said how much he looked like their father. Now the women were crying for a different reason. When they had reached the strongbox they had discovered it had been cleaned out. The American military police were informed and began their investigations.

By that time, Kathleen Nash had concluded her tour of duty and had returned home to America for discharge. She and Durant were about to be married themselves. They were arrested separately on 8 June 1946 and questioned by military and FBI investigators, who used newly introduced lie detectors to extract the story. Kathleen Nash broke down first. She told how they had brought most of their haul back to America and pinpointed the places where it had been hidden. They had planned to sell it selectively over a period of years. It was hidden in a number of locations, some of it in a house at Hudson, Wisconsin. Other less bulky items were stored in left-luggage lockers at a Chicago rail terminal. As police gathered up the haul, it was brought to the Pentagon where amazed military chiefs viewed the property as it was spread out on tables for an inventory to be prepared. The report of that day's work concluded that there were 'enough jewels to fill the windows of half a dozen shops on Fifth Avenue.'

Girl secretaries in the Pentagon modelled the items as military photographers took pictures to be produced in court evidence. They giggled and paraded through the Pentagon corridors wearing the Hesse treasures, which included tiaras, brooches, rings and necklaces set with the finest stones: diamonds, pearls, rubies and emeralds. Literally hundreds of other stones were loose in paper bags, having been prised from their settings to make them unrecognizable when sold. There were also various Hesse family heirlooms and memorabilia dating back to 1601 – including nine volumes of letters from Queen Victoria, bound in black leather edged with gold. As the military police spread out the Hesse property, they naturally gave a prominent place to what they considered one of their most important finds: a large Nazi emblem in solid gold. The total value of jewellery recovered was estimated at £1.5 million but at least another twenty per cent had already been sold off and was never retrieved. The family heirlooms, such as the Queen Victoria letters, were recovered intact.

The case against Nash, Durant and Watson was dealt with not in America but by a military court in Frankfurt, which began taking evidence in October 1946 – four weeks after the denial of an engagement in the British Royal Family. The case was adjourned on a number of occasions and was not finally concluded until May 1947. Watson got three years, Nash five and Durant, as the most senior ranking officer, was sentenced to fifteen years.[8] Strangely, the case received little publicity. The *New York Times* carried an initial lengthy report of the theft while *The Times* in London felt it merited very little of their valuable newsprint. No connection was drawn between Philip of Hesse and the British Royal Family, nor especially the relationship between the Hesses and Prince Philip of Greece, who was by now regularly in and out of the social headlines. Back in London, the royals must have breathed a sigh of relief.

There was, however, still the unresolved question of what would happen to Prince Philip of Hesse. He had still not been tried before any court of justice. The months during which he and his family awaited a decision on his eventual fate are surrounded in what can only be described as a convenient silence. Having been imprisoned by Hitler for eighteen months before the war's end, he was now in US military confinement where he was interviewed regularly and brought before examining lawyers from Nuremberg. Presumably the delaying tactics of the US Justice representatives mentioned by Attorney John Loftus were used. True, Philip of Hesse was an important Nazi, but more by association and title than actual deed. Alongside some of the horror stories, his contribution to the Nazi cause did not rank high.

However, he was held in custody for a further thirty months while the headlines relentlessly documented the deeds of some of his former colleagues in the inner sanctum of the Third Reich. He was eventually brought before the Denazification Tribunal in Frankfurt on 19 December 1947, one month after the wedding of Princess Elizabeth to Prince Philip of Greece (the two events may or may not be connected; there is simply no way of knowing from available declassified documentary evidence). The tribunal sentenced him to two years' imprisonment, ordered the confiscation of one-third of all his property and, because he had been 'classified as a Nazi activist he is therefore deprived of the right to vote, to hold office, or engage in any profession for a period of five years. He is also deprived of owning a motor car or firearms of any description.'[9]

Philip of Hesse, having already served more than the two-year sentence, was quietly – in fact in almost total silence – released to return to the family home. In England, his release was covered with a small news item in *The Times*; no connection was made between Philip of Hesse and Philip, formerly of Greece, who had just married the King's daughter. Mountbatten must have been well pleased. Not so Philip's German relatives. According to the Kaiser's daughter, Princess Victoria Louise, who died in 1980, 'other princely families suffered greater privations but none so undeservedly' as Prince Philip of Hesse.[10]

If all this was not sufficient to give King George VI many sleepless nights, then the thirty roles of microfilm found buried close to the German castle of Friedrichshof, along with a selection from the 500 tons of German documents being collected up by the Allies for sorting and examination, certainly was. 'King fussed about the Duke of Windsor file and captured German documents,' wrote Sir Alexander Cadogan in his diary on 23 October 1945.[11] Among the documents on German foreign policy were some relating conversations between the Duke of Windsor, when he was King, and his Nazi cousin Charlie Coburg. Others, of course, contained details of his contacts with the Germans while in Spain and Portugal and these were considered among the most damaging, relating to Hitler's attempts to woo Windsor into 'holding himself in readiness to return to the throne' – an ambition the Führer maintained until the end of 1943. George VI was shown examples of the contents. Prime Minister Clement Attlee and Churchill both took up the cause to have the documents – which Attlee judged to be 'of little or no credence' – destroyed or locked away. The Americans were joined by British historians in the campaign to have the documents saved for posterity, though it was finally agreed, as we now know, that their contents should not be released until 1954. King George, ironically, would not be there to oversee publication and, one month before his daughter's Coronation as Queen Elizabeth II in June 1953, Winston Churchill – by then back at Number 10 – wrote to his friend President Eisenhower. The memorandum, headed 'SECRET AND PERSONAL', implored the President to 'exert your power to prevent publication'.[12] Eisenhower replied, effectively telling Churchill there was nothing he could do. However, Churchill did succeed in getting the most sensitive documents suppressed until 1957. These related to the Duke of Windsor's treacherous contact with the Nazis in Spain and Portugal in 1940, while he decided whether to take Churchill's offer of exile to the Bahamas or to throw his lot in with Hitler for the 50 million Swiss francs which Schellenberg claims the Führer was willing to pay him to be ready to return to England as King. It mattered not whether the Duke was cast the sinner by those who believed he was in willing contact with Hitler or whether he was sinned against by over-ambitious memo-writers, as his apologists have claimed. The fact remains that highly damaging remarks were attributed to Windsor which everyone knew he was quite capable of making.

What other secrets brought back by Blunt and Morshead remain untapped will continue to provide speculation for historians, though the total rejection by the 'highest authorities' of Peter Wright's attempt to question Blunt in 1967 suggests that the contents will remain firmly under lock and key. Perhaps Philip Ziegler will yet reveal all.

There were other outstanding matters to be dealt with in the aftermath of the war. The King found himself having to consult with his ministers over his continued relationship with his European relatives and especially the former Regent of Yugoslavia Prince Paul and his wife Princess Olga, who were still languishing in South Africa and had become a thorn in the side of the authorities there. The Yugoslav government was demanding Paul's return as a war criminal but the South African government regarded him as a political refugee entitled to the normal rights of asylum. George VI held Paul in a rather better light than most of his ministers; he still saw him as an anglophile who could in no way be treated as a criminal. Moreover, for the forthcoming royal visit to South Africa, he sought governmental approval at least to acknowledge the man who was brother-in-law of his own brother's widow and also cousin by marriage to the man his daughter wanted to marry.

A response to the King's discreet request for guidance came through the Foreign Office in a note stating that it would be 'preferable if such a meeting could be avoided because it would be likely to give rise to unfavourable comment . . . and steps should be taken to ensure that neither Prince nor Princess Paul be present at any public function which Their Majesties may attend.'[13] This was indeed translated as an instruction to the King that he should have no public contact whatsoever with Paul and Olga and any meetings should be in private.

It was doubtless during these times of somewhat strained contact between the Palace and Westminster that King George gloomily pondered the future of the monarchy – thoughts which came more frequently now through the initially uncomfortable relationship he had with Clement Attlee. Although the King was supposed to be above political party, it was more difficult to be above class – though Mountbatten succeeded in cutting across the divisions – and the arrival of a Labour government in effect confronted the King with a new social order which, at its extremes, would eliminate the very system that supported the continued presence of a Constitutional monarch. 'Everything is going nowadays,' he said grumpily after learning that one of the great stately homes had gone to the National Trust. 'Before long, I shall also have to go.'[14]

This was all detail to which King George VI had access between 1945 and the end 1947 as Philip and Elizabeth were coming ever closer to each other, to the point that an engagement was being rumoured almost weekly. The devoted parents had so much on their minds as they watched their daughter falling more deeply in love and they continued to stress, for all the reasons we now know, the dangers of too much haste.

It was as one that they selected a play for the young sweethearts to see in London's West End one night when Philip asked permission to take Elizabeth to the theatre; it was called *The Hasty Heart*. Perhaps the King and Queen were trying to point a moral.

In October 1946 rumours started again when the first photograph of the couple together was flashed around the world; they were pictured side by side at the wedding of Mountbatten's daughter Patricia to Lord Brabourne. With such publicity, in the eyes of the nation's royal commentators there could be few remaining doubts about romance.

It was clearly serious enough for Mountbatten to consider his next move – an unprecedented step taken a month later when he made contact with senior executives of the Beaverbrook newspaper empire; the contact was unprecedented in that he and Beaverbrook were locked in battle. The newspaper proprietor had consistently castigated Mountbatten for 'errors' during the war and especially blamed him personally for the defeat at Dieppe when 900 men, mostly young Canadians, were killed in action and another 2,000 taken prisoner. From that moment, hardly an item appeared in Beaverbrook's newspapers which did not remind readers of the Dieppe fiasco, ignoring the views of war chroniclers that the guilt was equally borne by many others in the Allied command. Nevertheless, Beaverbrook continued to amass a file of Mountbatten misdeeds and wrote that he 'did not trust him for any public office'.

There can be little doubt, therefore, of Mountbatten's intentions of

28 November 1946 when he invited three Beaverbrook executives to his home in Chester Street: he wanted to take the wind out of their sails. Moreover, the meeting had echoes of the 1936 co-operation which Edward VIII achieved from the British press when Beaverbrook led the conspiracy of silence over the King's affair with Wallis Simpson, not a word appearing in British newspapers until a few days before the Abdication Crisis began. Headlines had raged around the world while at home the King's subjects remained blissfully unaware of his associations.

On a chilly winter's evening, the three newspaper men were ushered into the Mountbatten sitting room: Arthur Christiansen, editor of the *Daily Express*; John Gordon, editor of the *Sunday Express*; and E. J. Robertson, Managing Director of Express Newspapers. Mountbatten welcomed them with warm handshakes and grasped Christiansen around the shoulder as they walked in. Edwina was on hand to add her charm and style. Then the subject of this strange meeting, Prince Philip of Greece, rose from his chair, was introduced all round and dispensed the drinks before quietly resuming his place in the corner without pouring anything for himself. Mountbatten began his little exercise in sycophantic public relations by outlining his reason for inviting them along: to seek the advice of three such eminent communicators on the best way to handle his nephew's forthcoming application for British citizenship. What would be the feeling of the press and the British public? It was an odd enquiry.

Though Philip's name had been suggested as a suitor to Princess Elizabeth, it seems unlikely that the great British public would have cared much at all about the naturalization ambitions of an obscure Greek prince about whom they had, until recent months, heard virtually nothing – unless of course he really was set for the higher station in life which had already been denied; or unless there were background reasons that might publicly damage him, like having a couple of Nazi brothers-in-law.

Mountbatten always insisted that the meeting was purely for the purposes of discussing Philip's quest for British citizenship and that no mention was made of the young man's possible future role of consort. Nor was there to be any discussion of Philip's odd royal upbringing at the hands of his uncles; of his father's death in poverty, separated from his wife; or of his mother's having taken a nun's habit and dedicated her life to aiding the poor. Nor of the German connections.

John Gordon recalled that during the meeting Prince Philip

> told us frankly how deep was his affection for the Princess and hers for him. And that their engagement would be announced soon. Yet for weeks after that the Palace press office continued to deny emphatically that there was any foundation whatsoever for the suggestion of a marriage. An odd set up, isn't it?[15]

Mountbatten later furiously rejected the idea that any mention of an engagement was made at the meeting in Chester Street and continued to insist that Gordon's memory had 'played him false'. Such protestations were not unnatural for him as a disguise to his earlier indiscretions. Sincere or not, the fact remains that Uncle Dickie considered he had out-manœuvred three hard-nosed Fleet Street executives, who advised him there should be 'no problems' in view of Philip's war record and his very English appearance. Lord Beaverbrook, on hearing what had transpired, was said to be angry that his three top men had been so disarmed. Again, it seems odd that such feelings and bitterness should be aroused simply over Philip's attempts to become a British citizen. As far as Beaverbrook was concerned, the matter would not rest there.

It was a miserable winter, cold and snowy. At Christmas, Prince Philip was invited to join the rest of the Royals at Sandringham, which merely fuelled the open suggestions that, in its denials of a forthcoming engagement, Buckingham Palace was blatantly lying.

That had not been an unusual stance for Palace public relations officials in the past; nor would it be so in the future. Similar denials came when the Queen was pregnant, variously over Princess Margaret's romantic affairs and intentions, over the engagement of Princess Anne and other notable royal events in which rumour was subsequently proved correct. However, in this particular instance, there were more understandable circumstances. The King was still withholding his permission and now it would have to wait for at least another five months while the Royal Family embarked upon a major overseas tour – and, as we have seen, the resolution of the trial involving the Hesse jewel theft and decisions over the fate of Philip of Hesse.

In January the couple were together again at Chester Street when the King and Queen brought Princess Elizabeth to a family dinner with Dickie, Edwina, Philip and David Milford Haven, shortly before the Royal Family set sail for an important visit to South Africa. The Mountbattens were preparing to go to India, where he was to be the last Viceroy and oversee the nation's bloody progress towards independence.

On 1 February the King and Queen with their two daughters sailed away aboard HMS *Vanguard* – which Princess Elizabeth had christened during the war – leaving behind a nation in the grip of one of the worst winters for decades and with a tottering post-war economy that could hardly stand these added difficulties.

The King needed sunshine; the onset of the illness that would soon kill him could be seen in his face. It was an important and arduous tour as well: South Africa was touchy and unconcerned about remaining in the British Empire, which was still George VI's greatest ideal. The Royal Family's main task was to arouse the loyalty of the South Africans and persuade them to stay in the Empire. The King did not want the main thrust of his visit to be diverted by the marital aspirations of his daughter or her suitor's unsavoury relations. In fact, there were many long conversations between father and daughter as the *Vanguard* made its way to the Cape of Good Hope and the King's aide, Brigadier Stanley Clark, maintains that it was during this outward journey that King George finally realized that his elder daughter had arrived, almost without his noticing, at young womanhood. Clark said:

> The laughing girl with the lovely golden hair, wonderful pink-and-white complexion and beautiful blue eyes had been a child to him throughout the war years. Now she was suggesting full entry into the world. He was cautiously responsive . . . but had mixed feelings that his elder daughter was now ready to bear some of the burden of one of the world's most difficult jobs.[16]

That realization became clearer a few weeks later when, on 15 April, the Royal Family visited the grave of Cecil Rhodes in the Matopo Hills outside Bulawayo. At the top of the hill, after a steep climb, Princess Elizabeth stood alone for a moment, gazing across the bush country below. Her father watched her, then turned to one of his aides and spoke the incredibly prophetic words: 'Poor Elizabeth. Already she is realizing that she will be alone and lonely all her life; that no matter who she has by her side, only she can make the final decision.'[17]

Was it any wonder that the doting father was being so protective?

Chapter Eleven
Marriage

Whatever else Prince Philip of Greece might bring to a union between the future monarch and himself, his contribution could certainly not be judged in materialistic terms. Apart from his little car and a few personal possessions, he travelled light. Mountbatten's footman and valet at Chester Street, John Dean, remembers having to wash and iron his shirts and underclothes, which he usually brought home at weekends; he possessed few changes of clothing.[1] His naval uniform was in constant use – as Queen Mary once noted, 'he looks a bit shabby, that post-war look' – and of his two or three suits, one was an evening suit lent to him by Mountbatten and one a blue lounge suit salvaged from his father's possessions brought from Monte Carlo. Though the latter was slightly moth-eaten, Philip had the holes darned and the suit altered in shape to his slimmer build and he continued wearing it for a number of years. He also used his father's ivory-handled shaving brush daily.

These recollections, plus a prissy account of life with Prince Philip, right down to the style of his underpants, came into public view when Dean joined a number of other royal servants and associates who rushed into print with their 'secrets' both before and after the wedding, much to Their Royal Highnesses annoyance. It was a route to substantially more money than was on offer as a Palace servant which Philip quickly closed when he came to power! John Dean and royal governess Marion Crawford were the initial 'betrayers'. Others followed, until the threat of legal action and the requirement to sign a secrets declaration prevented further revelations. This did not, of course, include Philip's impoverished cousin ex-Queen Alexandra of Yugoslavia, who told all in her family portrait of the Prince.

Philip was surprised at the media attention he attracted and he hated it. Personal matters that he considered no one else's damned business came tumbling forth in abundance. We soon learned, for example, that his balance at the bank was about £6.10s and that his total income was

£11 a week from the Navy. He had no hidden wealth, no call on any funds or property on foreign soil and no bequests. Like Prince Albert, he brought nothing except himself and his ancestry.

Unlike Albert, his other main attribute, the prefix of 'Prince', disappeared at the end of February 1947 when he finally gained his naturalization and British citizenship, renouncing his claim to the Greek throne and becoming plain Lieutenant Mountbatten. The formality cost him £10 and was announced in the *London Gazette* along with the successful applications of 800 other post-war immigrants – a motley bunch that included German Jews who had fled the horrors of Hitler, some scientists who were going to show us how to build nuclear bombs, some Nazis who had changed their identities and found shelter, and some true European heroes justly rewarded with citizenship for their service to the British wartime cause.

The choice of Philip's name itself had involved discussions with the King, because as a member of the Greek royal house he did not possess a surname or family name. The College of Heralds was consulted and came up with the suggestion of Philip Oldcastle, based upon an anglicized version of one of the old dukedoms in his family tree, Oldenburg. But Oldcastle was dismissed by almost everyone; someone said it sounded like a Yorkshire brewery or a factory manager to whom trouble at t'mill is reported. Even the Home Secretary, Chuter Ede, got involved in the discussion and thought it should be something with a more substantial ring – 'grander and more glittering'.[2] Things had reached an important stage if a senior member of government was being consulted over a surname for a minor member of Greek Royalty.

The discussions continued. Uncle Dickie said not a lot until the crunch came and, unsurprisingly, the adopted name of Philip's mother's family was selected. It served the dual purpose of giving him a name and tying him firmly to Earl Mountbatten of Burma, a hero still to most of the nation (with the possible exception of readers of the *Daily Express*). So Philip Mountbatten it was and Uncle Dickie's eyes must have glistened with emotion at the prospect of a British Royal Family bearing his own family name, a prospect now within sight.

Ironically, one month later, Philip learned that he would have moved closer in line to accession to the Greek throne, unstable though it was. King George II died suddenly after the months of strain of the war and watching his country once again torn in civil unrest and political upheaval. He personally had led the campaign against the Communists but they had won by outlasting him. Paul succeeded to the throne with his Queen, Frederika. Courageous they were, but precarious times once more lay ahead for Greece and Philip must have been thinking to himself that he was as well out of it. Certainly his prospects were improving by the minute in England.

Engagement edged closer. HMS *Vanguard* sailed back through a storm, appearing out of the early-morning mist off the southern coastline of England. Princess Elizabeth danced a jig on the deck as they reached the shore and Princess Margaret's eyes were hardly deflected from their fixed gaze towards Peter Townsend.

Between the serious, very serious, business of delivering her first ever speeches of importance, the elder of the two sisters was talking young-woman talk, about Philip and marriage. Lovelorn, she could not wait to see him again. Lovelorn, Princess Margaret was looking longingly towards another woman's husband. The pair had been thrown together by circumstances; Townsend, by the nature of his work, was always around and was first choice – simply through availability and age – to accompany Margaret, or be at her side, at any of the many official duties they had all performed as a family business unit in the preceding months. What had begun between Townsend and Margaret was in all innocence, but by virtue of their enforced togetherness they were also being caught up in the wash of the romance of Philip and Elizabeth. Nothing could stop either developing. And in the end Philip would be the man who had to sort it out.

Expectancy filled the air. Philip was not among the gaggle of VIPs at the quayside to welcome the royal party home on 11 May – 'I can't see him anywhere,' said Princess Elizabeth as she peered into the crowds from the dock. But later that day he arrived at Buckingham Palace, where he had a brief meeting with the King who then made an excuse and left the room, leaving his daughter to discover her suitor waiting to greet her. In the coming weeks there were many meetings and outings, away from the prying camera lenses. Philip took Elizabeth to see his mother, now living at Kensington Palace; they went on outings to the countryside and managed to walk unnoticed through Richmond Park – he in dark glasses and she wearing a headscarf. Philip's cousin Marina, Duchess of Kent, provided them with private hospitality for lunches and dinner at Coppins, as did the Brabournes. The newspapers re-ignited the rumours that an engagement was on the way and the crowds shouted 'Where's Philip?' as Princess Elizabeth was launched into her own diary of public engagements.

The family waited with baited breath. Still King George withheld his consent. The Greek problem had long been resolved and to the public at large there appeared no other constraint to an engagement.

The King held back for another two months while the politicians and heads of Commonwealth governments were informed of the marriage plans. And then he discovered that his fears about Philip's reception by the British public were entirely justified when a newspaper poll[3] showed that forty per cent of those approached were opposed to Princess Elizabeth's marrying a foreigner. Philip was a foreigner, Greek, German or Danish – no one was quite sure. A veil was conveniently drawn across his itinerant past. A forty-per-cent vote against was bad enough. What would it have been if the nation and the media had been in possession of the wider knowledge of which only the King and a few of his politicians had been made aware?

Nervousness prevailed as the Royal Family proceeded, slowly but surely, to the point of finally announcing the engagement on 10 July 1947, when, according to the approved version of events recorded by the King's biographer Sir John Wheeler-Bennett, 'there could no longer be any question as to the wishes and affections of both parties, and their pertinacity and patience were rewarded.'[4] Philip had arrived at the Palace two days earlier with an engagement ring which included diamonds provided by his mother, who had given him her own engagement ring for restyling; he and Elizabeth had chosen the design themselves. At last the 'meandering', as Princess Margaret described the long wait, had come to an end and, despite the ominous opinion polls, a great display of public joy and affection for the young couple was soon being displayed. Crowds, thick and dense, went to the Palace gates, as they always do on such occasions, and when the couple joined the King and Queen at one of the scheduled Palace garden parties, all eyes were upon them.

The British people were indeed ready for some celebrations, but many politicians and public figures were of a mind to deprive them of it and use the money for more practical purposes, like homes and food and clothing. The nation had been starved of joyous moments; hundreds of thousands were trying to rebuild their lives. Widows whose dead husbands were buried somewhere abroad struggled through these austere days not knowing how they would manage to bring up their fatherless families. In every major industrial town the bomb sites were still being cleared, and scattered in the rubble of the Luftwaffe's devastation lay the remnants of a former life, a home where children's laughter once rang out. Poignant memories; desolation, poverty and even fear had only been made worse by the shivering, desperate months of the coldest winter on record this century, when factories ground to a halt and electricity supplies were intermittently shut down. In many respects, Britain was worse off than during the days of war; now its people faced the task of re-establishing life, though they knew things would never be the same again.

And now, stepping smilingly, happily through these traumatic times was the romantic image of Britain's best-loved young woman, displaying to the world her intended husband, tall, handsome and looking occasionally strangely out of place. His betrothal was secure, but those opponents who distrusted the arrival of 'another foreigner' into the midst of British Royalty – and there were many – would not let their opposition die. In the months leading up to the wedding and beyond, Philip faced the stark realities of being brought to the heart of the world's greatest throne.

As King Peter of Yugoslavia observed when Philip was presented at his first Palace garden party: 'They've wasted no time. It's rather like throwing him to the lions.'

The animal analogy was used, incidentally, by other members of his family. Philip himself is on record as noting after the first clutch of newspaper articles about him that 'I read about myself as if I were some animal in a zoo'. Queen Wilhelmina of The Netherlands reminded him that/with his engagement to Elizabeth he was 'entering the royal cage'.

His bride-to-be was, of course, well used to such a situation. Philip, conversely, had never been troubled by his royal prefix and his impatience with the protocol of it all was soon apparent. Arriving at Buckingham Palace one day, he discovered flunkies rushing to open the door for him and responded abruptly, 'I've got a bloody pair of hands, man.' There were those ready to remind him of Prince Albert's words as consort to Queen Victoria: 'A Royal consort should entirely sink his own individual existence in that of his wife . . . should shun all attention, assume no separate responsibility before the public.' And of Queen Victoria's own prophecy for her husband, that his 'path will be plentifully strewn with thorns'. Never again would Philip be able to so much as blow his nose in public without attracting attention, or travel on bus or tube, or call into the local pub unnoticed for a swift pink gin. Whatever he did from that July day forth would be observed and faithfully recorded by the ever-present onlookers, snoopers and peepers.

He had a quick experience of this when, dashing back to his shore-base at HMS *Corsham* one rainy night, his sports car skidded off the road and landed in a hedge. He suffered little damage personally, and any young officer other than himself would have escaped without note; but Philip starred in a mass of headlines reminding him to be more careful. There was more at stake now 'his well-being is essential to the happiness of the heiress to the throne'. Soon afterwards, there was another slight altercation when his car touched the side of a taxi at Hyde Park Corner. More headlines.

The snipers and critics were ready and waiting, and there would be plenty of ammunition to fire across the young couple's bows as Britain prepared for what Winston Churchill described as 'a flash of colour on the hard road that we travel'. Churchill was out of office but was called upon to second an Address of Congratulations in the House of Commons, in which he used a quotation from *Troilus and Cressida:* 'One touch of nature makes the whole world kin'. From the bottom of its heart the nation sent good wishes and goodwill 'to the Princess and the young sailor who are so soon to be united in the bonds of holy matrimony. That they may find true happiness together and be guided on their paths of duty and honour is the prayer of us all.'[5] Later, Churchill invited Philip to a private lunch to impress upon him 'how serious it was, marrying the heir to the throne'. The lunch was arranged at the suggestion of

Lord Mountbatten,[6] who thought it a good idea for a man of Churchill's stature to give the young man the benefit of his thoughts. Still Mountbatten was pushing!

Support or advice from any quarter was probably gratefully received, for at the time an unseemly row was being waged over the £50,000 required to make Clarence House habitable as the first home for the newly-weds. Hadn't Buckingham Palace with its 600 rooms enough suitable accommodation for them?[7] And then there was the question of their country home, a weekend retreat at Sunninghill which the King had given them as an engagement present. The grace-and-favour house close to Windsor had been used by the Army during the war and also required heavy renovations. In fact, the local council was on the verge of requisitioning the property for conversion into flats for the homeless, of whom there were many. As the controversy raged, fate – or some enraged saboteur? – played a hand. One night in August, the house at Sunninghill mysteriously caught fire and was burned to the ground.

Clarence House was nowhere near ready by the time of the marriage. It was so dilapidated after wartime use as a Red Cross centre that it would take almost two years to complete the improvements and in the meantime, just as the critics had suggested, minor modifications were made inside Buckingham Palace to provide an apartment for the couple, using Princess Elizabeth's existing and ample suite of rooms on the second floor. Philip was given a room close to Elizabeth's with a sitting room between his bedroom and hers. As far as Philip was concerned, anything that slightly resembled permanency was better than he had ever experienced.

His rooms at Kensington Palace, to which he moved after the engagement, with David Milford Haven in an adjoining bedroom, were incredibly spartan – just scrubbed floorboards with a few threadbare rugs; they were reached by stairs and a hallway with creaking floorboards which alerted Philip's grandmother whenever he and David arrived home late. More than once, the two of them clambered over the roof to their bedrooms to avoid waking her.

In the run-up to the wedding, the discussion continued over the privileges being shown to the couple in such dire times. Prime Minister Clement Attlee had many heart-searching talks with his cabinet over the expense. Left-wingers were all for a ceremony more in keeping with the ration-book syndrome of the late forties. Others thought that the public would welcome a great show of pomp and circumstance. Plans were considered to stage the wedding quietly at St George's Chapel, Windsor, but, even as these details were revealed, letters of protest quickly arrived at *The Times*. The *New York Times*, then an observant commentator on life in England, noted the need for 'a welcome occasion for gaiety in grim England, beset in peace with troubles almost as burdensome as those of war.' And so a major celebration it was to be, egged on by Mountbatten, ever the showman and ever ready to project his family at their best.

Two more delicate manœuvres remained. The King had been in correspondence with the Archbishop of Canterbury over Philip's Greek Orthodóxy. The Archbishop suggested a course of action to resolve any embarrassment and Philip duly arrived with Elizabeth at Lambeth Palace where the Primate performed a short private ceremony admitting Philip to the Church of England.

The second matter concerned titles. It could hardly be conceived that the heir to the throne should marry a commoner, which at that time is exactly what Philip was; he was without title, plain Mr Mountbatten. In consultation with Attlee, the King agreed to bestow upon his son-in-law on the eve of the wedding a grand array of ermine which would make him anything but common: Philip, Baron Greenwich, Earl of Merioneth, Duke of Edinburgh. As the King himself admitted, 'It is a great deal to give a man all at once but I know Philip understands his new responsibilities on his marriage to Lillibet'.[8] In doing so, the King gave Philip the prefix 'His Royal Highness', although the title of 'Prince' of the realm was not granted to him until 1957. They were titles lightly earned, though seriously thought out. They were a demonstration of the King's own power and influence, and were carefully chosen to cover the spectrum of Philip's new life: Baron, as the lowest in the order of nobility and usually connected with a town or village, was to reflect his naval connections; Merioneth provided him with a Welsh link; and for the dukedom King George turned to Edinburgh for the dual purpose of providing a Scottish tie and a family descendancy – Alfred, Queen Victoria's second son, had also been Duke of Edinburgh. Alfred, as we saw at the start of this book, would have been King of the Hellenes had he accepted the Greeks' offer back in 1863. Had he done so, of course, Philip would not have been there on that day accepting Alfred's old title. What strange turns of fate have administered themselves on this man's life.

In the midst of all this activity, Philip seems to have given thought to retaining at least some degree of 'private' life into which he could disappear without fear of publicity to escape the rigours of Buckingham Palace officialdom and the duties he now faced as consort to the heir. One of the escape routes he chose was to join with others in forming a 'stag' club where he and his friends could meet privately, swear if they wanted to, tell bawdy jokes, play games, let off steam, dine and drink in all-male company. Larry Adler recalls the formation of the group, which called themselves the Thursday Club; he believes he and Prince Philip are now the only surviving founder-members.[9] There were fifty or so men in the club, drawn from a fairly diverse collection of professions. Philip was brought into it by Baron Nahum, one of the preferred Court photographers, known to the world simply as 'Baron'; one day he was to hire as an assistant one Antony Armstrong-Jones.

Baron came into the royal circle through Mountbatten, who 'discovered' him in Malta in 1935 and won him his first royal commission by getting the Duke and Duchess of Kent to allow him to photograph them and their children. From then on, Baron became a Court regular and one of Philip's early friends there. Through him the young Duke was introduced to the high life of London in the forties and fifties, which, with hindsight, it might have been better to have avoided. Like anyone slightly flamboyant in post-war London, Baron was gathered up by the gossip columnists. Philip and his other best friend and party-goer David Milford Haven could hardly be ignored. Philip managed to stay out of the scurrilous little news items, though there were murmurings, as Adler recalls: 'There was already a lot of talk about an affair that Philip was supposed to be having with a French singer [Hélène Cordet] and there was supposed to be a child by her. It was before he got married, though.'[10] Philip continued to see Hélène, often, and had visited her in Paris in the spring of 1946 when she was distraught and penniless – he turned up unexpectedly one day and took her for a meal at the Ritz; then she moved to London again to be with her mother and their friendship continued.

Male-type gossip was one of the features of the Thursday Club; who was doing what with whom and where. But the real purpose of the Thursday luncheon was little more than a social booze-up in interesting company. Other members joining the merry band included the rumbustious actor James Robertson Justice; his friend the wit Peter Ustinov; the rascally artist Vasco Lazzolo; Donald Ogden Stewart, the American writer who won an Oscar for his screenplay of The Philadelphia Story; Harry Kurnitz, another American writer; Arthur Christiansen, editor of the Express, whom Philip had first met at Mountbatten's house; and his opposite number on the Mail, Frank Owen.

They gathered each week in the top room on the third floor of the famous Wheeler's Restaurant in Old Compton Street, Soho, where they paid a set price for lunch, wines and vintage port. There were no formalities, no protocol, no 'Royal Highness' titles observed. Philip was plain Philip, even after he had acquired his various titles. It was a fairly right-wing group, though Adler himself became known as the 'token Red', having been blacklisted in America during the McCarthy purges of Hollywood. Adler's memory of the lunches provides an insight into the humour that prevailed.

'I was arguing with Philip one day about the British public-school system which I considered virtual factories for manufacturing homosexuals,' Adler said.

'Good God, Adler,' roared James Robertson Justice, who never spoke quietly about anything. 'Are you on that dreary hobby-horse of yours

Φίλιππ

Traditional Greek costume for a young prince of the Hellenes but Philip of Greece, then five, was already living a nomadic life in western Europe following his father's banishment under threat of execution from the country of his birth. (Private collection)

Left: Philip's immediate ancestry on his father's side included a Queen of England. His grandfather, George I of the Hellenes, assassinated before Philip was born, was married to Grand Duchess Olga of Russia (pictured centre). George's sister, Alexandra (right) was destined to become Edward VII's Queen. (Hulton-Deutsch Collection) *Below:*The Battenberg line which produced Philip's mother began with the morganactic marriage of Prince Alexander of Hesse-Darmstadt to a commoner, Julie Hauke. He was banished as a result of the marriage until his brother repented and gave Julie a vacant title, Princess of Battenberg. (Hulton-Deutsch Collection)

Below: Alexander and Julie's first son was Prince Louis of Battenberg, pictured here with is own two sons – Prince Philip's uncles – Prince George (right) and Prince Louis (left), who were to become the Marquis of Milford Haven and Earl Mountbatten of Burma respectively and also the major influences on Philip's life. (Popperfoto)

(Inset): Philip's father, the handsome Prince Andrew of Greece, pictured on his twenty-first birthday when he was an officer in the German military. *(Popperfoto)* *(Main picture):* First picture of Prince Philip in his mother's arms in 1921. Soon afterwards, the child was being packed into an orange box as his parents dramatically fled the country. (Daily Mirror)

Above: With an unsettled home life, Prince Philip often found solace with his Continental relatives. Here, in 1928, he was holidaying in Rumania with his sisters and cousins: left to right, Princess Theodora of Greece, the boy King Michael of Rumania (his father had just been de-throned after trouble over a mistress), Crown Princess Helen of Rumania, Princess Irene of Greece, Princess Margarita of Greece, Prince Philip and Prince Paul of Greece. (Camera Press) *Left:* Philip with his mother and father, Prince and Princess Andrew, at Berck-Plage in 1927. (Private collection)

Opposite page, top: Philip's grandmother, the chain-smoking Princess Victoria, Dowager Marchioness of Milford Haven (second from left) with her daughter and son-in-law, Prince and Princess Andrew of Greece and their two eldest daughters, Theodora and Margarita who both married German princes, taken in November 1923. (Press Association)

Below: The third of Philip's sisters, Princess Cecilie, married George Donatus, Grand Duke of Hesse, pictured here with their family in 1937. Tragically, the Grand Duke and Grand Duchess and their two sons were killed soon after when a plane carrying them to England for a family wedding crashed. Cecilie was expecting their fourth child at the time, and the baby in arms in this picture also died later. (Daily Mirror)

Left: Philip's second eldest sister Princess Theodora married Berthold, Margrave of Baden who became Philip's headmaster during his brief stay at the German school of Salem from which Kurt Hahn was evicted by Hitler. Hahn later founded Gordonstoun and Philip was among his first pupils (Popperfoto)

Right: Prince Christopher's brother, Prince Philip of Hesse was another of the German princes closely allied to the Third Reich and became a member of Hitler's inner circle and his personal contact between other European Royal houses. (Keystone)

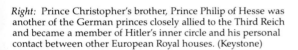

Left: The youngest of the Greek princesses, Sophie married Prince Christopher of Hesse, a devout Nazi and close associate of Goring. He was killed in a plane crash in 1942. (Daily Mirror)

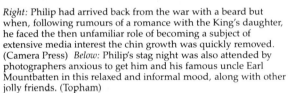

Left: A charming informal picture of Princess Elizabeth and Prince Philip in the grounds of Earl Mountbatten's home at Broadlands where they spent part of the honeymoon besieged by photographers. (NPA Rota Picture, *The Times*)

Right: Philip had arrived back from the war with a beard but when, following rumours of a romance with the King's daughter, he faced the then unfamiliar role of becoming a subject of extensive media interest the chin growth was quickly removed. (Camera Press) *Below:* Philip's stag night was also attended by photographers anxious to get him and his famous uncle Earl Mountbatten in this relaxed and informal mood, along with other jolly friends. (Topham)

The wedding of Princess Elizabeth and the newly-enobled Duke of Edinburgh on 20 November 1947, came at a time when Britain was suffering from the deprivations of post-war austerity. But the nation put on a happy face and rejoiced in the most public wedding of the era. (Press Association)

Philip often enlisted prominent figures from the world of showbusiness in his work for charity, notably for the National Playing Fields Association. *Below:* He found himself surrounded by showgirls at a charity gala evening in theatreland in 1948. (Topham) *Right:* He chats to American star Rhonda Fleming prior to dinner at the Empress Club sponsored by the Variety Club of Great Britain. (Topham)

Below: He ignored criticism from establishment circles that he was lowering standards by allowing himself to be photographed with Frank Sinatra and his wife,, Ava Gardner, who accepted the invitation to appear in a Midnight Matinee gala on 8 December 1951. The result was that the Playing Fields Association benefitted with a very substantial donation. (Topham)

Above: Boats, planes and horses became three of Philip's prime interests in the fifties and photographs of him became a familiar aspect of daily newspapers. Here is an unusual one. Taken on board the 20-ton yacht *Sea Breeze*, Philip is sitting astride a horse-riding saddle which had been fitted for his comfort by his friend Uffa Fox while they competed in the Britannia Challenge cup at Cowes in August 1955. Next to the Duke is his then private secretary, Michael Parker. (Topham)

Above: Another great passion of the era was polo, to which he was introduced by his uncle, Lord Louis Mountbatten. At this moment, between matches in 1952, Philip is sharing a joke with a young spectator who asked, "Are you really a Duke?". (Topham)

Left: Flying became another obsession. Here, in flying helmet, he is seen at the controls of a Blackburn Beverly transport aircraft in April 1956. (Topham)

Left: The Canadian press noted that he was having a "dandy" time during a Royal visit to Canada and Philip certainly joined in the party when he donned jeans and a checked shirt for a square dance in Ottowa. (Topham) *Below:* The world tour carried out by Prince Philip in 1956/57 as his personal contribution to the Commonwealth ideal attracted considerable criticism over the expense and length of time he was away from his family. As usual, he disregarded the opposition and gave an unfaltering account on television, including a demonstration of this interesting spinning wheel he picked up in Tristan da Cunha. (Camera Press)

At the time, they still shot tigers for fun in India and Philip proudly poses with Queen Elizabeth II in front of the 9 foot 8 inch animal he killed on a tiger hunt during the Royal tour of India in 1960. (Camera Press) It would return to haunt him in future years as he became one of the world's leading conservationists, as (*left*) when he became president of the World Wildlife Fund and expressed the view, beneath the photograph of a threatened panda, that conservation was man's moral duty. (Camera Press)

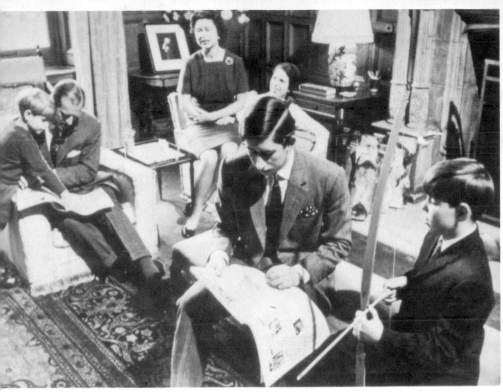

Above: Media interest in the Royal family was heightened considerably by a television film which received worldwide acclaim. It showed them, in 1969, as a family group and in a way that no previous Monarch had allowed. This photograph, of the Queen and Prince Philip with their children, Charles, Anne, Andrew and Edward, released in April 1969, typified the new image. (Fox Photos) In contrast, almost twenty years later, the informal scene is repeated this time with the grandchildren. (Sunday Mirror)

Left: The Goon Show comedians, Harry Secombe, Peter Sellars and Spike Milligan, were always firm Royal favourites and especially with Philip and Prince Charles. This moment of hilarity was captured in 1972 with Lord Snowdon, Princess Margaret and Princess Anne joining the fun. (Topham)

Right: In more familiar pose . . . Philip is at the side of the Queen during the traditional carriage ride at Ascot in 1987.

Left: And for the Trooping of the Colour, Prince Philip is accompanied by Prince Charles (left) and the Duke of Kent (right). (Camera Press)

Above: The balcony scene: Philip has been there for the big moments of Monarchy for half a century, adding cheer and ice-breaking jokes for these special family moments. (Sunday Mirror) *Right:* An informal greeting which shows the fondness that exists between himself and his daughter-in-law, the Princess of Wales. (NPA Rota, Daily Express) *Below:* Old comrades of his uncle Dickie, the surviving members of the Burma Star Association were in good humour for this meeting at the Cenotaph in April 1986. (Press Association)

The rock of monarchy and the epitome of consort, Prince Philip adopts his familiar constitutional position for a state opening of Parliament. (Mirror Newspapers)

again? Look, I was buggered in my first week at Eton. Did it do me any harm?'

To which Adler retorted, 'I suppose everyone had to watch – so that Justice was not only done but seen to be done.'[11]

On another Thursday, Philip and David Milford Haven, also a member, waged a £5 bet with Baron that he could not photograph the cuckoo coming out of the clock at precisely 3 p.m. At 2.58 Baron was poised with his camera, but on the stroke of three, Philip and David threw two smoke bombs into the fireplace. There was a terrific bang and the room filled with soot from the restaurant chimney, which had not been cleaned for years. Adler said the police outside in the street heard the explosion and rushed upstairs to find what looked like the cast from a well-dressed black-and-white minstrel show. 'It took a lot of explaining,' said Adler, 'and even more diplomacy, to keep the incident out of the papers.'

And was that the same day of another incident in Trafalgar Square? They were all walking towards The Mall from Soho when Donald Ogden Stewart lay down full length beside Nelson's Column and asked a passing pigeon 'Any messages?'

Somewhere in a bank vault, there may lie some rather disgusting caricatures of Philip. One of the members was a gifted caricaturist and used to sit through lunch making drawings of fellow members in imagined compromising situations. The drawings are thought to have been locked away with the club records but no one seems to remember where they were deposited. Anyone seeing them now could well get the wrong impression.

Innocent fun, they all agreed, though somewhat schoolboy in its nature. But really, what would the starchy courtiers of Buckingham Palace have to say? Philip did not seem to care, or even to give it a thought. Adler said he would not allow protocol of any kind to get in the way of his lunchtime enjoyment. 'I think he liked it and felt that it was a relaxation that was good for him. We all liked him; he was just a damned nice fellow.'

More worrying were the parties at Baron's flat; soirées and dinner parties which were not generally for the likes of his Thursday Club friends – though some did attend – because of their sexual connotations. Girls dressed only in Masonic aprons featured regularly as waitresses and hostesses but, though he had been a regular guest at Baron's for dinner, the Prince is unlikely to have risked his reputation. David Milford Haven, however, had no such qualms.

Back in the real world, the grumblers grumbled on. Attlee's Minister of Health, Aneurin Bevan, declared that under no circumstances would he wear an evening suit to a pre-wedding party at Buckingham Palace and left-wing MP Richard Cobden wrote to the King to 'remind you that any banqueting and display of wealth would be an insult to the British people at the present time.'

That did not stop the continuing worldwide display of affection. By now the wedding presents were arriving by the truckload, some of which noticeably reflected the concern of overseas onlookers that the royal couple might be short of clothes. A man from Milwaukee sent Philip a duffle coat trimmed with beaver; his old skittle team, the Methuen Moonrakers at Corsham, sent a pair of flannel trousers – a welcome addition to his depleted wardrobe; someone else sent Princess Elizabeth a mink coat, while another clearly had one eye on the make-do-and-mend philosophy by despatching a sewing machine to her. Mahatma Gandhi had taken to the thread himself and sent a piece of cloth he had personally crocheted from cotton that he had spun on a traditional Indian spinning wheel. (Queen Mary wasn't impressed. She hadn't liked Gandhi since his supporters gave her son David, when he was Prince of Wales, such a hard time during his Commonwealth tour of India in the twenties. Philip was courageous enough to disagree, and said Gandhi was a man to be respected. Stoney faced silence came back from the old Queen.) Others were less practical and displayed some opulence that still existed elsewhere, like the Shah of Persia's magnificent Persian carpet – what else? – and a Maharajah's ivory table, ideal for displaying some of the silver ornaments. There were 1,500 gifts in all.

Prince Charming he wasn't. Wedding-eve nerves had got the better of Philip, along with the realization of what lay in store. First, he had attended a brief family ceremony when his prospective father-in-law touched him on the shoulder with a sword and officially bestowed upon him his new titles. An additional investiture made him a member of the Most Noble Order of the Garter, an honour which King George had given to his daughter eight days earlier to ensure her seniority. Then Philip left for his stag night, putting on a jolly front for the press horde who had been invited to photograph his party at The Dorchester. It was followed by a stag night proper for members of the family and close friends.

Two days earlier, there had been a 'secret' stag night organized by Baron and his chums from the Thursday Club; they wished they hadn't bothered. True, it was a robust and ribald occasion with Philip the butt of their humour and drunken antics. Philip himself did not enjoy it. Larry Adler remembered him being 'too scared; he just looked so damned frightened. There was a kind of constraint the whole evening because of it. He seemed terrified of what he was getting himself into.' David Milford Haven, as best man, was naturally also present at the 'secret' party. He was elected 'Cunt of the Week' at the next meeting of the Thursday Club for selling his account of it to the *Daily Mail* – an act which Philip considered one of betrayal, the unwritten rule of never talking officially to newspapers having been broken by the very man he trusted most in his own world.

Uncle Dickie, back from the strife of India and under renewed attack from certain sections of the press,* was on hand to help see his nephew through his last hours of bachelorhood. Mountbatten also provided a piece of dynastical symbolic weaponry for the marriage itself by loaning Philip his father's bejewelled, ceremonial sword to wear with his uniform; thus the link to the Battenbergs was maintained visually as well as in spirit.

Philip was up bright and early for the big day, 20 November 1947. No hangovers. He had imbibed moderately the night before, unlike Milford Haven. Down at Claridge's, The Dorchester and Brown's, various members of European royal houses were having their tiaras and finery polished. In the stately homes of England, the ermine and blood-red capes of their lordships had been dusted down for the procession to Westminster Abbey. It was a great display of pomp such as only Britain is capable of providing, even in impoverished times; yet there was a touch of pathos. As they paraded in, the commentators identified them: the King and Queen of Denmark, the King and Queen of Yugoslavia, the King of Norway, the King of Romania, the King of Iraq, the Queen of the Hellenes, Queen Helen of Romania, the Princess Regent and Prince Bernhard of The Netherlands, the Prince Regent of Belgium, the Crown Prince and Crown Princess of Sweden, Queen Victoria Eugénie of Spain, the Count and Countess of Barcelona . . . It was the largest gathering of the monarchies for ten years, but in that time their greatness, their influence and their importance had been diminished beyond recognition. Where once any one of them would have merited a State occasion for their very arrival, they trooped in through the great masonry of the Abbey somewhat dispirited. Only memories of past glories remained as they watched the marriage of a young couple in whose hands rested the survival of the last great monarchy on earth.

---

* A view not entirely shared by the public – he was cheered one night when he was spotted during the interval at a performance of *Annie Get Your Gun* in London's West End.

Chapter Twelve
Hopes and Realities

Any hostility towards Prince Philip among the establishment who blamed Mountbatten for consorting with 'the enemy' in the partition and disposal of India was outweighed by the avalanche of public support and happiness for the bride and bridegroom. Ten thousand telegrams, the wedding presents and the cheering crowds on the streets spoke volumes. The glamour of the wedding, as one writer put it, jerked the British out of their one-candlepower lives and tossed them into dreamland.

Mountbatten recognized the intensity of feeling against him among the old aristocrats who thought his handling of the Indian situation 'traitorous', yet he was desperate to be among his nephew's supporters:

> This was a great moment in the history of our family, yet such was the state of affairs in India in November 1947 that I had grave doubts whether I ought to go to London for the wedding. Of course, I wanted to badly and the Indian government settled matters for me by saying that if I didn't it would make the atmosphere of crisis in India appear even worse. For me, it was a splendid interlude in the midst of the hardest work I have ever done in my life . . . and then it was' back to India where the crisis atmosphere was still intense.[1]

His arrival also gave food for thought to those enemies who believed that he would, through his nephew, now begin to stage-manage the monarchy. It was no idle consideration and one which would certainly not have escaped Mountbatten's own thoughts as he weighed the future for his protégé.

There were still rumblings from the left of the Labour government over the expense and extravagance. Wasn't the rest of the nation toiling hard, regardless of the marriage? Another unpleasant little incident arose over whether the wedding day should have been declared a public holiday. 'Certainly not,' said Clement Attlee. 'The nation cannot afford it.' A school holiday was thought appropriate, however, and Attlee sent a Cabinet official to Buckingham Palace to broach the question with the King, suggesting that it might be announced that Princess Elizabeth herself had wished there to be no public holiday. The King refused to accept the idea. It would throw upon his daughter's shoulders the responsibility for a decision which, if expressed in such a way, might arouse criticism.[2] By the time of the wedding, Attlee had introduced various austerity measures to tighten further the nation's slender belt.

An example of the extremely sensitive and political nature of all things connected with the 'happy couple' occurred when it became known that silk for the Princess's wedding dress was coming from abroad rather than from home production, thus avoiding the clothes rationing. The King ordered his Private Secretary to write personally to Attlee to explain that

> the wedding dress contains silk which originally emanated from Chinese silkworms but was woven in Scotland and Kent; the wedding train contains silk produced by Kentish silkworms woven in London. The going-away dress contains about four to five yards of Lyons silk which was specially imported but was part of a stock held by the dressmaker (Mr Hartnell) under permit.

And that wasn't all. The King's missive pointed out that earlier, when the Palace had asked for guidance over where 'ornaments' necessary for the wedding dress might be purchased, the Board of Trade itself had suggested a firm called Pompadour Products, run by an Austrian woman who had only just become a British subject – a 'recommendation which threatened us with an appreciable amount of embarrassing publicity.'[3] If they were getting into a flap about a former Austrian national supplying decorations for the Princess's wedding dress, little wonder that Prince Philip's continental connections had been cause for concern. What would they have said about Philip of Hesse?

In a week when the meat ration had been further cut to a shillingsworth per person, the wedding breakfast was classed as an 'austerity meal'. But the Palace chefs had been sufficiently imaginative to provide such dishes as Filet de Sole Mountbatten, Perdreau en Casserole, followed by Bombe Glacée Princess Elizabeth, served on the Palace gold plate by dozens of footmen in their scarlet-and-gold uniforms and washed down with liberal supplies of champagne. There were also twelve wedding cakes – made, it was hastily pointed out, from ingredients sent from the Commonwealth; the one that was to be cut by the Battenberg sword was a 9-foot-high creation covered with icing and with sugar-painted panels carrying the Arms of both houses and the bride's and groom's monograms; a slice of it would have consumed the week's sugar ration for the average family. The bejewelled and medallioned guests sat around fifteen circular tables; the 'top' table took the bride and groom, the King and Queen, along with the Kings of Denmark, Romania and Norway, Queen Mary, Princess Margaret and the groom's mother, Princess Alice, who on this special day had been persuaded to discard the grey nun's habit which was now her sole garment and don a flowing gown more suited to such a grand occasion.

It was Princess Alice's deepest regret that none of her three surviving daughters, nor their German spouses, was asked to the wedding. The King's advisers had remained firm: it would be unwise to invite them. They would have to make do with a complete set of the wedding photographs taken by Baron, which Marina, Duchess of Kent, and Queen Frederika of Greece took secretly to Germany four days after the wedding. The Duke and Duchess of Windsor, whose absence – also through lack of invitation – was noted, sat across the water growling to one another. No snapshots were sent to them. They would have to be content with newsreel and press coverage to get a look at the nuptials.

Happy families! The feud continued; past sins too great to be forgiven yet.

The bagpipes swirled and the toasts were made. The King was slightly melancholy that his elder daughter had been taken from him; he set his thoughts down in a letter he wrote to her just before her honeymoon:

> Our family, us four, the 'Royal family', must remain together with additions of course at suitable moments!! I have watched you grow up all these years with pride under the skilful direction of Mummy who as you know is the most marvellous person in the world in my eyes and I can, I know, always count on you, and now Philip, to help us in our work. . . . I can see you are sublimely happy with Philip which is right, but don't forget us in the wish of – Your ever loving and devoted Papa.[4]

It was a touchingly simple letter, which to this day remains one of the most revealing indications of the way in which the King and Queen viewed their own lives and the great burden of responsibility which rested upon their shoulders.

The realities of Philip's task were yet to confront him, but the first indications were lying in wait as the couple reached the first stop of their honeymoon, Broadlands, the Georgian mansion at Romsey in Hampshire owned by the Mountbattens, which Uncle Dickie had insisted they use for their honeymoon. Unhappily, they discovered reporters and photographers surrounding the place, even hanging from trees to get a better view. A peaceful, private honeymoon it would not be. However, the surroundings were lavish enough for the gilded couple; the mansion had all the old-style opulence of the eighteenth century: a sumptuous country house dripping luxury, its warm ceilings decorated with the paintings of Cipriana and Angelica Kauffmann, the walls with their Dali sketches and the rooms furnished with Georgian and Louis XV pieces, handed down through the years to Edwina Mountbatten who was born there.

She had placed her own suite of rooms at the disposal of the honeymooners – the Mountbattens had begun their honeymoon in the same room, for, like Philip, Lord Louis had little money to speak of when he was married – where they could relax after such a hectic, unbelievable day in the soft, homely, pink-flowered chintz and pale-blue décor. Outside, the police force, overwhelmed by the influx of press and visitors, had to enlist Broadlands gamekeepers to patrol the 6,000-acre estate.

There was no let-up from the prying eyes and it soon became clear that the choice of honeymoon venue had been a mistake. They should have hidden themselves away somewhere quiet, said Philip, who was becoming angrier by the minute at being nothing short of the subject of a peep show, surrounded by clicking lenses and people with binoculars. At church on Sunday morning, a thousand people clammered for seats in Romsey Abbey; others jostled for position among the tombstones, walking over graves and creating an unpleasant scene. Philip and his Princess, who would normally have taken their places in the raised pew reserved for the Mountbattens, chose less conspicuous seats at the head of the nave. They were pleased to get away on the second stage of the honeymoon to Birkhall, near Ballater in Aberdeenshire. They discovered that the chilly Jacobean house where they were to stay was surrounded by deep snow and Philip had developed a severe cold. But, save for a host of servants, they were alone at last.

A frosty reception awaited them back in London, where the King was hoping that His Majesty's government would show seasonal goodwill to the newly-weds and grant their allowances from Civil funds without undue fuss. He was to be bitterly disappointed. On 17 December the House of Commons degenerated into an unflatteringly familiar rumpus in which the topic of wrangle[5] was the amount to be awarded to the Princess Elizabeth now that she was married, and the separate sum to go to the Duke of Edinburgh, as he was to be known. The King had even taken the unusual step of sending a message to Parliament making known his feelings that he was 'relying on the liberality and affection' of his faithful Commons. Affection, however, did not come oozing out of the government, many of whose members were totally against paying the couple a single penny. In fact, the Prime Minister sent his Chancellor of the Exchequer, Hugh Dalton, for discussions at the Palace. The King argued that, while he accepted the need for economy, he attached the greatest importance to the traditional procedures being maintained. He

127

explained to Dalton that he could not provide for the couple indefinitely and the Chancellor agreed that it was 'a delicate matter from so many different points of view.'[6] Attlee had earlier set up a Select Committee to investigate the vexing issue and it had recommended that the Princess should get £40,000 and her husband £10,000 per annum. The King felt that neither sum was either liberal or showing any particular display of affection. Had not Prince Albert, Victoria's consort ninety-three years earlier, been given £30,000 a year? At the time Philip was on 26 shillings (£1.30p) a day, with an extra 18s 6d married man's allowance – a good salary for a young man, and in line with a million and one similarly placed young couples throughout the land.

The rumpus became a mêlée in the House. Chips Channon, who once sycophantically allowed King Edward VIII to flick cigar ash into his hand because there was no ashtray, was critical of George VI and thought that the Royal Family had received a 'deserved jolt'.[7] The debate lasted four hours. The Socialists were in favour of substantially reducing the amount to be paid. Many still maintained that Philip should get nothing – suggesting that if indeed the King's new son-in-law required financing to such a degree, then the Royals should dip into their own fortune, or sell off some of their finery. It would never have happened, said Channon, if the MPs had all been invited to the wedding in the first place! Mr William Callacher, a Communist, lashed the newly-weds in a manner to which they would become accustomed: 'If I can live on £1,000 a year, including expenses, why is it necessary for this couple to have £1,000 a week?' Sir Stafford Cripps, who had recently succeeded Dalton as Chancellor, hoped that Parliament might have managed to hold the debate without causing the couple 'any undue distress'. It was essential, he added, that the Duke of Edinburgh must be given an allowance so that he 'may enjoy a proper degree of independence in financial matters'.[8]

When the average family man in Britain earned less than £10 a week, the couple's joint allowance could hardly be seen as modest, especially when the King gave them a further £100,000 – which again was money from the State, having been saved from his Civil List. This was just the start of years of critical analysis of royal finances in which Philip would evolve as a central figure and aggravation. Up to that point, money had been of little concern to him. He had never had any to start with, and anything that came his way in terms of expenses for the job – enabling him to buy a few suits, a decent pair of shoes or two and a nice new Humber would be a pleasant change.

He had never had a home of his own either and the prospect of living with the in-laws at Buckingham Palace was not what he might have hoped for; the King did, however, agree eventually to their taking over a small house in Kensington Palace, known as the Clock House, for two or three months. They also found a country retreat, a house called Windlesham Moor near Windsor. It was owned by financier Philip Hall, who suggested to Princess Elizabeth's secretary John Colville (before he went to Churchill) that the couple might like to rent it. They duly turned up for a tour and became more excited as they moved progressively through the sparkling marble-floored reception hall with its green marble pillars, into the Chinese-style study opening on to a sun lounge, then into a dazzling 50-foot drawing room and onwards up the pine staircases through the seven bedroom suites with fitted wardrobes and dressing tables and with the walls covered in mirrors, all overlooking the immaculate grounds of 50 acres. Next to the existing miniature golf course, Philip could imagine a fine cricket pitch.

It was just what any couple starting out in life would dream of! Nothing changes, as was witnessed in the seventies by Anne and Mark's Gatcombe Park, Charles and Diana's Highgrove Estate, and Andrew and Sarah's much-criticized £5 million home in Berkshire in 1990.

They started married life just as they meant to go on, enjoying all the privileges of their privileged position, regardless of the uncomfortable lives which their subjects, by and large, were forced to accept.

Did they give it a thought? Probably not. They were excited about it and one can hardly imagine even the caring Princess turning to her husband and saying something like, 'Do you think we should have another home like this when so many of our loyal subjects are living in poverty?' The King and Queen agreed they should have it, especially since the house required virtually no work; it had been completely redecorated in 1944. Windlesham became their first real home together. Six resident staff were employed for the house in addition to the Duke's personal valet, John Dean – whom he had brought from Mountbatten's staff – and the Princess's own attendant.

Philip liked getting away from Buckingham Palace, where he was ill at ease with the formalities of Court and their rigid traditions of 'dos and donts' – religiously upheld by staff who jealously and snobbishly guarded their rank and duties as if the world depended upon them. The rules of etiquette were stiff and firm, a hangover from the days of George V and Queen Mary, who were sticklers for propriety and the observation of all aspects of Court protocol. After a brief lapse in the eleven-month reign of Edward VIII all this had been reimposed by George VI, carried to the point where, immediately after the wedding, the King instigated an inquiry into why a certain distinguished admiral among the guests had failed to wear his ceremonial sword.[9]

In the less formal surroundings of Windlesham, Philip could do as he pleased and say what he damn well liked without much fear of upsetting anyone. They had small private dinner parties for their closest friends and at weekends would often go over to Windsor Great Park to ride. Philip also made great efforts to keep fit; first thing he would put on several heavy woollen sweaters and go for a long run around the grounds, just as he had done years before at Gordonstoun, which amused his bride immensely. "I am sure Prince Philip is mad,' she commented to his valet Dean one morning as he returned perspiring profusely.[10]

That Christmas of 1947, Philip joined the rest of the Royal Family at Windsor for the traditional celebrations – his first as a true member of the family. He learned some of his father-in-law's little eccentricities – never to be taken lightly – such as the custom of male members of the group wearing a kilt. Philip didn't have one, so George VI offered to lend him one of his late father's; Philip chose the prestigious Stuart hunting tartan. The King was not amused when Philip made his entrance and gave a mock curtsey. It was the first time he had worn a kilt and he attempted to overcome his embarrassment by humour, without appreciating the seriousness with which the King treated his attire for each occasion. Philip wore a kilt many, many times after that but never again, after receiving his father-in-law's stern rebuke in good old-fashioned Navy language, would he joke about it.

The turn of the new year saw the beginning of what many would term the era of 'Murgatroyd and Winterbottom' or, alternatively, the advent of the 'terrible twins'. It was signalled by the arrival on the Palace staff of Philip's old friend and fun-seeker from the early days of the war Captain Michael Parker, whom he appointed Private Secretary. Murgatroyd and Winterbottom were silly nicknames invented by Philip for himself and his new man as a rather immature disguise. They were adopted from the popular wartime radio programme, ITMA, as Mike Parker's wife Eileen recalled,[11] at times when the two men were seeking relaxation away from the Palace – 'Murgatroyd and Winterbottom will be home late tonight' or 'Murgatroyd and Winterbottom will be going for a stroll', which usually meant they were going off to the pub or to the West End with other friends and might not return until after midnight.

Parker's appointment seemed a good idea at the time. He received a letter from Philip shortly before the wedding suggesting that he might like to become his 'general nanny and factotum'. He grasped the opportunity with both hands, having gone through months of unhappiness since leaving the Navy, working for his wife's grandfather as a salesman in their rope-making company. He suffered gossip about being kept by his wife's family – ironically, his new employer was about to experience the same thing.

Philip's choice of Man Friday caused a few raised eyebrows at the Palace. Parker had no experience whatsoever of royal matters nor, for that matter, of mixing with the kind of high society of State into which his old chum would now be plunged. That was probably the precise reason Philip had picked him.

Philip was surely aware that he would face resentment from certain factions within the Palace who knew as well as anyone that King George would really have preferred his daughter to have married some wealthy, upper-class male drawn from a strictly noble English family and heritage. Such a man would have adapted easily to the ways of the British monarchy, sliding unnoticed into place alongside the establishment and the aristocracy, without critics, questionable background or controversial relations. Such a man would have spoken the language of courtiers, he would have experienced life in the shires and the country mansions, he would have had his own set of friends drawn from a conventional education at Eton or Harrow, Oxford or Cambridge, Sandhurst or the Diplomatic Corps. He would have had an 'in' to the right people.

Prince Philip had none of these. Of course, he was experienced in Palace life. He had been closer to it than most since childhood, but, in an odd way, he was still the outsider. He had few friends, virtually none within the hub of the Royal Family.

When Princess Elizabeth and Philip took possession of their country retreat in January 1948, Mr and Mrs Parker were invited to Windlesham for a getting-to-know-you luncheon. Eileen Parker tells us that she found the Princess warm and welcoming but, of course, always the etiquette had to be observed. She and Mike had been well briefed: they should never speak until spoken to; all members of the Royal Family should be addressed as Your Majesty or Your Royal Highness initially and by the title of Sir or Ma'am thereafter. Men should bow on entering or leaving royal presence and women should curtsey. Only when he was alone with Philip was Parker allowed to let the formalities drop – and then it was back to Murgatroyd and Winterbottom. Philip was far more relaxed when he turned up at the Parkers' flat one day for lunch. All they had was macaroni and cheese, but Philip had brought a bottle of Gordon's gin to make pinks.

Mike Parker's main role would be in helping to arrange Philip's work schedule as he and Princess Elizabeth settled to their increasing workload of official duties and public engagements, though Philip had by no means given up thoughts of pursuing his own naval career. His role as a naval instructor was hardly in keeping with his new royal status and on his return from honeymoon he was moved temporarily to a new job at the Admiralty which he found 'utterly boring . . . pen-pushing and shuffling papers'.[12] He could not have viewed his immediate prospects with any great relish. The King was, after all, only fifty-two years old and the likelihood of Princess Elizabeth becoming Queen in the foreseeable future could not even have occurred to any of them.

The King listened sympathetically to Philip's concern over his career. He too had been wrenched from naval duties when faced with his brother's Abdication. The upshot was that Philip would transfer to the Royal Naval College at Greenwich to undertake a hefty course which would take him towards higher rank and assure him of a continued career – a determination he shared with his Uncle Dickie, who was equally adamant that after his term of office as Governor-General of India had ended he would return to the Navy.

Whatever course Philip eventually took, there were built-in difficulties, echoed some thirty years later by his daughter Princess Anne when she was discussing the identical problem facing her own husband, Captain Mark Phillips. She said:

> I think there is a special difficulty. After all, we normally still think of the husband as number one and his wife as number two, whereas in the case of a royal female who has public duties to perform it's rather the other way about. There has got to be a problem, hasn't there? My father had a naval career and eventually had to give it up. My husband had an army career – he didn't have to give it up, but he would never be allowed to serve in his regiment to the extent that he should and to do the service he joined to do . . . that in itself is a difficulty. [13]

Furthermore, Philip soon discovered that public duties seriously interrupted his work, studies and private life. The engagements began to pile up: the pair were extremely good ambassadors for Britain in terms of the overseas publicity they attracted and at home they raised morale with their round-Britain tours. Apart from the endless stream of relatively minor appearances – opening things, cutting tapes and launching the occasional ship – there were more demanding and nerve-wracking formal occasions. In April 1948 Philip found himself thrust into another 'first': a ceremony of great pomp and pageantry to mark the 600th anniversary of the founding of the Order of the Garter. It was at this hugely elaborate occasion that he and the Princess had the insignia of the Order officially bestowed upon them in the Throne Room of Windsor Castle, along with five wartime leaders who had also been given the Order: Alanbrooke, Alexander, Montgomery, Mountbatten and Portal.

This new insight into the significance and inner workings of monarchy preceded a happier family occasion: the silver wedding anniversary of the King and Queen, although once again the festivities became caught up in the machinations of the politicians. A small committee had been formed the previous February to arrange the anniversary celebrations, which unfortunately fell during a new economic crisis, the handover of power in Palestine and the ongoing bloodshed in India. In addition to the continuing issue of 'austerity' for which Attlee seemed determined to go down in history, Home Secretary Chuter Ede was concerned about the security of the Royal Family during the anniversary procession to St Paul's Cathedral. The King remained firm, demanding a public celebration in the tradition of such occasions, and Attlee again went to the Palace to discuss it. The Prime Minister wanted the official celebration to be held on the Sunday nearest to the day of the actual anniversary so that the working classes would not feel that the Royals were having another party. The King refused to budge and on a superbly sunny day, 26 April, they drove through the streets of London in a state landau amid cheering crowds and, happily, no hint of attempts upon their lives.

Throughout these early months, the first major public engagement for Princess Elizabeth and her husband had been under discussion and the massive amount of political involvement it invoked illustrates once again how worried Attlee was about all matters royal, and conversely how concerned the King was over the attempted restrictions politicians wanted to place on their lives.

This post-war period, with its grave economic situation coupled with Attlee's worry over the workers – surely he could not have feared revolt? – had placed the Royal Family under the closest scrutiny it had received since the First World War. Never in recent history – with the exception of the Abdication period – had a ruling monarch and his family laboured, under such strait-jacketed conditions, which might well have threatened the very continuance of monarchy had George VI been an Edward VIII. It was bad enough as it was. While the nation loved George and Elizabeth for their wartime heroics of just being there, there was still a considerable amount of agitation around over their bountiful lives.

Philip, the new boy used to direct naval discipline rather than contrived political influence, found it difficult to accept. When, for instance, he and Princess Elizabeth began talking about making an official visit to France as soon as possible, it was the signal for interjection from Whitehall. The suggestion was put forward through the usual channels by the Princess's Private Secretary John Colville, who personally felt the excursion was merited by the public interest shown in their wedding throughout free Europe. The King liked the idea, though he felt the tour should have a definite object, such as the opening of an exhibition of English life which was being staged jointly by the British Council and the Foreign Office in Paris in May.

A royal visit to France, however, was a touchy subject for several reasons. The first involved the Royals personally. The Duke of Windsor had made his home in Paris and was still sniping at the King for refusing to recognize the Duchess as Her Royal Highness. Windsor had also been berating all who would listen – including Churchill, Beaverbrook, Attlee and the Foreign Secretary Ernest Bevin – about his 'untenable' position as an ex-King without a job, and about being continually shunned by all and sundry. He was a resident embarrassment that the British Ambassador to Paris, Sir Oliver Harvey – who was bound to invite him to Embassy functions – could do without.

Second, Bevin had been given Intelligence reports of mounting Communist activity in several European countries that could lead to possible *coups d'état* in the spring of 1948. More discussions . . .

Eventually it was agreed that the visit should go ahead and in the third week of May they duly arrived in Paris, where they drove among vast crowds down the Champs-Élysées and through the Arc de Triomphe. The welcome was so moving that tears glistened on Princess Elizabeth's cheeks.

Philip adopted the stance: two paces behind his wife wherever she went and at her shoulder, slightly to the rear, as she surprised everyone by delivering her speeches in perfect French. Ernest Bevin had himself taken an interest in their programme in Paris and had ordered that they should be allowed to visit some of the surroundings, such as Fontainebleau, Versailles and Vaux. He called for a report on the visit from Sir Oliver Harvey, who wrote in glowing terms:

> By this visit Their Royal Highnesses have performed a fine service in the cause of Franco-British friendship. What began as a warm welcome . . . turned in a few hours to a universal expression of personal affection and admiration. It was an unusual experience to see townsfolk of Paris cheer an English Princess from the Place de la Bastille.[14]

Prince Philip played no small part in the success of the visit. Already it was being noted that he was a man who was respectful of his wife's position but did not allow it to transcend the fact that he had a mind of his own.

Their return from Paris was marked by more conjecture. It had been openly suggested while they were in the French capital that Princess Elizabeth was expecting her first child and the rumours travelled back with them to London. And, indeed, it was soon confirmed that a child was due in November. The Princess was advised to curtail her diary for the remainder of the year and this in turn placed greater demands on Prince Philip's time, with engagements mounting up to almost one every day of the week. For the moment his career would have to wait.

During the spring and summer, they also took the opportunity of meeting the politicians who were so involved in their lives. They dined with the Attlees at Number 10 and the following month they met the Chancellor and his wife, Sir Stafford and Lady Cripps, at Number 11.

There were family matters to catch up on too. Though their presence had not been welcome at the wedding, Philip's sisters were invited privately to the seclusion of Windlesham Moor. Princess Sophie was the first to arrive with her two teenage daughters, the Princesses Christina and Dorothea of Hesse. They came quietly into London to a warm welcome from Philip and his wife. They talked children. Sophie had five by her first marriage to Prince Christopher of Hesse and had recently produced a son by her second marriage to Prince George of Hanover. Unseen by the prying eyes of the ever-vigilant press, Princess Elizabeth took her sister-in-law shopping in Knightsbridge and Princess Sophie was the first to present Elizabeth with gifts for the expected arrival. Later that summer Philip's other sisters, Princess Theodora and Princess Margarita arrived with some of their children. If the German faction had felt troubled about being left out in the cold for the wedding, normal family relations were now resumed.

Chapter Thirteen

A Certain Silliness

Throughout this period the King was suffering growing discomfort, which was kept from his daughter for fear of upsetting her during her pregnancy. As they all moved to their Scottish retreat for the summer of 1948, the King and his aide Peter Townsend went for walks during which his troubles were particularly noticeable.

'What's the matter with my blasted legs?' he kept saying to Townsend. 'They won't work properly.'[1] Within a couple of months, the complaint was diagnosed as arteriosclerosis and, with the threat of gangrene developing, the King feared that he might have to have his right leg amputated. The news remained a secret, known only to the King's medical team and the Prime Minister.

The world was concentrating on news from the nursery as the day of the royal birth approached; the new child, second in line to the throne, was being heralded with great public interest. All details emerging from the Palace about the room the Princess had chosen for the nursery, the décor, the staff, the cradle with its 'draped head curtain trimmed in peach satin, covered in cream net' were all feverishly reported to the waiting millions at their breakfast tables. Philip discovered, to his horror, that after being a star performer in the most glamorous wedding for several decades, he was now the husband of the world's most publicly pregnant woman; he was astounded by the intensity of interest.

It was perhaps as a diversion to all this that he sought occasional private enjoyment in a stag environment. The realization that he was now a very public person does not appear to have sunk in. Even when it did, it would not necessarily affect his attitude to privacy. Those who were close to the royal circle consistently noted that the relationship between Philip and Elizabeth was one of 'true love'; their devoted affection for one another, especially in private, unguarded moments, was there for privileged observers to witness and we have been provided with many published examples of such recollections. Yet Philip's former

136

bachelor traits, carefree and seemingly unhampered by the requisites of Court protocol, were also apparent and in the first year of his marriage certain events brought his judgement into question.

When in Northern Ireland, for instance, during his naval course, he and a group of chums decided to cross the border to try out some Eire pubs, disregarding the sensitive nature of the British government's current negotiations with the Dail over the Republic of Ireland Act, and the obvious reflections on all persons royal. At the time, the government of Eire was planning a ceremony to raise its flag from the Post Office at Dublin on the next Easter Monday, anniversary of the 1916 Rising on exactly that spot.[2] With Philip on the Irish trip was Richard Sharples, future MP and Home Office minister, who recalled,

> There were fourteen of us in the taxi going south and the Duke was somewhere under the pile. We drank quite a lot of Guinness in a small town and he thought he wouldn't be recognized. But when we came out, the whole population had gathered. We had to take evasive action to dodge out through the back of the pub.[3]*

Fun, games and sport with the yachting fraternity also brought Philip a mass of pictorial publicity in the newspapers as he entered the sailing world with his own craft. That year, 1948, saw the formation of many friends in that world, including the magnificently rollicking, Falstaffian character Uffa Fox, who was one of the many who crewed on Philip's newly acquired Royal Dragon class yacht, *Bluebottle* – his favourite wedding present. The yacht was launched on 10 July 1948 and took third place in the Royal Yacht Squadron race on the same day. Realizing that he would not have sufficient time to do justice to the yacht himself, the Admiralty provided a sailing master for *Bluebottle* in one of Philip's friends from his youth, Lieutenant Commander Michael Crichton, who took charge during his off-duty time. Others who crewed included Michael Parker, Peter Scott and Clive Smith. Philip himself raced *Bluebottle* for the first time at Lee on Solent on 5 September and came sixth out of fourteen. New experiences, new friendships and extra moments of relaxation. If Philip required a safety valve from the rigours of public life, he found it among his new yachting friends at Cowes and elsewhere that year, and in many years to come. Uffa Fox became a great chum. He was noted for his rumbustious stories, nautical language and parties. At his 300-year-old boathouse overlooking the River Medina at Cowes, he had a sign bearing the legend 'Respectez ma Solitude'.

---

* That wasn't half as bad as the Duke of Windsor, who sent his friend and confidant Kenneth de Courcy to Dublin in 1948 for a meeting with Eamon de Valera to ask if he would mind if the Duke and Duchess made their home in Eire; the Mosleys were already there. De Valera advised against it, de Courcy told the author in an interview in 1987.

Princess Elizabeth did respect Philip's solo appearances at Cowes and seldom, in all the years of his visits there, did she join him. She accepted these outings with the yachting brigade as merely an addition to 'Philip's funny friends' in whose midst, as Eileen Parker soon discovered, wives were unwelcome.[4] Revelry and humour, childish though it may have been at times – like the old joke of putting a rubber car-horn under a cushion, to be repeated one Christmas holiday years later when Captain Mark Phillips produced a fart cushion – were in vogue in that set. It was all pretty harmless, even for the husband of a future Queen awaiting the birth of a future King.

Rather more questionable were excursions during his wife's pregnancy to London's theatreland and night clubs, where incidents occurred which, forty years later, would still keep bubbling to the surface every time someone went to write the definitive story of the 'women in his life'. Following the ever-present inferences over Hélène Cordet, actress and entertainer Pat Kirkwood became the second of the famous young females with whom he was to be linked. The day of Prince Charles's birth was not far off when Philip went out with the photographer Baron, who at the time was having a fling with Pat Kirkwood and had arranged to collect her from her dressing room at the London Hippodrome where she was starring in a show called *Starlight Roof*. Pat had gained a reputation as leading lady in several hit musicals, which eventually led to a Hollywood contract and, like Hélène Cordet, fame on television. Baron and Philip had been out to lunch and had continued on into the evening – quite a regular occurrence after the Thursday Club meetings.

They arrived at the Hippodrome at 11.30 p.m. to pick up Pat, then went on to Les Ambassadeurs, which was packed with other famous theatre people like Michael Wilding, Jean Simmons and Margaret Lockwood. Later they moved on to the Milroy Nightclub where Philip whisked Miss Kirkwood, highly noticeable in an orange fluorescent dress, on to the tiny dance floor and swirled around vigorously. The news travelled like wildfire, of course. Diners from downstairs were soon crowding in to watch the husband of the nation's première Princess dancing and laughing with the actress. Baron had got the sulks and disappeared, though he returned later to drive them all back to his place for scrambled eggs before delivering Pat back to her mother's house at 6.30 a.m.

By then the damage was done. The gossips were gossiping and soon Pat Kirkwood and Philip were the talk of London. Wild stories of an affair developed and later, years later, it was ridiculously suggested that he had bought her a white Rolls-Royce as a silencing present. Kirkwood reflected:

Certainly, it was a fun evening. We danced for about two hours, waltzes, sambas, the lot. I admit that if he hadn't been married, I might have developed a crush on him. He was great company and there was a lot of joking and laughing. But despite all those rumours, we did not have an affair.[5]

Forty years later, in 1988, Miss Kirkwood was preparing memoirs of her showbusiness life and four marriages and wrote to Prince Philip at Buckingham Palace to request his approval to mention the incident. She says he replied immediately, encouraging her to 'put the record straight'.[6] She said she fully intended to do so, recognizing that at the time it became 'very embarrassing for all concerned' and even after so many years have passed 'many people still think I was his mistress.'

Knuckles were rapped over the incident. According to Miss Kirkwood, Philip was summoned to his father-in-law's study where he was asked for an explanation and an assurance that such behaviour would not occur again. Elder courtiers who frowned on the pursuits of the newest member of the family were saying he needed to be brought to heel. But Philip still required the facility for 'letting off steam' outside the repressive atmosphere of Buckingham Palace, which he apparently hated so much.

His association with the Thursday Club continued – less frequently perhaps, but he was still very much a part of that little stag gathering. Larry Adler remembers an occasion when they all went back to Mike Parker's house for a drink, there to find the Greek millionaire Aristotle Onassis and the opera-singer Maria Callas waiting patiently for Philip and Parker to arrive. Onassis and Parker disappeared for a conversation about an aircraft – it seems that while acting as Philip's Private Secretary Parker also had part-time employment as an agent for Lockheed Aircraft Corporation and was trying to sell Onassis a jet.

Adler also recalled a special Thursday Club dinner to which Philip brought Prince Bernhard of The Netherlands as a guest. Bernhard had to leave early to catch a plane and when he got up to go Philip got out of his chair, dropped to his knees, salaamed to Bernhard and said, 'Please give my regards to Her Imperial Majesty.' Adler said the two consorts had been making the point about their respective roles all evening – Philip comparing his own with Bernhard, who, he said, had a free life because no one recognized him. 'You can go where you like, see who you like and even have affairs and no one knows,' said Philip, 'whereas I am known everywhere and I am constantly being trailed by secret service men.' Adler said Philip moaned regularly about his 'moral straitjacket and felt really bitter about the position in which he found himself, especially walking behind his wife. He didn't like that; he just didn't like it at all.'[7]

He may well have felt confined both during the eighteen-month wait for his engagement and after his marriage, but it did not entirely prevent him from seeking pleasurable interludes. During the late forties, Baron's parties were becoming notorious. It was the age of breaking out from the constraints of the war, the time of that peculiar mix of London life where girls in cheap utility dresses and American nylons hung around the nightclubs, which attracted a cross-section of clients from the rich and famous, the fun-seekers, the goodtime girls like Ruth Ellis, right down to a few notorious thugs from the East End.

It can only be considered unfortunate that two members of the Royal Family, Philip and David Milford Haven, should have come into contact during this decade with one who was to become an infamous figure in London society in the next. Dr Stephen Ward, though not a member of the Thursday Club, came as a guest on a number of occasions. Larry Adler remembers Ward being brought in by Baron,[8] whose friendship the society osteopath and provider of girls had deliberately cultivated as his route into the avenues of higher society. Through Baron, Ward became friendly with David Milford Haven, with whom he shared an interest in pornography. Milford Haven, it has been said,[9] had acquired a large collection of risqué photographs dating back to the twenties and thirties. He was both a keen giver and attender of parties, especially those which developed into sexually deviant encounters of the kind which he gave at his apartment in Grosvenor Street.

A scan through the gossip columns of the era provides an illuminating insight into the social activities of Milford Haven, Baron and the rest, and the Court photographer's parties at his Piccadilly flat achieved a certain notoriety, which continued until his death in 1956. By association Prince Philip unfortunately found his name plunged into a self-feeding spiral of rumour.

If one excursion had been sufficient to bring the wrath of King George upon him, a second or third must justify a challenge to his common sense. Yet we have been told by Summers and Dorrill[10] that Ward left a memoir in which he claimed that Prince Philip had once, possibly twice, been a guest at parties at his flat in Cavendish Square where he was seen with 'a very attractive girl called Mitzi Taylor', although we are provided with no indication of the dates of this alleged happening and Ward was eventually branded among the legal profession as a notoriously unreliable witness. It was sufficient however for the attachment of a stigma that would arise again with the outbreak of the Profumo Affair in 1963.

In the meantime, David Milford Haven managed to embarrass his cousin still further by having the audacity to marry an American divorcee named Mrs Simpson. It was made known that his presence at the Court of Windsor would no longer be welcome and would he kindly not bring that woman anywhere near Buckingham Palace. The marriage didn't last. A succession of romantic liaisons conducted with high profile through the gossip pages and his equally embarrassing Mexican divorce were followed by an affair with actress Eva Bartok, which ended with her making some publicly hostile comments about his sexual demands on her.

All this, even by mere association, provided the critics with a store of ammunition – true or false – on which they would draw for many years to come. It must, with hindsight, be considered a period of exuberant misjudgement on Philip's part. To suggest that he was out on the town with his 'funny friends' at every possible moment was, of course, a gross exaggeration. These were brief interludes to his mounting royal workload – but, as he learned to his cost, such stories have a habit of being handed down. Mud sticks and events of this phase of his life would return with regularity to haunt him. Perhaps he should have paid more attention to what Stanley Baldwin once described as 'the cruelty of modern publicity'.

The Palace was taken by a curious mixture of joy and worry in the autumn of 1948, with the anticipated arrival of the baby and concern over the state of the King's health, which was still being kept from his daughter. The Princess went happily to the pictures on 10 November, to everyone's surprise, since the birth was imminent. Not a public picture house, of course, but to Alexander Korda's private cinema at the film tycoon's home in Picadilly.*

On 12 November Professor James Learmouth, Regius Professor of Clinical Surgery at Edinburgh University, was called to the palace by the King's medical advisers for a second opinion on his leg troubles; the Buhl Room at the Palace was cleared of its lavish furnishings and turned into a temporary medical centre for the dual purpose of the King's examination and the birth of his grandchild.

On the 14th, Princess Elizabeth went into labour and was given a light sedative before she was wheeled along the corridors from her own room to the Buhl Room by Philip and a doctor. Philip, tense and pacing, went off to play squash in the Palace court with Mike Parker, followed by a swim in the Palace pool and then another game of squash. He was still playing when the news came that he had a son. He dashed over to see the King and Queen in their sitting room and then to see his wife and son. She was just recovering from a post-birth slumber when he arrived, still in sweater and flannels, clutching a bunch of carnations and a bottle of champagne to share with the medical team.

A week later, the seriousness of the King's illness was revealed when the projected royal tour of Australia in the New Year was cancelled. His doctors issued a bulletin which said that he required complete rest to help rectify an obstruction in the arteries of his legs and this treatment would last for a prolonged period. Queen Elizabeth blamed the Windsors, and Wallis in particular. The doctors seemed to concur. There was

* All members of the Royal Family went to Korda's private cinema regularly; they loved to watch themselves on the newsreels and laugh and joke about their own mistakes . . . 'Look at the funny face Mummy's pulling' . . . 'Doesn't Lillibet look stern', and so on. Then they'd collect fish and chips from a favourite shop on the way home and eat them back at Buckingham Palace.

'no doubt that the strain of the last twelve years has appreciably affected his resistance to fatigue.'[11] Things went haywire at the Palace. In addition to the lingering crowds outside the gates trying to catch a glimpse of either of the new parents, plus mail-van loads of presents which needed to be sorted and distributed to the needy, there now came letters of concern and 'get well' messages for the King. Twelve girl temps were hired to help get the regular Palace staff out from under the deluge.

King George was kept informed of matters of government by diligent reports from Clement Attlee, and the start of 1949 saw some major developments of particular interest to him and his family. They centred around what was really the start of the New Commonwealth, in which Princess Elizabeth and Philip would have such a great part to play. It had always been the King's ideal that the Commonwealth should be fostered; the Royal Family recognized that it was their last international power-base. Attlee warned the King, 'It is vitally important to take every step possible to prevent any matter affecting the Crown becoming a subject of political controversy'.[12]

The improvements to Clarence House, the young couple's new home, could hardly be seen as a political matter; but they soon became one. Philip sighed wearily. Didn't they have any sympathy at all? None whatsoever. Clarence House, after the public euphoria of the royal birth, became the focus of a great deal of discussion and Philip's attitude did not help during his regular visits to his new home to see how the work was progressing. He wanted to be in there – and out of Buckingham Palace – just as soon as possible.

He had made a close study of the plans drawn up by the Ministry of Works and was naturally able to inform the workers just where they had strayed from original intentions and how they could rectify their errors.

Princess Elizabeth mixed the paint to get exactly the right shade of apple green for the dining room. Philip saved a bit of money by finding someone who could make gilded light brackets that looked as genuine as other George III fittings in the house. He used the white maple panelling sent to him as a wedding present by the Canadian Pacific Railway to line the walls of his study, and other wedding presents were liberally scattered through the house. (The study, by the way, was designed like Mountbatten's bedroom in Brooke House, to be decorated like a ship's cabin.) Other notable gifts came in handy. Philip's combined dressing room and bedroom came as a gift from the City of Glasgow, created after consultation with the Prince by Scottish designer Neil Morris. The room had fourteen items of furniture, including a divan bed – thoroughly modern, then – which fitted snugly into a recess between the bookshelves and writing desk, all trimmed to the wall linings of white sycamore over hidden cupboards.[13] Like his Uncle Dickie, he had a relish for gadgets and installed some of his own inventions in his bedroom so that when he pressed a button, an unseen cupboard door opened.

Princess Elizabeth's rooms on the first floor overlooking St James's Park – definitely the best suite – were more warmly furnished in rosewood, with drapes of red rose and cream on thick satin, and rose-pink walls. Her other favourite room was the Lancaster Room, one of the main reception rooms, which came complete as a gift from the people of Lancashire.

With so many gifts, how could the repairs to Clarence House be over budget? They were, and very much so! The House of Commons went into uproar again and Labour politicians, quite correctly in view of the circumstances prevailing in the world outside, claimed that the cost had soared to £250,000 against the original estimates of £50,000 which the government had approved. Now it was costing more than the amount required to purchase 400 prefabricated homes for desperate families living in squalor and over-crowding.

Philip brushed aside the criticism. He said all estimates were always exceeded by actual cost and he reckoned that the costs for their new home would come in at under £60,000. Mr Norman Kennedy, secretary of the London district committee of the Amalgamated Society of Wood-workers, made headlines by refusing to believe denials of the extensive overspend and challenged Philip to meet him to discuss it; the Ministry of Works supported Philip, whose fury had been aroused by Mr Kennedy, and said the costs would exceed the original estimate by between £5,000 and £8,000. All very tiresome, no doubt, and the King didn't like his daughter taking the brunt of this awful criticism. In the end, he dipped into his own funds to save any further embarrassment.

Good works. That's what Philip needed, said the King early in the New Year; something to get his teeth into. They were all figure-heads, one way or another. Colonels in chief of various regiments, patrons of this, presidents of that; Philip as yet had no such titles or attributes. The King himself suggested one: the National Playing Fields Association, of which Lord Mountbatten was President. Mountbatten was hiked out of the job and it was handed over to his nephew. As one Palace observer described it, he went at the task 'like a bull at a gate'. After some discussions with Mountbatten, he came up with the idea of a £500,000 appeal fund to finance the building of new playing fields and sports facilities throughout the country. He even jarred the cranky Palace officials by agreeing to go on film with the appeal, which was shown at every cinema throughout the land. He wrote his own script – another aspect of the new ways that struck fear into the hearts of timid courtiers, for ever worried that, in his quest to appear to be speaking 'off the cuff' and without notes, he would say something that would cause offence. He would, and it did, and it all became very much a part of Philip's developing style. Convention went by the board.

Who else in the Windsor family, for example, with the exception of the Duke and Duchess of Windsor, would let themselves be photographed in a nightclub with a recently divorced actress and her new lover, a popular singer? Philip did. He danced the samba with Ava Gardner and chatted with Frank Sinatra. In the late forties, such hobnobbing was an affront to the socialites and courtiers. It was, after all, only a short while ago that, under the strict regime of King George V and Queen Mary, no divorcee should be allowed in their presence.

Following his uncle's lead in showmanship, Philip talked Sinatra into donating the royalties from two of his best-selling records to the playing-field fund and the singer flew over to England specially to give an eight-minute show when Philip staged London's first post-war midnight matinee. In the middle of it all, Ava Gardner's jewels were stolen from her hotel and Philip said how sorry he was. The Playing Fields Association benefited, however, with a £14,000 profit from the appearance of the two American stars – a fact which was somewhat lost in the public furore over Philip's common touch. Sinatra rallied to his support: 'I have found him always terribly kind, most interesting and highly intelligent. He has what I consider to be the most important attribute in a man, a great sense of humour.' British children, whose parks and swings had been melted down for gun metal in the war years, had the best laugh. The Playing Fields Association reached its appeal target within four years – in days when £150,000 was sufficient to finance 400 playing fields, it achieved this sum in the early fifties and still had more than £300,000 in hand for future projects.

As he became more confident, Philip began writing his own speeches, which traditionally were prepared by a Palace aide and given the personal touch by whichever member of the Royal Family was making them. The speeches tended to be merely gracious and formal, without a hint of controversy. Undaunted by the raised eyebrows of courtiers and the King's warning about being too outspoken, Philip pressed on with his campaign for 'more meaningful' speeches and encouraged his wife to do the same. Later in the year, she shocked everyone and Philip's influence was said to be the cause. At a Mothers' Union rally in London, she spoke of the 'age of growing self-indulgence, of hardening materialism and of falling moral standards. Some of the very principles on which the family, and therefore the nation, is founded are in danger.' The sanctity of marriage must be upheld, she said. 'But when we see around us the havoc which has been wrought, above all among children, by the break-up of homes, we can have no doubt that divorce and separation are responsible for some of the darkest evils in our society today.' At the time, the Princess's speech was headlined as one of the most outspoken from any member of the Royal Family in living memory. Reaction from around the world was immediate and generally in support of her views, though there was trouble from the Marriage Law Reform Committee who viewed her words 'with regret'. Divorce and separation themselves were not responsible for the evils to which she referred. Other causes, such as inadequate housing, led to the break-up of marriages. The Princess had stepped straight into a hornet's nest. Politics. Divorce. Poverty. Dangerous topics for Royalty, especially for two who were about to move into their sparkling new home. Forty years later, the rediscovery of these words had a touch of irony.

They soldiered on regardless, not knowing where all this openness would lead. Philip and Princess Elizabeth visited Lancashire in March to say thank you for the Lancaster Room at Clarence House; then they went to Wales and Belfast before returning to London, where the Princess took her first Trooping of the Colour, deputizing for her father on 9 June. The following week, Philip went off alone aboard the HMS *Anson* for a tour of the Channel Islands, which were still clearing away some of the reminders of wartime occupation by the German forces. The two of them resumed their tour of Britain on his return and, midstream, they moved quietly into Clarence House; the noisy protests about royal extravagance had died down and occupation of their new home was noted by no more than a change of address on the Court Circular. And then they took a couple of months off for their traditional summer holidays.

The King looked better and was feeling stronger. Philip was thinking about resuming his career as a result of his promotion after the course at Greenwich; in the early summer he had taken the opportunity of having a word with the King about going back into the Navy. Would there be any objection? These tours were all very well but the thought of a constant round of shaking hands and watching parades and little children presenting flowers and boottees to his wife brought more than a passing yawn. His naval career was still important to him. Lord Mountbatten had already done something about his own life on their return from India: he had requested a more active role than going into the Admiralty to push papers about and lunching at the club, and had been fortunate enough to get the post of Commander in Chief of the British Fleet in the Mediterranean. Philip wanted to join him.

Word leaked out in the summer and there were a few nasty little digs in the gossip columns that Philip could take royal life no longer and wanted to return to the Navy; expressions like 'getting away from it all' were used. There was more than an element of truth in that statement. He had made it plain from the beginning that, although he would temper himself for his job in the crucible of royal precedent, he would not be knocked totally out of shape. Captain Mark Phillips had the same view when he married Princess Anne. In their different eras both Princesses supported their husbands and wanted them to resume service life. In

Philip's case, both he and his wife knew that it must end eventually, but later rather than sooner, they thought. And, of course, there was no pleasing everyone when Philip went back to work. His 'unearned' promotion brought a few comments.

Meanwhile, Malta was agog because the Princess made it known that she would be joining her husband there as often as her own work permitted. This became even more applicable when Philip's ship, HMS *Chequers*, to which he was assigned on 12 October as First Lieutenant was to be dry-docked for some months.

In those days, before antagonism set in and the British fleet left, Malta enjoyed the presence of the Royal Navy base and visiting members of the nobility. The Mountbatten clan had been residents on and off since the days of Prince Louis of Battenberg's charge of the Mediterranean Fleet. The imminent arrival of Princess Elizabeth pleased the Mountbattens no end and sent the island's hostesses dashing to London for new cocktail dresses and gold-embossed stationery on which to send out their party invitations. But enjoying, as he did, doing exactly the opposite of what was expected of him, Philip shunned the smart set and was more often to be found in dungarees down at the docks.

He was back in the sea-salt air at last and the kind of fun he enjoyed was being arranged by Uncle Dickie. He was booked for Mountbatten's Malta polo team for next season and his brand new yacht, *Coweslip*, was brought out by aircraft carrier. He also equipped himself with a nice little runabout, a Sunbeam Talbot, which was rather more down to earth then the motor transport he had been used to of late.

His wife flew out in November to celebrate their second wedding anniversary and caused a flurry of excitement. The Governor arranged a special ball in her honour and there were crowds everywhere when she went out with Philip or went shopping. Almost by instinct, she was soon performing public duties, visiting schools and hospitals. They stayed with the Mountbattens in their rented villa, Guardamangia, where the Princess joined the usual social round for which her husband's uncle was famous.

Prince Charles usually remained in the London nursery with plenty of attention from his grandparents, Philip's mother and the King and Queen. Princess Elizabeth continued with an overloaded diary, which she interspersed with occasional visits to Malta, matched by infrequent return trips by Philip. In mid-April 1950 Britain was beaming again with the news that had been rumoured for weeks: she was expecting her second child in August. Just as a reminder of how important this event was at the time, it should be recalled that Royalty was rather thin on the ground in the late forties compared with the late eighties and the nineties. The King was often out of action, which left the Queen, Princess Elizabeth, now pregnant, Princess Margaret, the Duke and Duchess of Gloucester and Princess Marina to carry the workload.

Her engagements were cancelled from May so that she would not be in the public eye during the later stages of her pregnancy, though that did not stop her going to the races, for the Derby on 27 May and Royal Ascot in June. Philip was also in the news in July, when he returned home on special leave for the birth of their second child – and it was revealed that he had been promoted to Lieutenant Commander. It was speculated that he would get his first command and a pay rise when he returned to Malta.

Mountbatten arranged the promotion to be timed with the birth of Princess Anne on 15 August; Philip was given command of the frigate HMS *Magpie*, again at Malta. Mountbatten himself was already preparing to leave. He had been appointed Fourth Sea Lord back in London, and as a very public sign that she intended to spend plenty of time in Malta, Princess Elizabeth took over the lease of the Mountbattens' villa and forty packing cases of clothes and personal effects were sent ahead of her.

Philip was piped aboard the *Magpie* on 5 September and told his 186 crew that he intended to make her the 'cock ship'. He worked his men hard and, being a commander with such connections – and the added attention drawn by the visits of his wife – the activities of the *Magpie* attracted rather more interest than most others in the Mediterranean command.

All eyes were on him, and his subordinates, which is probably why he pushed them that bit harder, especially in Navy sporting competitions. Later memories of his command from the ranks were not always complimentary. 'He stamped about the ship like a ——ing tiger' was one recollection.[14] Another said he worked his men like hell but treated them as gentlemen. But probably the most biting were comments that he treated the ship as if it were his own private yacht, calling on various members of foreign Royalty who could be reached via Mediterranean ports, including a call at Athens to see King Paul and Queen Frederika and a stop at Corfu to revisit his birthplace. True, it was something of a personal visit, since Princess Elizabeth was tagging along aboard the frigate HMS *Surprise*, fitted out as the flagship and placed at her disposal. It was by way of a surprise, in fact, that Philip had made all the arrangements himself and when the little convoy sailed towards the Greek coastline, he ordered the guns to give their salute. King Paul drove the couple himself in an open car to the family home at Tatoi and the weekend was filled with sightseeing adventures, in which Philip was able to show his wife his homeland for the first time.

As well as his Greek relatives, Philip also began to reacquaint himself with those in Germany. Although protocol prevented the Royal Family's setting foot in the country until the monarch had made a State visit, Philip secretly began journeying back and forth as often as he could to keep in touch, especially enjoying the shooting weekends which his brothers-in-law and cousins arranged for him in the countryside around Darmstadt.

In between times, there were fleeting visits back to England for official duties – and the christening of his daughter in the Music Room at Buckingham Palace in October – and to become involved in the arranging of a forthcoming overseas tour with his wife. He had also been in at the start of the plans for the Festival of Britain, in which he and Mike Parker took a great interest; it was Britain's great effort to show the world that, regardless of the post-war crises and austerity, the nation was fighting back.

In spite of the Princess's official duties in Britain and these occasional excursions back home by Philip, his two years in Malta provided them both with a life which was perhaps the closest they ever came to anything near 'normal', although they did have to endure running press criticism that they were both spending too much time away from their children – to which Philip replied, 'They're quite well enough without being fussed over by their parents.' He also had to put up with 'special treatment' for being the King's son-in-law; former colleagues say he disliked any kind of preferential distinction, though naturally he enjoyed certain perks that came with the royal job – like the new Rolls-Royce that was delivered to Buckingham Palace for him in 1950, a Phantom Four 5.7-litre straight eight with the new-fangled screen washers and electric demisters. But for all that, when she was in Malta the Princess became an officer's wife and they all liked to think she would be treated as such, though it was never possible. It was a happy time for both of them.

It would end all too quickly.

Chapter Fourteen
The House of Mountbatten?

Lord Mountbatten's greatest dream, that a Battenberg wife should take the throne and bring his family name into the heady realm of the ruling houses of the United Kingdom, was within sight. It was, of course, an event that he had been anticipating since long before King George's health deteriorated. Now, though everyone hoped and prayed that the King would recover, his volume of Mountbatten lineage, lovingly and laboriously researched, was ready to be crowned.

The doors of the 'cage' closed upon Philip midway through the last full year of King George's reign and all his hopes of a continued naval career were finally dashed. He joined the rest of the family in the opening ceremonies for the Festival of Britain in May, which had been designed to coincide with the anniversary of the centenary of Prince Albert's Great Exhibition of 1851. A busy year was in store, but events took a dramatic turn at the end of the month when it become known that the King had a shadow on his lung which in the end proved to be cancer. IRA threats against the lives of 'foreign Royalty' during the King's planned visit to Northern Ireland set for 30 May only added to the consternation. The IRA blew up Belfast police station to show they meant business. In the event, the King was too ill to travel and the Queen courageously went with Princess Margaret, without any violence occurring.

However, Princess Elizabeth and Philip increasingly found themselves deputizing for the monarch as he spent the next few months as a semi-invalid. Philip was granted indefinite leave from his naval duties and never returned. As he left his ship, he was piped away by his crew, their whites gleaming in the Maltese sunshine. 'The last eleven months', he said, 'have been the happiest of my sailor life.'[1]

It was over. The longed-for career in the footsteps of his grandfather Prince Louis of Battenberg and his uncle Earl Mountbatten of Burma had ended. New tasks lay straight ahead. He had, for instance, just accepted the Honorary Presidency of the British Association for the

Advancement of Science and spent hours while still on HMS *Magpie* swotting up and drafting his first major speech. He showed it to the King, who advised him to delete some of the more controversial passages. Still, he criticized British industry for not making enough use of scientific progress and made what was described the next day as an 'impassioned. plea' for mankind:

> Scientific knowledge has reached a point where it can either free the world from drudgery, fear, hunger and pestilence or obliterate itself. . . . it is clearly our duty as citizens to see that science is used for the benefit of mankind. For what use is science if man does not survive?

The speech stunned his audience. Their reaction stunned Philip. They gave him a standing ovation, while the newspapers cautiously welcomed his first major pronouncements to the world, with the odd murmuring of 'Who the hell does he think he is?'

At the beginning of September, a series of tests was performed on the King and it was suggested that he should undergo an immediate operation for the removal of the whole of his left lung, where the cancer lodged, though apparently the word itself was not used in the King's presence. Princess Elizabeth and Philip were due to embark on their most important tour so far, to Canada and America, on 25 September, sailing aboard the *Empress of Canada*. The King's operation was set for two days prior to their departure and this gave the family and His Majesty's ministers a problem. The couple did not want to leave England so soon after the King's operation. Philip suggested a way out: why not fly across the Atlantic and thus cut out the time of the sea journey? Palace old-timers and government alike stood back in horror. There was great nervousness about the heir to the throne flying such a distance, especially at such a delicate time. Attlee took the unusual step of consulting the leader of the Opposition, Winston Churchill, who replied, 'It would be, in my opinion, wrong for the Princess Elizabeth to fly the Atlantic. This seems to me more important than any of the inconveniences which may be caused by changing the plans and programmes in Canada.'[2]

Attlee did not let it rest, prodded no doubt by someone at Buckingham Palace responding to Philip's own nudges. When the King's operation was declared a success, Attlee called the Chairman of the British Overseas Airways Corporation to discuss the possibility of a flight. He was told that a BOAC Stratocruiser was a comfortable and safe aircraft which had completed many uneventful journeys on the route. After a Cabinet meeting on 27 September, Attlee agreed to let them fly.

Elizabeth and Philip took off on 7 October and in the next thirty-five days they completed one of the most arduous and acclaimed royal tours since the twenties when Lloyd George sent the young Prince of Wales (Duke of Windsor) on his tour of the Dominions. They travelled across the American continent twice, completing 10,000 miles in Canada alone, and were met by cheering crowds everywhere, thus setting the tone for dozens of repeat performances in future years. Philip came into his own, and steeled himself for his future job. When photographers popped their flashbulbs too close to the Princess, he growled disapproval and they backed off apologizing; in Montreal he complained that his wife was expected to eat lunch 'under the gaze of a thousand people'; at a reception in Ottawa he discovered that through bad organization some people were being presented twice in a never-ending queue of outstretched hands and abruptly ended it all by saying, 'This is a waste of everyone's time.' These were small asides; the crowds loved them. President Harry Truman summed it up in a letter to George VI: 'We've just had a visit from a lovely young lady and her personable husband – Their Royal Highnesses, Princess Elizabeth and the Duke of Edinburgh. They went to the hearts of all the citizens of the United States. . . .'³

While they were in America, a British General Election was held. Attlee had called the poll after discussions with the King in August, when it was still assumed that he and the Queen would be making their much-planned five-month journey by sea to East Africa, Australia and New Zealand in 1952. Attlee lost the election and Winston Churchill was restored to power. Mrs Truman commented to the Princess, 'I'm so glad your father's been re-elected.'⁴

The King, though successfully recovering from such a major operation, was still in no condition to make the Australian tour and, to avoid the costly arrangements being scrapped yet again, it was agreed that Elizabeth and Philip should go instead. In preparation, and as a mark of the King's pride and thanks, Elizabeth and Philip were both sworn in as members of the Privy Council on 4 December 1951, thus becoming members of what, in times when the monarch had real power, had been the King's council of personal advisers. Now, of course, it had become an adjunct of government and all members of Cabinet were sworn in as Privy Councillors for life. Though the business of the Privy Council is not publicized, no undue secrecy surrounds it either. Strange, therefore, that the records of the day of Elizabeth and Philip's ceremony at the Public Record Office at Kew carry a 'seventy-five-year' stamp, which means that they cannot be made public until the year 2026.

During the Christmas celebrations at Sandringham, the King told everyone not to worry. It was two months since his operation and he felt stronger and well. Elizabeth and Philip were put at their ease and felt less anxious about their forthcoming tour, the longest any member of the family had been faced with in many a year. They were already well versed in the route; they could be found on their hands and knees with maps spread over the sitting-room floor as they spent their free time studying their journey. The Queen meanwhile talked happily about her own trip, a convalescence cruise to South Africa with the King in March; purely relaxational, with no officials or duties.

They were all together for the last time on 30 January when the King and Queen took Princess Margaret and Elizabeth and Philip to the Drury Lane Theatre to see *South Pacific*. At noon next day, on the cold and bitter last day of the month, the King was on the tarmac kissing his daughter goodbye and shaking hands with Philip as they boarded their aircraft bound for Nairobi, the first stop of the tour. Three days later the Princess and her husband were at Sagana Lodge, a timber bungalow given to them as a wedding gift by the people of Kenya, where they were planning to stay for five nights, with a break on the night of 5 February when they had been invited to stay at Treetops, the famous observation spot. That evening, they were to observe animals in the wild. Philip, rifle in hand, walked beside his wife as they went to a spot where, just a few yards away, they saw an elephant and its calf; then they climbed the ladder to the hotel in the tree and watched an endless stream of animals arriving at the waterhole.

It was probably at that moment, while the Princess was taking pictures with her cine-camera, that King George VI died peacefully in his sleep at Sandringham. As the register at Treetops recorded for posterity: 'For the first time in the history of the world, a young girl climbed into a tree one day as a Princess and next day as a Queen. God bless us.'

A tear rolled down Winston Churchill's cheek as he stood on the Heathrow tarmac with the Mountbattens and the King's brother, the Duke of Gloucester, to welcome their new monarch back to London. Queen Mary, now eighty-four years old, waited at Clarence House to kiss the hand of her granddaughter and curtsey deep in the formal, stylish manner of protocol which the old Queen herself had done so much to maintain. Centuries of it were suddenly swept up into a neat pile for the new reign and it must have hit Philip rather forcefully. Those around him at the time recollect his manner as stern-faced, and not just through the sadness which surrounded the Court. The realization of how it affected him personally must have been running constantly through his mind in between the times he and his wife were actually discussing how they would cope with the premature arrival of this awesome responsibility. In normal circumstances, it might not have come to them for another twenty or twenty-five years.

The Queen herself faced an enormous task, which, falling as it did on one so young, would require the rock-like support of her husband. The accession of Elizabeth II brought into focus a very real crisis in Philip's life and career: that of an exacting, often frustrating, separation by status of husband and wife brought about by the fact that the Queen held the highest position in the land and represented the highest authority, while Philip himself had none – not a single jot of power. Constitutionally, he did not exist. And this was never more evident than when, after the first meeting of the Privy Council, the Queen got up to leave the room and walk to another part of the Palace. Philip instinctively followed, only to find the door slammed in his face. Protocol ruled it that way: a mere husband – Duke or not – could not breach such tradition. If there are ghosts in Buckingham Palace, Prince Albert must surely have been gazing and chuckling at his luckless successor, who would be for ever compared with him.

What Philip had to achieve, personally and quite apart from his supportive role as husband to the world's most important woman, was a job of his own. He had to seek out an avenue for his immense energies, and in this he would rapidly run up against those who still related to the reigns of the Georges V and VI. Nothing at all had changed since Albert wrote despairingly about being the 'husband but not the master in the house'. In fact, Philip gave his own interpretation of that saying when he reflectively reviewed his situation prior to and after the Queen's accession: 'Within the house and whatever we did it was together. I suppose I naturally filled the principal position. People used to come to ask me what to do.'5 All that quickly changed. Suddenly, it was her house, her servants, her soldiers – even her children.

No wonder he was walking around with a face as long as a wet weekend in Bognor. But there's no point in making too much out of his 'fear' of what lay ahead, as newspapers filled countless inches of eulogy for the late King and almost hysterical conjecture for the new reign. Philip's route through a maze and haze of protocol, etiquette and political intrigue in this ancient institution was to make himself into the iron foundation of the new monarchy while disregarding the old-fashioned ways of the courtiers. We are told that this is exactly what he set out to achieve; but if he were to give advice to his wife, it would have to remain strictly behind closed doors, for herein lay an immediate problem. It is summed up in one word: Mountbatten.

There were background noises ironically similar to those heard when Prince Albert joined Victoria. Then, there were whispers about Albert's Uncle Leopold, King of the Belgians – who was also Victoria's uncle – and the arch-plotter Baron Stockmar, wielding an unhealthy influence upon the young Queen and her consort. Even Victoria complained that Leopold 'is given to believe that he must rule the roost everywhere.'

Concern that history would repeat itself was very quickly apparent with the fears that an ambitious uncle was keeping a close eye on how his protégé was developing. There were plenty of whispers, if not loud noises off, among Mountbatten's enemies, who were alert to the dangers of his gaining and exerting too much power over the Queen through her husband. Enemies abounded, particularly in the echelons of high conservatism. Churchill and Beaverbrook were among them, and the Queen Mother, still grief stricken at the loss of her husband, certainly did not trust him. She of all people at the Palace could remember that Mountbatten had been a supporter of Edward VIII right to the last, when he suddenly switched sides with a grovelling letter to the Duke of York.

In the immediate wake of King George's death an odd situation developed. Mountbatten recognized that he was already being cast in the role of wicked uncle. Barely two weeks after the King died he was writing to Edwina about 'London buzzing with rumours' that he was to be offered an immediate post abroad to remove him from being able to 'influence Lillibet through Philip'.[6] There were people around with loud enough voices to broadcast the widely held view that Mountbatten was a dangerous man to have so close to the monarchy.

Concern, Mountbatten heard, was also being expressed that Edwina's extreme left-wing views – she now veered towards Communism – might be passed on. Their daughter Pamela had already caught the bug and, though not a member of the Communist Party, was a declared supporter of Communism. This alarm over the politics of the Mountbatten household was merely heightened by the regular presence of the homosexual socialite Peter Murphy, a card-carrying Communist who had been one of Mountbatten's closest friends and regular 'secretary' for thirty years. They had first met at Cambridge, where Murphy had been struck by Mountbatten's good looks and incredible charm, which he saw as second only to that popular idol the Prince of Wales himself. Their association continued until Murphy's death in September 1966. Murphy was preaching a new social order for Britain when they first became friends and, despite the fact that Mountbatten had just lost several relatives in the Russian Revolution, he was intrigued to the extent that, as Philip Ziegler has told us, Murphy 'opened Mountbatten's eyes to what he believed to be inherent flaws in the capitalist system.' Murphy was astonished to find a member of the Royal Family 'so free of prejudice and reaction'[7] and, although he did not perhaps indoctrinate his young friend with the principles of Socialism, he certainly influenced him towards questioning the values of the alleged superior class to which he belonged. In their long-term relationship, Murphy also brought a calming influence to bear on the Mountbattens' oft-troubled marriage. His advice and mediation was sought by both. Their children came to regard him as a permanent fixture and indeed Mountbatten took him on to his personal staff in official duties on numerous occasions. He was at his side, for instance, during the traumatic transfer of India to independent status. Murphy and Noël Coward, back in the days of the pre-war Mediterranean service, often came to visit Mountbatten on his ship HMS *Wishart*. Prince Philip knew him well.

It surely cannot be coincidence that in the very month after Queen

Elizabeth II succeeded to the throne, British Intelligence began to take an interest in the leftish connections of Mr Murphy, following indiscreet suggestions in Westminster that he was in fact a Russian agent. If that were indeed the case, the Soviets would have had two infiltrators within the royal circle, though the treachery of Anthony Blunt – Surveyor of the Queen's Pictures – was as yet unknown. Murphy and Mountbatten both strenuously denied these affiliations and Mountbatten claimed that he personally instigated an investigation of Murphy by the security service in the wake of the allegations against his friend. Their findings, in a report to Mountbatten later in that year of 1952, confirmed that Murphy was a homosexual but could find no evidence that he was a Russian spy[8] and that seemed to end the matter. Those who recall the general fear of this man deep in Mountbatten's confidence would later point to the fact that, at the time, the British Intelligence network was rather well endowed with traitors; it was barely six months since Burgess and Maclean were tipped off by Kim Philby to make their exit to the Soviet Union. Nervousness prevailed – unsurprisingly in that era when the onset of the Cold War and the McCarthy purges on American public life, which had recently reached their peak, brought a manic fear of anything prefixed with Communist (and especially Communist with homosexual undertones). So, in retrospect, account must be taken of the prevailing world hysteria.

There was no doubt, however, that the presence of Murphy within the Mountbatten entourage was an embarrassment at this sensitive time and the 'no smoke without fire' syndrome took hold when an American, writing in the international Bulletin of Information Services, edited by Ulius Amos, spoke of the 'Red aura' hanging over the British throne. The piece pointed to the Mountbattens' close contact with Communists and their sympathizers, and reported the belief that Mountbatten thought capitalism was on the way out – which he certainly did – and was considering some sort of regency for when the monarchy was disenfranchised. 'Some rumours go further and allude to the bizarre possibility of a future Marxist King Louis of England,' said the article.[9] It seemed a silly, incredible theory but, unlikely though it may have been, it found support among a large number of people – especially the Americans, who failed to appreciate that there was very little space left within the system for a monarch's view to have any sway at all on British life, let alone influence a government minister. And, incidentally, the whole question of suspicion that Mountbatten had a spy in his camp seemed to be torpedoed when, ten years later, two Prime Ministers, Macmillan and Wilson, successively offered him the top job at the Ministry of Defence (which he refused). Mountbatten himself said the theory was wicked and fantastic; none the less, the theme of his underhand influence was already being hinted at in the British press and in government circles to the point that he found himself in late February stating that 'the Duke of Edinburgh has got his head screwed on the right way . . . [he] certainly stands in no need of advice from anyone least of all his uncle.'[10]

The uncle was no better trusted at Buckingham Palace than he was among the establishment – a fact that was to become crystal clear very soon, largely through Mountbatten's own doing. If, with hindsight, it may be thought nonsensical that he had political ambitions via the monarchy – though these cannot be entirely dismissed in the light of later developments – the same could not be said of his dynastical aims. At the beginning of April he was heard boasting that the British throne had been occupied by a Mountbatten since 7 February; the House of Mountbatten had now been established. This view was confirmed in a newspaper article by L. G. Pine, editor of *Debrett's Peerage & Baronetage*, with whom Mountbatten had been in touch over the preparation of his family lineage. Pine made the point that, by adopting his mother's anglicized family name when he was naturalized, Philip had upon his marriage effectively replaced the Royal Family name of Windsor with his own new surname.[11]

This possibility had not gone altogether unnoticed by the King when he was alive, but it had been left untidily unresolved. A week before the birth of Prince Charles, for instance, George VI issued Letters Patent under the Great Seal[12] ordaining that any children born to the Duke and Duchess of Edinburgh should have the title of Prince or Princess and the style of Royal Highness. Otherwise, the first son would have been known as Charles Mountbatten, Earl of Merioneth – and would subsequently have become a Mountbatten king – because when George VI gave Philip his bagful of titles, he deliberately omitted the inclusion of 'Prince'.* If the first baby had been a girl, she would have been merely the Lady Anne Mountbatten. Charles was christened Prince Charles of Edinburgh. Princess Anne's arrival in 1950 created rather more confusion, demonstrating that the question had still not been resolved. She was not registered until nine days after her birth and the official documents now contain a deliberate omission: that of her surname. This awkward situation remained until the week of Mountbatten's boast about his family having taken over the House of Windsor.

His jubilation was not shared by Queen Mary when she learned what had been said. Outraged at the thought, she furiously retorted to her informant that her husband had founded the House of Windsor *in aeternum* and 'no Battenberg marriage', however solemn and effective in English law, could change it.[13] The old Queen moved rapidly to ward off this threat to her husband's memory. Churchill was contacted

---

* This was only conferred upon him by the Queen in 1957 in recognition of ten years of service to the Crown.

immediately and the delicacy of the situation showed when it was brought to a private Cabinet discussion. Churchill and his ministers – well aware of the undercurrent of unhappiness over Mountbatten's close proximity to the throne and the disquiet that future kings might bear his name – unanimously agreed with Queen Mary: that Queen Elizabeth II should be advised that the name of the British Royal Family ought to stay the way it had been since 1917, regardless of her marital status. Churchill himself tactfully explained this view to the Queen. And so it was that, on 21 April 1952, it was officially proclaimed by Order in Council that it was the Queen's 'will and pleasure She and Her Children shall be styled and known as the House of Windsor.'

Ructions followed at the Palace. 'An amoeba . . . I'm just a bloody amoeba!' raged Philip as his name was deleted from the family tree.

Mountbatten was equally furious, but would not be outdone. In his own family tree, now taking shape as 'The Mountbatten Lineage', he recorded what was to him a most memorable, significant and important sentence relating to the accession of 'Elizabeth Mountbatten'. It states: 'The House of Mountbatten reigned for two months but historically it takes its place among the reigning Houses of the United Kingdom'.[14] This self-congratulatory claim was also self-delusion, and, in purist terms, quite false. He had usurped Philip's credentials to bolster the Mountbatten lineage, when in reality the credit ought to have gone back to the House of Glücksburg.

Mountbatten did not give up his quest; he persisted with his lobbying. Twelve years later the Queen changed the family name to Mountbatten-Windsor. He had won, at least, partial victory but, as we will discover, it was not one that would permanently attach his name to the ruling house.

Regardless of the name-game, Philip was cast in his uncle's shadow and there he would stay for many years to come. In terms of any political influence, it was a ridiculous thought. While Mountbatten's own views may well have veered left of centre, his nephew's certainly did not! Whatever else he faced, the question of the name merely served to highlight the difficulty of Philip's situation. The strain was evident early on, when he was laid low for three weeks with jaundice. He was confined to a rather uncomfortable room on the ground floor of Buckingham Palace, since the Queen Mother had, naturally enough, shown no hurry in vacating the main living rooms of the building. He had his own bed and television moved over from Clarence House, which, just months after the completion of their tailored and high-profile renovations, had now become redundant as the family home. In fact, Philip discussed with the Queen the possibility that they might continue to live there while conducting royal business from Buckingham Palace, but Churchill would not hear of it.

So the Palace it was – and all those musty traditions, curious people, corridors of power and stern, timbered doors that kept slamming in his face. Philip must have felt out on a limb when he sought advice from his only living comparable role-model, Prince Bernhard of The Netherlands, who told him bluntly:

> You probably don't realize what you are up against. Practically everything you do will be a subject of criticism. You can't ignore it because some of it may be justified. It may be politic to heed it . . . but don't let it get you down. In this job, you need a skin like an elephant's.[15]

The Queen attempted partially to resolve his vague position within the Constitution by declaring that 'His Royal Highness, Philip, Duke of Edinburgh, henceforth and on all occasions . . . shall have, hold and enjoy Place, Pre-Eminence and Precedence next to Her Majesty', which at least brought him from the shadows of ranking lower than other royal dukes, and even lower than his own children. Parliament, after the usual heated exchanges that had become tradition on any mention of money, eventually and begrudgingly raised his income to £40,000 a year, subject to tax.

This in itself was taken by the Royals to be a rather miserly award to the man at the side of the monarch; it was as if he were being put in his place by Parliament – advance warning that he should never stray from his position, billeted firmly two paces behind the Queen, from whence he should act with quiet restraint and not interfere. If that was the case, they were asking rather too much of him, as time would very quickly show.

In those pre-Coronation months, he also collected a few military accolades and decorations which were, embarrassingly for him, totally unearned. The Queen approved his appointment to supreme positions in each of the three services – Admiral of the Fleet, Field Marshal and Marshal of the Royal Air Force – all of which ranks had been taken by King George VI upon his accession and which were all still held by the Duke of Windsor, who fell back in rank behind Philip.

What must Windsor have thought of that?

Chapter Fifteen

First Gentleman

The newspapers had started to call him the 'First Gentleman', largely through want of a better term. As one writer of the day put it, Philip faced the world's most contradictory role. He was strong, masculine, self-assertive; he had more natural capacity for getting around and meeting people than any member of the Royal Family since the former Prince of Wales, though that comparison might not have pleased him. Yet he had no position of any authority. He was officially neither a prince nor a consort, nor anything other than the Queen's husband – so if she was the First Lady, it followed that he was the First Gentleman. He sort of lived up to it – or tried to – by his deliberate decision to adopt a position very much in his wife's shadow during the early years of her reign, though the humiliations were clear to see. At the first State opening of Parliament he attended with her, for example, he could hardly believe what they had done to him. Whereas Queen Elizabeth had sat alongside King George on a similar throne under the sovereign's canopy in the House of Lords, it was wrongly believed that Philip, without the official designation of Consort, could not be allowed to do the same. The consort's throne was therefore removed and, while the monarch's throne remained lofty and alone, a chair for Philip's use was placed outside those few square feet of hallowed floor space. He was furious, and it did not happen again.

Those surrounding the Queen were, in any event, deliberately trying to keep him out of both her and their affairs. Encircled as she was by the old-time courtiers and inherited advisers who had served her father and even her grandfather, Philip's scope for involvement was extremely limited. There was a very definite and organized campaign to exclude him from any active role within the true function of the monarchy.[1] The 'gnarled men' who gathered daily around the Queen and bowed to her every need presented a set of hostile faces to her husband.

To take one example: Philip suggested that certain lesser matters of

Palace life might be brought to him for decision. He could see that his wife had been under immense pressure during the first months of her reign, meeting all the foreign statesmen who craved audience with the new monarch, signing documents, giving audience to her ministers, dealing with the important and with the mundane. Philip wanted to lighten her load by having some of these burdensome tasks rerouted to his office. After all, he argued, when the Queen Mother was the King's consort, staff had come to her for some decisions and King George himself had involved her in a much wider way.

What was then known as 'the old guard' at the Palace would not have it. Philip was kept out and in this they were aided by politicians. Basil Boothroyd, in his informal biography of Prince Philip, referred to the 'crusted old operators' tending the Constitutional juggernaut who closed ranks, hoping that it would rumble on without any tinkering from a newcomer 'for whom there was literally no place.'[2] Since Philip authorized the biography and provided an office at Buckingham Palace for Boothroyd to do his research, one must assume that these words summed up his feelings entirely!

Another observation neatly pinpoints the feelings of politicians and takes account of the suspicions surrounding his uncle. Philip was a Mountbatten and 'no Prime Minister would be caught dead acting in accordance with what he said'.[3]

Philip's answer was to stay out of the mystical aspects of the monarchy; since the Constitution forbade any active participation, he also distanced himself from such formalities as Privy Council meetings. As his biographer later wrote, Philip was not mad about the bows and scrapes of Royalty; he saw himself as a man first and a prince second.[4] With the loss of his career at sea, he began to extend his own diary, arranging official visits to coalfields, factories and scientific workshops. The Queen approved his proposal to take up flying – though Churchill as usual objected on the grounds of risk – and he obtained his wings in May 1953. But at least flying gave them a topic of conversation at a rather frigid luncheon when the Duke of Windsor came to visit his sick mother. As Philip said, he could hardly hold the rank of Air Marshal without being able to fly a plane. As with everything, it was a touchy topic with the Duke of Windsor, who had been there before him and indeed had introduced air travel to the monarchy, installing its own small private airline. And he did not need to be reminded that the initials 'ER' appearing on everything once stood for Edward Rex!

These events were insufficient to take up Philip's time. He had overseen their removal from Clarence House and had had his white maple panelling taken down from his study and re-installed in his new apartment at Buckingham Palace, the same study used by King George. Elizabeth preferred not to take that room and moved instead to the day rooms used by her mother. These minor matters of detail took but a few hours to organize. The Queen rescued him to a degree by appointing him Chief Ranger of Windsor Great Park – a title which caused some mirth among his relatives – but from that position he was able to begin an assessment of the operation of the royal estates. More topically and urgent, the Queen also made him Chairman of her Coronation Commission, which raised a few more greying eyebrows, especially since it was to consist of no less than thirty-six diplomatic representatives from Britain and the Commonwealth. In between times, he visited the Olympic Games in Helsinki, and raced their yacht, *Bluebottle*, during Cowes Week while the Queen went off to Goodwood races to watch one of her string of fourteen racehorses in action. To balance her heavy workload during the first half of the year, she and Philip retired to Balmoral on 8 August and remained there until 13 October.

By then the Coronation plans were well advanced. Queen Mary asked Philip to keep her informed of the arrangements and was able to chip in with a few suggestions herself, recalling her husband's ceremony and her own role as Queen Consort. This was the sixth reign of her life, but she would not see the crowning of her granddaughter. On 9 February 1953, a cold and miserable day, she went for a drive along the Coronation route and saw the stands being erected in the London streets. As if struck by some prophetic knowledge, she made a last self-effacing gesture to the British throne to which she had devoted her entire adult life: that should she die prior to the Coronation, her passing should not be allowed to interrupt the proceedings. That outing was her last. She died on 24 March. The Queen, it is said, arranged for the St Edward's Crown to be brought in secret to Marlborough House so that she could pay homage to her grandmother; she also approved a lying-in-state for Mary's body at Westminster Hall, and the old Queen thus became the first royal consort in modern times to be given this honour. The British public responded in their thousands by queueing day and night for the seventy-two-hour vigil.

Queen Mary had been – next to her father – the most influential person in moulding Elizabeth II's character. More importantly for Philip, her death thrust the helm of the matriarchal system of Buckingham Palace into the control of Queen Elizabeth, the Queen Mother, who had spent the last year mourning her beloved Bertie and was coming out of it with an irritable, if not angry, edge to her normally warm and wonderful public persona. The death of her mother-in-law and the forthcoming crowning of her daughter had introduced family difficulties which Philip would now observe first hand. He had already seen the edginess of his wife and others when the Duke of Windsor came to call; suddenly a more delicate matter was at hand. Queen Mary had resolutely refused to receive the wife of the Duke of Windsor – who in the confines of the Palace was never, at this stage, even afforded the title of Duchess. Windsor would be expected for the funeral and there was a good deal of speculation over whether Wallis might be accepted into the fold now the old Queen was dead. Quite the opposite happened. The Queen Mother was equally, if not more aggressively, opposed to the reception of 'that woman'. This determination was only aggravated by Wallis's incredible behaviour during Court mourning for Queen Mary. Windsor had been apprised of the fact that his wife was not welcome at the service so he left Wallis in New York, where, on the very night of the funeral, she was to be found dining and dancing with her homosexual playmate and occasional lover Jimmy Donahue, the exceedingly rich Woolworth's heir. This unseemly display of Wallis's lack of feeling towards her husband's relatives – which was entirely reciprocated, one might add – merely confirmed to the Queen Mother that she was still unacceptable to the Royal Family. She spoke to her daughter and Philip about the Windsors and the Coronation; before he left the Duke was informed that he and his wife would not be invited to the crowning ceremony.

There was better news for Philip's own relatives, however. The tenseness over matters Germanic had eased with the changing of the political situation. Germany was no longer a country full of ex-Nazis; the great powers of the West, now engaged with Russia in the Cold War, saw Germany as the buffer zone and, far from antagonizing them, they desperately required their help and co-operation. Philip's three sisters and their families were invited from Germany to the Coronation. Philip also arranged for them to stay at Buckingham Palace. Although they had all visited Britain in the past, it was the first time that their existence was 'officially' recognized through their presence being requested by royal warrant.

Otherwise, not a lot was different from the last time. The Queen viewed the Coronation as a repetition of her father's; she kept referring back to her mother and advisers about whether he would have done it this way or that; like her father she took it all very seriously. As the day came nearer, she was struck with nervous anticipation and, oddly, a distinct lack of self-confidence in private. Many a day of endless official duties or rehearsals at the Abbey ended in tears of nerves and exhaustion. She was a worrier in these early days, especially over minor detail. She worried over everything from the new postage stamp to the high cost of carpeting and curtains for the royal apartments.[5] She worried on days when Philip went flying and, if the telephone rang while he was out, she would wait anxiously until she discovered that the news was not about him. She worried about the Coronation and protocol, and about the suggestion from some of her advisers that Philip should not be allowed to ride with her in the Gold State Coach. They suggested he should go in a separate coach or ride on horseback alongside. There was no precedent, because Victoria was unmarried when she was crowned and Queen Anne, whose consort was Prince George of Denmark, was carried by chair to her Coronation. Finally, they decided to travel together. But the tension was building up, day by day.

It was not eased by the thought that she would become the first monarch in history whose Coronation would be seen by many millions around the world through the miracle of television – a plan which Mountbatten implored them to adopt. Churchill advised against allowing live television cameras inside Westminster Abbey with these words to his Cabinet: 'I don't see why the BBC should get a better view of my monarch than me.'⁶ For once the newspapers – even Beaverbrook – agreed with Mountbatten. Rather than attack the Prime Minister, John Gordon of the *Sunday Express* hit out at the 'tight-knit group of Palace officials whose determination to keep people as far as possible away from the throne never diminishes. What a bunch of codheads to run the Queen's business.'⁷

Philip could not have put it better himself!

Mountbatten, in the wings, continued to press for a televised ceremony and the Queen eventually made her decision and relayed it to Churchill: the burden of cameras in the Abbey was something that she could and should bear for the sake of her people.

The effect of television on this gloriously British occasion would not be realized for some time to come. For one thing, it brought to the world closer understanding of British Royalty; *Time* magazine, for instance, said the whole world was Royalist now.⁸ But did anyone realize exactly what they were letting themselves in for? Had they dismissed too quickly the protestations of the old guard who said the mystique and magic would disappear through the tube, regardless of the highly respectful commentary of Richard Dimbleby? The old guard was probably right. This, the Coronation, was the beginning of mass-market monarchy on a scale matched briefly only once in their history, with the Abdication. On that day, Tuesday, 2 June 1953, the British Royal Family moved into the realm of global celebrities.

While the Queen was, of course, the star of this particular world-wide extravaganza, the Royals were also seen together as a family once again and they all basked in the afterglow of their own magnificence. But in all the excitement, they had failed to take action over a problem of mammoth proportions zooming towards them on the inside rails: Margaret was in love.

Perhaps they could be excused for the simple reason that so much had happened in such a short space of time. The deaths of the King and of Queen Mary followed by the Coronation might well have been enough for anyone, yet these were only the beginnings of a succession of events which would test the Queen to the absolute limit. Suddenly, it was all turning sour.

The Margaret problem had been with them for some time; the Queen had been told in April 1953 that Margaret wanted to marry Peter Townsend, who had recently divorced his wife Rosemary. Margaret brought the news herself and found her sister sympathetic yet riven between the choice of Margaret's personal happiness and the very serious Constitutional and Church issues involved. The Queen Mother was in tears as they anguished over the situation confronting them, and Margaret, some years later, was to say that if it had been ended there and then perhaps the whole damaging business would have gone no further.

As it was, Sir Alan Lascelles, the Queen's Private Secretary, read them quotations from the Royal Marriages Act of 1772. As a veteran courtier of the Abdication Crisis, he knew it by heart. Haunted by Wallis Simpson, he was personally deeply opposed to even the thought of Margaret's marrying a divorced man, but told them a marriage was none the less 'not impossible', though she could not marry anyone without Her Majesty's permission before she was twenty-five. In his view, permission should be withheld.

But Lascelles did more. Presumably with the Queen's approval, he alerted the government to this impending problem through Press Secretary Richard Colville, whose cousin Sir John Colville was now Winston Churchill's Private Secretary.* Lascelles, a dour but honourable man steeped in the total formalities of the Court, was absolutely convinced that a rerun of the Abdication Crisis, albeit to a lesser degree, was in the making.

Over lunch at Chequers, Sir John Colville revealed all to Churchill. The Prime Minister did not immediately see the point and commented, 'What a delightful match.' As Colville explained the implications, Clemmie Churchill interrupted and said 'Winston, if you are going to begin the Abdication all over again, I'm going to leave! I shall take a flat and go and live in Brighton.'[9]

Churchill pondered and eventually came to the decision that Lascelles had been seeking; through him, his Cabinet should advise the Queen that any question of her sister's marriage should be postponed until she came of age under the Royal Marriages Act in eighteen months' time.

It was, with hindsight and bearing in mind the furore that followed, a bad decision. But Churchill was not a well man. It was one of the last major decisions he would make before his next stroke, in July of that year, and if any blame were to be attached, it should more likely be hung on the door of Buckingham Palace where Lascelles, the single most influential man behind the throne, was pulling the strings and trying to avert the haunting return of an Edward VIII-like débâcle.

Hope sprang eternal because no one actually said, 'You can't . . . and let that be the end of it.' The Queen talked to Margaret and persuaded

* John Colville, as we have seen, was previously Private Secretary to Princess Elizabeth.

her to wait. As usual, the information was passed on to the press by one of their Palace spies and was hinted at in continental newspapers. The British papers, though they knew of it, dared not touch the story without some official comment and Commander Richard Colville, the Queen's Press Secretary, would not even discuss it, preferring to sweep aside any embarrassments and allow comment on only the nicest aspects of Palace life – much the same policy as exists today.

What he had not noticed was that the press had been keeping a close eye on the lovers. The moment they secured the 'evidence' came on Coronation Day itself. One reporter in the annexe of Westminster Abbey noticed Margaret flicking a loose thread from Townsend's lapel – an instinctive gesture that occurs between two people who are close to one another. And the very day after the Coronation, an American newspaper brought it all out into the open. The writer spoke of the 'astonishing familiarity' between Margaret and Townsend – 'the officer held out his hand and Margaret almost fell into his arms, a half embrace.'

The route to printing such revelations in the British newspapers was well established. Perhaps the best example was given by the *Sunday People*, which demanded indignantly that 'these scandalous rumours' circulating abroad should cease. The paper then went on to explain exactly what the rumours were – and thus the story was turned from cautious toe-dipping to a full-blown, up-and-running account with every dot and comma. In the seventies and eighties the preamble was still used, as Princess Anne, for one, would find to her considerable annoyance. One paragraph can change lives.

The *People* took the quasi-moralistic tone:

> It is high time for the British public to be made aware of the fact that newspapers in Europe and America are openly asserting that the Princess is in love with a divorced man and that she wishes to marry him. This story is of course utterly untrue. It is quite unthinkable that a royal princess, third in line of succession to the throne, should even contemplate a marriage with a man who has been through the divorce courts.[10]

One cannot help feeling sorry for Peter Townsend, and one must also spare a thought for his wife Rosemary. He was in that band of royal aides whose life for the past few years had revolved entirely around the needs of their masters; he knew no set working hours, no nine-to-five existence, no pattern of home life. His marriage, according to Townsend, had been over in real terms for about two years when Rosemary wisely decided to discover more appreciative company. He divorced her in December 1952 on the grounds of her adultery with John de Laszlo, son of the artist who painted one of the most praised portraits of the Queen Mother. Not much was said at the time and the Royal Family remained quietly sympathetic, knowing, perhaps, that the demands of his job may well have contributed to the marriage break-up. He was described as the innocent party and as such he could continue his employment at the Palace, although the rule of 'guilty' parties in divorce proceedings not being allowed at Court was still being loosely applied to those at the centre of the machinery.

If the Queen's own advisers had had their way, however, Townsend would have been drummed out of the Palace long ago. They blamed him for allowing the romance with Margaret to develop; he was the one who should have put a stop to it either by removing himself from service or by telling Margaret, or perhaps Philip as her brother-in-law and possible counsellor, that the affair had no future. When he turned to Sir Alan Lascelles for advice he, not surprisingly, looked him straight in the eye and said, 'You must be either mad or bad, or both.'

The Queen's own sense of morality and virtue was as strong as her grandmother's and she would soon be reminded, by way of the newspapers, of her speech some time ago to the Mother's Union when she used the words 'divorce and separation are responsible for some of the darkest evils in our society'.

Townsend was well liked by the family, with the exception of Philip. King George had been heard to say once that he would have liked a son like Townsend. Churchill called him pleasant and courteous and gallant. When George VI died, the Queen Mother appointed Townsend Comptroller of her Household when she and Margaret finally moved into Clarence House in May and came to rely on him for his quiet, modest strengths. She needed that kind of male support from someone; unlike Queen Victoria or Queen Mary when they were widowed, she had no son to come to her side, except Philip, who had yet to win her complete confidence.

Princess Margaret's contact with Townsend was frequent; she had been only fourteen, after all, when he first came to the Palace. She had a crush on him from the outset and it developed. They were discreet and he seldom joined her socially, unless as a chaperon. The Princess Margaret 'set' included a number of well-heeled bachelors who would have made eminently suitable suitors and the King had always hoped she might fall for Johnny Dalkeith, Earl and inheritor of vast acreages on three estates in England and Scotland. In fact, Colin Tennant told Nigel Dempster that if the King had lived a few months longer, he would have made Margaret marry Dalkeith.[11] By then, she only had eyes for Townsend and Dalkeith drifted off into the arms of a model.

In other circumstances, the Queen Mother might have seen the warning signs. But both she and her younger daughter painfully missed the presence of the King. Philip and even the Queen herself could not, surely, have failed to notice the affection building up between Margaret and Townsend, both vulnerable for different reasons and in need of reciprocal affection. Presumably, in the welter of activity that had consumed them all, this budding problem was overlooked; perhaps they thought it would go away. But it didn't.

They hoped against hope that Fleet Street would not follow its American and continental counterparts and run the story. But Fleet Street was straining at the leash and eventually, ten days after the Coronation, the *People* broke the silence. Could the royal courtiers really have believed they wouldn't? This time there was not going to be any press silence. The pages of the popular newspapers were suddenly full of it. They revealed what Margaret's relatives had apparently failed to acknowledge: true love. Religion, divorce and Mrs Simpson were all trotted out in abundance.

Philip was flippant, then angry. Townsend was not among his favourite people. True, as Townsend recalled in his autobiography, they fought each other to a standstill on the squash court. Yet Townsend said that he 'never got to know Prince Philip well'.[12] For one who had been so close to the family for almost ten years and who had joined Philip and Elizabeth on many occasions, both formally and socially, it was an odd thing to say. Others have preferred to believe that he was being coy about the real antagonism between the two men, dating from the time of Philip's arrival as suitor to the future Queen. As one of Margaret's biographers noted, 'When Peter and Philip brushed against each other, it was like ice floes passing in the arctic.'[13] This, it is said, stemmed from Philip's certain knowledge that Townsend did not approve of him as a husband for the future Queen, a view he had made known to King George. Townsend leaves us only with the comment that he found Philip a 'genial, intelligent, hard-hitting extrovert'.[14]

In yet another family conference, it was finally agreed that the only way to take the heat out of a horrifically public situation was to despatch Townsend to Brussels on a trumped-up posting and replace him as the Queen Mother's Comptroller. Margaret joined her mother on an official visit to Africa at the end of June – a journey on which Townsend should have escorted them. His place was taken by the new man, Lord Plunket. But that did not solve a thing. The headlines continued, Margaret was the woman of the moment and every camera lens pointed at her. In July, one month after the Coronation, the *Daily Mirror* conducted a poll of its readers to ask: should Princess Margaret be allowed to wed Peter Townsend? The paper announced the result with a huge headline which stretched halfway down the front page: one word – YES. The vote in favour was 98.81 per cent.

If the Royal Family ever needed a father-figure, it was now. But did Philip provide no shoulder to cry on for his lovelorn sister-in-law? Certainly not. He had sided with the anti-marriage lobby and felt that the Crown had been drawn into a damaging public debate. He firmly believed that Margaret had let the side down. His principal concern was getting the whole business quietened and out of the headlines. The cruel fact of the matter remained, however, that by the very absence of a definite 'no' to the marriage and merely a postponement until she was twenty-five – when it would be reviewed if she were still of a like mind – both she and Townsend could read into it that they might eventually get government approval to marry. And so the lovers went blithely on believing that time and patience would solve all; eighteen months wasn't a lifetime, nor was Brussels the other side of the world. They continued to write and speak on the phone. Their parting had solved nothing.

There was one postscript to the first phase of the Margaret fiasco that affected Philip's Constitutional position. Churchill, again prompted by Lascelles, respectfully drew the Queen's attention to the fact that if by some accident the Queen were unable to carry out her business – or, worse, if she died or were killed – Margaret would take over. The Regency Act of 1937 ordained that the person twenty-one years or older who is next in succession to the throne should become Regent until the heir to the throne reached the age of eighteen. Churchill proposed a new Regency Act of 1953 and for this the Queen herself requested that 'in the event of a Regent becoming necessary in my lifetime, my husband should be the Regent and charged with the guardianship of the person of the Sovereign.'

Effectively, Margaret was relieved of her most important Constitutional role and Philip assumed it. At least he had been given some modicum of power which he would not have achieved without Margaret's unwitting assistance. Margaret would have begrudged him that; according to Lady Selina Hastings, relations between them were never the same and she thereafter referred to her brother-in-law, with her acid wit, as 'con-sort'.[15]

After the Coronation came the tours. England, Scotland, Northern Ireland and Wales were all visited to allow Her Majesty's subjects to display their undying devotion. Then it was repeated with an expansive tour of the Commonwealth, which took them away for almost six months in a complete journey around the world. The Queen, whose Prime Minister had, at the start of her reign, rearranged the time of his weekly audience so that she could bath the children, wept as she kissed Charles and Anne goodbye. In the eighties, she would have been castigated for leaving them alone for more than a week. They flew across the Atlantic to Canada, then on to the Caribbean. The refitted liner *Gothic* – the new royal yacht *Britannia* was still having its final trials – was waiting at Kingston to take them aboard for their onward journey and the most spectacular and relaxed royal tour in history. The first thing the Queen did was to radio back to England on the ship's high-frequency radio system to talk to her children. Philip was in his element back at sea. Everywhere they went, the new Queen and her handsome consort were given rapturous welcomes, and always Philip was the rock she would need so desperately. He came into his own on that tour as the man in her shadow, though he went out of his way to do the follow-up handshakes after the Queen. There was line after line of outstretched hands, row after row of dignitaries, one banquet after another; it was 173 days of an endless sea of faces in fifteen countries; exhilarating, exhausting, shattering times on a journey of 50,000 miles, but at least it gave the Queen, and Philip for that matter, new confidence. They had brought wavering loyalists back into the fold and increased the standing of monarchy no end. All was not lost.

It was left to the mischievous Windsors to spoil their Coronation year. The pair arrived in London two days after the Queen and Philip left and began doing the rounds and making sarcastic comments about the Queen Mother, whom Wallis called the Blimp.[16] Then they took off for New York, where on the last day of the year they were photographed in El Morocco nightclub for what would become the most famous of their ridiculous, deliberate poses – that of the nomadic couple wearing paper crowns. All of which did not escape the attention of the Queen, Philip and the Queen Mother.

The cheek of them! But truly it was a symbolic contrast as the picture went around the world. On the one hand, the Queen and her consort doing everything that could possibly be expected of them in the face of their 750 million loyal subjects inhabiting a quarter of the world's surface. On the other, the ex-King and the woman they wouldn't let become a king's consort, adrift in a sea of champagne as they lived out their worthless, purposeless lives.

Chapter Sixteen
It All Goes Wrong

Six months is a long time to be away from home. The media and the nation were almost suffering withdrawal symptoms by the time the Queen and Philip returned from their spectacular tour. On their return to London there was another afterglow to bask in and, after the initial welcome home, the new monarchy, of which Britain had seen remarkably little, went through another honeymoon period with relatively calm waters. Philip took off on his own for a three-week tour of Canada at the end of July 1954, visited the Empire Games, travelled in the Yukon and met some Eskimos in the Arctic Circle who were very pleased to see him; they never did receive any visits from Royalty.

But all the time there was an air of anticipation, an uncanny foreboding, among those close to the Court and those royal-watchers in touch with the inner workings of Buckingham Palace. The root of the seething was Princess Margaret and her association with Peter Townsend. The story had not, and would not, go away and every news editor in the land had pencilled in his diary the date of her twenty-fifth birthday when they and she believed it might be possible for her to announce her intention to marry her beloved divorcee.

In the meantime, she and he continued to be followed and observed. Any possibility of a reunion, any rumour of a telephone conversation or the briefest contact between them was quickly snapped up and faithfully delivered to the next morning's breakfast table. This constant surveillance operation not only brought Margaret and her 'set' under permanent scrutiny; it brought the whole House of Windsor within the scope of unflattering headlines.

Bearing this in mind – or was it the cause of it? – the timing of changing the rules for entry of divorced persons into the Royal Enclosure at Ascot could hardly have been more inviting. On 8 October the Duke of Norfolk, as the Queen's representative, announced that at the new, bigger and renamed Royal Enclosure at Ascot the Court rules which prohibited the admission of 'guilty' divorcees would no longer apply. They would, however, continue to apply for admission of divorced persons to a smaller area which would be known as the Queen's Lawn. Sensation!

The countdown to Margaret's birthday had begun and the desperate muddle caused by the ineptitude of politicians and courtiers signalled dire consequences all round, not least for Philip, who suffered in the aftermath – though he requires no sympathy. He was as much to blame as anyone for the débâcle that was about to emerge upon the public stage with an unwelcome display of dirty washing. All Palace activity – all the good works, the endless engagements, Philip's admonitory speeches and the popular pastime of photographing the Royals in off-duty moments – were covered during the ensuing months with a heady air of anticipation, for the *real* story was due to break any time after Margaret's twenty-fifth on 21 August. And as things turned out, the newspapers were to play a much greater role in the developing drama than their proprietors and editors could realize at the time; another precedent was about to be set and lessons learned. Or were they?

Come August, Margaret told the Queen she still loved Townsend with all her heart and wanted to marry him. A 'what shall we do now?' conference between the Queen, Philip and the Queen Mother produced a stop-gap agreement to allow Margaret and Townsend to meet to discuss their feelings, although these had been well expressed in the letters they had been writing to each other for two years. The Queen did not want to force her sister into any decision at that stage; her happiness was as important, then, as the issues entailed in the prospect of her marriage and the bond between the sisters was as strong as ever. The Queen would never forget her sister's support during the long delay in the announcement of her own engagement.

Philip was still against it. The Queen Mother had been persuaded by her friend Lord Salisbury, an influential figure in government, that her husband would have resolved the delicate situation simply by firmly prohibiting them to meet again. Someone in the family forum needed to be firm, and it was Philip. Margaret, if the gossips are to be believed, retaliated in one tearful confrontation by blurting out to the Queen some of the stories circulating about Philip's stag outings and the parties that followed the Thursday lunches at Baron's studio. One source said she even 'repeated a rumour that Philip had been involved in a car accident when driving an unnamed woman'[1] and it had been hushed up. The Queen, it was said, refused to believe anything that was said and was furious with her sister for listening to, and repeating, what she felt was slanderous gossip.

However, the Queen agreed that Townsend could return from Brussels. It was a decision which, by its implications, meant that the new Prime Minister, Anthony Eden, who had replaced Churchill on his retirement in April, would have to be told. But it was also a fair decision. How else could the couple, and Margaret especially, decide upon their actions?

The Constitutional issues, which would insist that Margaret renounce her right to the throne and her Civil List income, and also the attitude of the Church of England, were important enough. The Queen and Philip also had to consider the family itself. Marriage would almost certainly mean that her sister would be outcast for some years; she would have to live abroad, just as the Windsors had done and, though the family would not be split in such a bitter way as had occurred in 1936, the Queen had no wish to see another damaging era of disunity.

Townsend duly returned to London, where he was joined by Margaret and a very large contingent of reporters and photographers on 12 October. Whatever else was happening, the Queen had insisted on kindness to Townsend and enlisted the help of some very close friends to try to give the couple enough privacy and time to make their decision. One of them offered accommodation in Knightsbridge but it proved to be too accessible to the press, who laid siege outside every entrance and followed his every move – went to his tailor's in Bury Street to buy a new suit; went to another tailor's in Conduit Street for a pair of breeches; went to a cake shop in Chelsea for a box of fancies; went to Clarence House for a two-hour visit. Whole front pages were being devoted to the saga.

The Queen's plan was going badly wrong, largely through the under-estimation of media activity. The dour Commander Colville, whose own contribution was questionable, had to issue a statement to try to calm the nerves of news editors by saying that no announcement was contemplated.

Anthony Eden, in whom Margaret had misplaced hopes of sympathetic guidance since he was also divorced and had two other divorcees in his Cabinet (Thorneycroft and Monckton), went to discuss the situation with the Queen on 18 October. He spelt out his own view. Of course he had every sympathy for them, but realistically it was just not on. He was sure that because of the Queen's position as head of the established Church, the marriage would do irreparable damage to the standing of the Crown. Lord Salisbury, Conservative Leader of the House of Lords, had been kept informed by his contacts at the Palace and was already threatening to resign if the marriage were allowed. It was a strange matter of conscience that he invoked, one that allowed him to serve a divorced Prime Minister but not a monarch with a divorced brother-in-law. It was classic establishment hypocrisy, and only the beginning of it.

No better example was a solemn, sermonizing editorial in *The Times*, which really brought matters to a head. Its editor, Sir William Haley, believed, as its old editor Geoffrey Dawson had done during the Abdication Crisis, that his newspaper reflected the view and the wisdom on which Parliament, the Church and the nation should act when it said: 'The Princess will be entering into a union which vast numbers of her sister's people, all sincerely anxious for her life-long happiness, cannot in conscience regard as a marriage.'[2]

The newspaper mustered every ounce of its high-flown emotion and continued. 'There would be profound sympathy with the Queen who would be left still more lonely in her arduous life of public service in which she needs all the support and co-operation that only her close kindred can give.'

Philip had now been sidelined in the dispute. He could merely offer a broad pair of shoulders to help the Queen through this critical period. Politicians, churchmen and the media had taken over; Margaret was under intense pressure from all sides.

The Archbishop of Canterbury, Dr Geoffrey Fisher, was having his say and the Duke and Duchess of Windsor were being used in evidence. Philip maintained the view he had held all along: that they should not be allowed to marry. He feared the worst. Unswayed by romantic sentimentality, he correctly assessed the possible damage that a divorce entering the heart of the Royal Family might cause to the sacred nature of monarchy and its religious affiliations; the political implications which would certainly result, such as a major split in Eden's Cabinet; and, finally, the effect in the Commonwealth, which, as *The Times* kept on pointing out, was an important consideration.

Oh well, they seemed important issues at the time. And we all know the result.

Margaret and Townsend decided not to marry and *The Times* patronizingly congratulated her: 'all the peoples of the Commonwealth will feel gratitude to her for taking the selfless royal way which in their hearts they had expected of her.'[3]

What they were saying was that, unlike her uncle, Princess Margaret had put duty before self. Was it worth it? Of course not. Would our Commonwealth countries have resigned *en masse* from British affiliation if they had married? And would it have mattered if they had? No, on both counts. They had much more important problems of their own. The *Manchester Guardian* was prophetic in its assessment:

> her decision . . . will be regarded by the great masses of people as unnecessary and perhaps a great waste. In the long run, it will not redound to the credit or influence of those who have been most persistent in denying the princess the same liberty that is enjoyed by the rest of her fellow citizens.[4]

She kissed her lover goodbye and he went off and married elsewhere. She took the Queen's shilling and would never let her sister, and especially Philip, forget her sacrifice. She married Antony Armstrong-Jones on the rebound and they were divorced two children and eighteen years later in a blaze of scandalous publicity over her other relationships, damaging the standing of the monarchy to a far, far greater degree than her marriage to the gallant, handsome but divorced hero, Peter Townsend, might have done.

The gloves were off! The editors of popular newspapers were astounded by the way the 'Will She, Won't She?' story had riveted the nation, and the world. It was suddenly open season on the monarchy. Matters personal, once taboo unless raised officially, came in for a continuous barrage of scrutiny and attack. Philip was an obvious target, and not least of the admonitions came from the mass-selling papers that had supported Margaret, including Cecil Harmsworth King, nephew of the newspaper barons Northcliffe and Rothermere, who had become Chairman of the Mirror Group in 1951 and was yet to be totally overcome by his delusions of grandeur.

King and his chief lieutenant Hugh Cudlipp – both of whom came into regular contact with Mountbatten – were in favour of a more open monarchy, a people's Queen – a view totally opposed by *The Times* and the establishment. This kind of press comment, relatively unimportant but moving towards greater things, moved 'stuffy reactionaries', as the *Mirror* described them, to criticize the intimate manner in which the popular press was discussing the Royal Family. It was the beginning of a greater stridency in the way the Royals were reported and we now know how that developed.

Can it therefore have been wise for Philip, at that very sensitive time, to have been planning his next major contribution to mankind? He had been invited to open the 1956 Olympic Games in Melbourne, Australia, in November. Around this one single event, which under normal circumstances might have occupied his attention for a fortnight at the very most, he built a 40,000-mile world tour which he said would become his 'personal contribution to the Commonwealth ideal'[5] and which would take him and a small group of his friends to the west coast of America, Australia, New Zealand, Papua New Guinea, the Falkland Islands, the Galapagos Islands, Antarctica and Africa. The very fact that this incredible journey would take him away from Court for more than five months appeared not to have given Palace advisers any lack of sleep. If it did, and if they raised any possible pitfalls, we must assume that he countermanded them. And who was to know when the trip was being planned that Britain, and the Queen, would be plunged into a disastrous international crisis? And who could have predicted that his dream journey would end on the shirt-tails of yet another divorce scandal?

The Suez trouble was already looming. On 27 July Colonel Nasser seized the canal. The Queen was at Goodwood races at the time and it was in a private room in the Duke of Richmond's box that she read an urgent document from Eden, requesting her signature on a proclamation calling out Army reserves. She signed and put Britain on a war footing with Egypt.

No matter: Philip pressed on with his plans, with the continued co-operation of the Palace team of arrangers who seemed only too willing to provide him with enough rope! During the summer months that year there was a relaxing diversion at Cowes and other yachting events, where he was able to try out another new toy, the 24-foot yacht named *Fairey Fox* which had been designed, as the name might show, by his friend Uffa Fox. It was a fast craft and Philip was able to give King Faisal of Iraq a demonstration. In fact, the young King, who was staying with Philip aboard *Britannia* – moored conveniently nearby – was one of the crew when Philip raced her, with Uffa Fox and Mike Parker. Another of his yachts, *Coweslip*, was also doing well with a local crew and the third, *Bluebottle*, was on its way to Australia where it was entered in the Olympics.

The year rolled by, with a lot of planning meetings and a trip to Australia by Mike Parker for the preliminary arrangements. A foreboding note came on his return when his wife expressed concern over their marriage; she suspected him of having an affair and was pretty fed up with the hours he kept and his weeks away from home.[6] He might just as well have been married to Philip, she said.

October came and all was ready. A 400-page loose-leaf folder of foolscap pages detailed the itinerary and check-list. Bags were packed and trunks marked 'WOV' (wanted on voyage); Philip's brand-new Lagonda (wanted for private use at ports of call) was stowed aboard *Britannia*, which was sent on ahead, to be joined later by Philip and his personal entourage of friends, photographers and naturalists, who joined at various points of the tour. They included Mike Parker, artist Edward Seago, two girl secretaries and, later, the crew that was to race *Bluebottle* in Melbourne. As Eileen Parker put it in her memoirs, Philip and 'the funny friends were afloat'.

Another shot across the bows: one week before they left the *Daily Mirror* decided it was an opportune moment to re-examine the state of the monarchy and asked: is the New Elizabethan Age going to be a flop? Cecil King, through the editorial, argued that after the Coronation the nation had been longing for a more open sort of monarchy in which 'kings could mix with commoners and all the protocol surrounding royalty could be swept aside. The leader went on: 'The circle around the throne is as aristocratic, as insular and – there is no more suitable word for it – as toffee-nosed as it has ever been'. It was time for a reappraisal; the Queen and her husband should get off the 'dreary roundabout'.[7]

Philip doubtless agreed with the *Mirror*'s sentiments; before long it was being said that one of the underlying reasons for his long trip was to get away from it all and leave behind the frustrations and humiliations of his job. And so with the royal yacht *Britannia* under the command of a rear admiral, and with a crew of 275 officers and ratings already heading east for a later rendezvous, a distinctly subdued royal party made its way to Heathrow airport on the afternoon of 15 October 1956. There a VC-10 of the Royal Air Force, suitably adapted for the requirements of its important passenger, was parked on the runway with its four engines purring smoothly, ready for take-off. Philip was not asked to present his passport (he has the distinction of holding Passport Number One) and the Queen, Prince Charles – whose eighth birthday Philip would miss, just as he had the first five – and Princess Anne, aged six, kissed him goodbye. The Queen, it is said, looked noticeably apprehensive and hardly managed to raise a smile, a fact which would be used later when the sensation-mongers began to talk of a 'rift'.

Philip had hardly begun his round-the-world visitations when the Queen was caught in the worst crisis since the war. It was as well he was away, she is supposed to have confided to one of her attendants, otherwise he would have been 'impossible to live with' in the coming weeks and months.

The Suez fiasco had engulfed British and Western politics; diplomatic manœuvres were in full swing. While their attention was diverted, Russian tanks opened fire for the first time on Hungarian freedom-fighters in the 23 October Uprising; the Poles also looked menacingly troublesome and Khrushchev flew to Warsaw to warn of the repercussions. Meanwhile, also on 23 October, fifteen died in anti-British riots in Singapore and Anthony Eden was comparing Colonel Nasser to Hitler for his insistence on controlling the Suez Canal. On 31 October, RAF Valiants and Canberras took off from Cyprus and bombed Egypt as a forerunner to an Anglo-French invasion.

The Queen was on permanent standby during this activity. Philip and his friends, meanwhile, were having a hectic but enjoyable time.

There was uproar over Britain's handling of Suez and large-scale demonstrations. The United Nations sent in a peacekeeping force and demanded the withdrawal of Anglo-French and Israeli troops. America threatened to pull the plug on financial aid to Britain and, reluctantly, Eden ordered the evacuation of forces in the face of international condemnation.

No such withdrawal in Hungary, where 1,000 Russian tanks finally crushed the Uprising on 5 November and Radio Budapest was cut off after its last dramatic appeal: 'Help . . . Help . . . Help . . . Help . . .'

A similar plea was being made by Eileen, the wife of Mike Parker. She made an appointment to see Richard Colville at Buckingham Palace and explained that she was going to sue her husband for legal separation as a prelude to divorce.[8] Since he had joined Philip's staff, said Mrs Parker, her husband had progressively seen less of her and the children. Par for the course, perhaps, said a sympathetic but terribly formal Colville. Aghast at another divorce scandal hitting his nerve-centre, he implored Eileen at least to wait until Parker returned from Australia. He, like half the café society of London – which Philip hated – had already heard the nasty rumours of a troubled marriage between the Queen and Prince Philip and it would be better to avoid any untoward publicity at the moment. Mrs Parker agreed, although she warned that she fully intended to pursue the action upon Mike's return; she instructed her solicitor accordingly.

The Queen fell unwittingly into a constitutional crisis as accusations of Eden's duplicity emerged over the way he handled the Suez affair; he later maintained that he kept the Queen informed all along of each step, but a nasty taste remained that she had become his puppet and rubber stamp. Eden himself was taken ill as the crisis subsided and exited stage left to recuperate in Jamaica, leaving R. A. Butler in charge, and the Queen, as she viewed the volatile international situation, stunned, worried and fearful of whatever was going to happen next in her first major role in an issue of world importance.

Philip, meantime, shot a huge crocodile right between the eyes in Darwin and had it skinned and stowed on board *Britannia* to bring home to be made into handbags for the Palace womenfolk. He had a particularly busy schedule, flying here, there and everywhere, opening things and shaking hands with many people who showed him their 'heartfelt thanks' for his presence. He received an equally warm welcome when he declared the 1956 Olympic Games open. He stayed for the duration, especially pleased to see his own yacht *Bluebottle* take a bronze in the Dragon class. He was also noticed in some high-profile off-duty moments with Michael Parker. Then he reboarded *Britannia* and headed for more of the same in New Zealand. The final part of his tour took him to Antarctica to visit some of the seven British scientific stations, a journey which in retrospect can only be described as self-indulgent. The recorded highlights are of capturing wildlife on film and canvas, of watching icebergs float past, of having a beard-growing contest, watching whale-boats catch their quarry, having a football match on ice, visiting a few thousand far-flung Commonwealth citizens and a rather larger number of penguins.

He was able to make a broadcast from Antarctica on Christmas Day to link up with the Queen's from England, and afterwards they wished each other a Happy Christmas. From the Falklands, where he attended sheepdog trials and a farmers' luncheon, to Ascension Island, where he watched sea-turtles, they travelled on to Gambia, the tiny African colony which was to be the last landfall of the tour. Boy Scouts and nomadic tribes chanted their welcome, and later they were able to repeat their

Darwin crocodile hunt. Philip finished off one especially large specimen which had already been shot four times by Mike Parker but was still snarling and thrashing about.

The remaining two weeks had been planned as a lazy period of swimming and relaxing in the Canary Islands, away from the public glare after such hectic times, and then on to Gibraltar for a brief unofficial visit before meeting up with the Queen in Lisbon for a State visit to Portugal on 16 February. But in those early weeks of the new year, tension had mounted back home.

Eden resigned in January 1957, placing the Queen at the centre of a major and controversial Constitutional issue over the selection of a successor. It was supposed to be the Queen's choice and sole prerogative, and was indeed a situation filled with pitfalls from which only she might emerge the loser. In fact, far from making a personal selection, she asked her mother's old friend Lord Salisbury, the Lord President, to advise her. It was arranged that he and another of the Conservative Party's elder statesmen, Lord Kilmuir, the Lord Chancellor, should interview Cabinet ministers one by one to take a straw poll. She also saw other ministers, and her old friend Sir Winston Churchill. Harold Macmillan succeeded against Rab Butler, amid quite loud protests that the Queen had allowed herself to be bullied into selecting Macmillan. The Labour Party protested strongly that the Queen had been wrongly involved in party politics. She was even rebuked by the Lord's Day Observance Society for receiving her new Prime Minister on a Sunday.

Those days of exceedingly tense, high-level consultation must, in themselves, have left the inexperienced, occasionally naïve, Queen with furrowed brow and, in a parliamentary scene awash with post-Suez intrigue, she found herself at the centre of an unholy backlash. And all this at a time when Philip was away and unable to offer his support.

What happened next could only exacerbate her general feeling that the monarchy had been placed on a knife's edge. Philip and the *Britannia* were sailing towards Gibraltar when Eileen Parker's solicitors gave gossip columnist Rex North of the *Sunday Pictorial* a scoop: Philip's best friend and wife had parted. She intended to sue for divorce on the grounds of adultery.

A couple of decades later such an event would have been recorded without much fuss on an inside page of the popular newspapers and with probably no more than a paragraph in the quality papers. In the wake of Princess Margaret and all the other tensions in which the Queen had become embroiled, it became an 'exclusive sensation' which ran and ran beneath banner headlines in all the mass-selling newspapers in Britain and the rest of the world.

But there must have been some reason for this massive over-reaction to the marital problems of a relatively minor member of the Buckingham Palace entourage?

Indeed there was. The continental press had been hinting for some time that the marriage of the Queen and Philip was itself 'on the rocks'. Such stories had appeared in Italy, Germany and France in colourful magazines like *Oggi*, *Stern* and *Paris Match* whose writers had been posing such outrageous suggestions that Philip maintained 'a bachelor apartment close to London's Berkeley Square' and that his stag parties 'in the infamous Soho district' led to other more daring adventures. And since Mike Parker had been Philip's inseparable companion on these jaunts, the link was easy to make: his wife had become fed up with the philanderings and wanted out.

It was seen by the foreign journals as confirmation of what they had already suggested and Parker was cast in the role of Philip's willing partner in certain boisterous behaviour on their world tour. They did their best to imply that if one had been adulterous, then so had the other, blissfully unaware that the separation move had already been set in motion by Mrs Parker before they set sail and delayed only to allow her husband to return home.

The panic among the Queen's advisers at the Palace has been well documented. None had had the gall, it seems, to warn either the Queen or Philip about the bubbling speculation on the Continent and both were totally unprepared for the avalanche of outpourings that followed. Mike Parker resigned immediately to save the Palace any further embarrassment and there were some lengthy telephone conversations between Philip and the Queen over whether they should accept. Some newspapers tried to offer counsel with a snap poll of readers, who voted largely in favour of allowing Parker to stay on.

He didn't, and they all carried the picture of Philip and his departing aide shaking hands – 'silently' according to the *Mirror* but with emotion according to the *Sketch*, which reported Philip as saying, 'Good luck and God speed, Mike, whatever happens to you.'

Exit Mr Parker amid a barrage of black type. And could there possibly have been a mischievous telephone call from a certain duchess chuckling her heart out in Paris to prompt a malicious piece soon afterwards in the *Baltimore Sun*? The Duchess of Windsor's hometown newspaper had long taken an interest in the affairs of her relatives-in-law. An article signed by a Miss Joan Graham was typical of the journalistic creativity of the period. She suggested that Parker's resignation was linked inextricably to the rumours that Philip 'had more than a passing interest in an unnamed woman and was meeting her regularly at the apartment of the royal photographer, Baron.'[9]

In response to the welter of enquiries which followed, the Queen's most senior adviser, her own Private Secretary Sir Michael Adeane, took the unusual step of intervening and made a statement denying that anything was wrong in the royal household – totally forgetting that old adage by which the world and his wife chooses to assess such denials: 'No smoke without fire.'

And to use a tabloid word, Philip was fuming!

The Queen put on a brave face, flew out to meet him for a much-heralded reunion and said, 'How can they say such cruel things about us?' Philip's contribution, said the eagle-eyed reporters, was to wear a tie covered with red hearts. In fact, it was the official tie of the Hawkes Bay Regiment and the 'hearts' were actually stags' heads. However brave they were, and however much they appeared publicly unaffected by this absolutely daunting tirade of verbiage and conjecture, the mud was sticking.

The incident became a focal point for a new round of scrutiny and would indeed be referred to for many years. When Eileen Parker wrote her autobiography twenty years later, for example, she hinted strongly enough that there had been more to the troubles than met the eye: 'My first instinct was to blame sheer panic for Mike's abrupt decision [to resign] but then upon reflection I started to wonder if his resignation was a smokescreen for something, or somebody, else. . . .'[10] It was another throwaway line that would be used to inspire idle gossip.

Chapter Seventeen

Sweeping Changes

In the aftermath of Suez, Eden's resignation, Macmillan's selection and Philip's long absence, the monarchy faced several months of unprecedented attack which verged on a national debate over its future. The criticism was the worst the Queen and her husband – even the institution of British monarchy itself – had ever faced and it left its mark. At the end of the year, Philip was heard to make a classic understatement: 'We ought to take account of this.'[1]

Ironically, it was also to be their busiest year since the accession with more engagements and overseas visits crowded into the monarch's diary than in any single year in history – largely through their heavier use of air travel; official tours of Portugal, France, Denmark, Canada and the United States were planned in addition to a vast list of home appointments. And unlike the early days, when the Queen had the wit, warmth and wisdom of that great old statesman Churchill to advise her, she now had as head of her government a new man who had his own problems.

The visit to Portugal was carried out under far greater glare than would normally have been the case and the travellers returned, somewhat apprehensively, to face the music. The Queen, apparently anxious to demonstrate her own feelings upon the immediate situation, granted her husband the title 'and titular dignity of a Prince of the United Kingdom' on 22 February and declared that henceforth he would be known as the Prince Philip, Duke of Edinburgh. The Mountbattens, ever ready to put on a show of normality, gave them a party and arranged for them all to see a West End show, *At the Drop of a Hat* with Michael Flanders and Donald Swan who sang their famous 'Hippopotamus Song' loud and clear – without realizing, surely, the significance of the words:

181

'Mud, mud, glorious mud. Nothing quite like it for cooling the blood . . .'*

Philip appeared at a luncheon at the Mansion House on 26 February to deliver the speech traditionally expected after a world tour and clearly designed to answer his critics. He insisted, incidentally, that his former Secretary Mike Parker come to the lunch, along with others who had been in the Prince's party; Parker was placed as close to the top table as possible.

'I find it difficult to realize that I have been around the world and covered nearly 40,000 miles since October 15th last year,' Philip began.

> It would be quite easy to claim that this journey was all part of a deep-laid scheme but I am afraid I have to admit that it all came about because I was asked to start off the Olympic Games in Melbourne. In fact, it would have been much simpler to have flown out and flown back but had I done that I could not have visited several remote communities who are loyal members of the Commonwealth and I could not have inspected some of our bases in the Antarctic. I might have got home for Christmas but I could not have entertained nearly 1,400 people in the Queen's yacht from Australia, New Zealand and those remote communities at 26 lunches, dinners and receptions and thereby strengthened, I hope, the close links which exist between the Crown and the people of the Commonwealth.[2]

He went on to give graphic details of his trip and pointedly ended with reference to his homecoming: 'and finally, as you know, this adventure ended where it began at London airport with a very happy family reunion.' He also spoke of the sacrifice he had made in undertaking the trip and being away from home for so long: 'I believe there are some things for which it is worthwhile making some personal sacrifice and the British Commonwealth is one of those things. . . .'

It was a valiant effort. But sacrifice? What sacrifice? Those who inspected his itinerary in detail would have marvelled at its content but baulked at its inspiration. Was it not, after all, the Queen they all wanted to see in the colonies and Commonwealth, rather than her husband? Could there really have been any justification for such an expensive jaunt for the sake of a few thousand handshakes and some far-flung communities, many of whom didn't even know who he was?

Others supported him but agreed he had also had a good time. Sir

---

* The occasion was an echo of 1926 when the Mountbattens themselves faced a similar situation, returning to England after a trip to America to face persistent rumours that their marriage was over. Noël Coward arranged for them to sit in conspicuous, hand-holding togetherness in the front row on opening night of his new play, *The Vortex*.

Raymond Priestley, Antarctic explorer and former President of the British Association, remembered:

> The tour did a lot of good. True, it was a chance for the Prince to enjoy himself in informal company, doing things he wanted to do. It was all his idea and he was as enthusiastic as a schoolboy. He would have liked to have got closer to the South Pole but we faced the prospect of being iced in for months, so we did not go too far. He asked to sail in a whale catcher . . . and saw a large [whale] being killed at close quarters. I'd say he came away on the side of the whales. Overall, he made the tour a pleasure cruise for his close companions. I started one game by giving us all bird names. He was the Royal Crested Philip. I became the lesser Polar Backchat.[3]

What fun!

Another questionable aspect of the trip was the shooting of crocodiles in Darwin and the Gambia and the whale Philip saw harpooned. The League Against Cruel Sports gave him a stern lecture, the first of dozens; as far as they were concerned, he was as unable then as in the eighties satisfactorily to explain the paradox of supporting the preservation of wildlife while disposing of assorted creatures in pursuit of country sport. But more of that later.

On the back of one criticism came another, and then another. Articles arrived thick and fast, especially at Express Newspapers, and, where initially it had been the Prince who had been the target of attack, very soon the spotlight turned dramatically to the Queen herself. First, Leonard Mosley had them under the microscope in an article headed 'THE SUBTLE RELATIONSHIP OF THE QUEEN AND THE MAN SHE LOVES', in which he posed the case of a mythical tycoon's daughter richer and more influential than the man she married. He would probably spend the rest of his life, said Mosley, (a) persuading her that he really did take her for love not money, (b) trying not to resent the power of her bank account, (c) quelling the suspicion of his enemies that he would never have got anywhere in life if it had not been for the influence of his wife.[4]

Beaverbrook took them to task again a short time later, attacking them for their lack of culture and failing to offer sufficient patronage to the arts. Of course, it was quite true that the Queen would rather go to the races than view an exhibition of modern art; Philip certainly preferred polo to opera and once said to an artist he had just met, 'Oh yes, we bought one of yours, you know – had a nasty spot on the wall to hide.' Princess Margaret liked jazz better than an evening of chamber music and the Queen Mother was more than happy with a night out at the London Palladium, listening to the Crazy Gang's dirty jokes. It was also true that Philip didn't care for being 'highnessed' – just plain 'sir' would do – and preferred a half of bitter to a glass of champagne; he hated pomp and 'zoo teas' (Princess Margaret's expression) where they ate and people watched.

So what was Beaverbrook's case? First, it must be borne in mind that he had recently been painted by Graham Sutherland, who complained that he had yet to be invited to paint the Queen. Second, since his newspapers' circulation hardly represented the mass of the nation's élite and highbrow, there must have been an ulterior motive. Read on: 'No one in their senses', said the *Express*, 'wants a pompous, pedantic family of intellectuals round the throne. But more than anybody, they could set the stage for a grand flowering of talent on the highest level.'

Beaverbrook believed that Philip Mountbatten, as he insisted upon calling him, had been let off too lightly and he had not been entirely pleased with the general performance of the new monarchy so far. Beaverbrook chose to ignore the triumphs and would return to the attack in a bigger way later in the year; but it did appear that his legendary attacks on Lord Mountbatten were being inherited by Prince Philip. Some believed he had conducted an unwarranted vendetta against the Mountbattens. A. J. P. Taylor, Beaverbrook's biographer, thought this to be an exaggeration since Beaverbrook's views went up and down. He consistently attacked Mountbatten over Dieppe, spoke of his dislike of 'what I believe to be the betrayal of Burma and refusal to let the Dutch back into Indonesia', and labelled Mountbatten 'the man who gave away India'. Almost until his death in 1964 he held the firm view that Mountbatten was 'a man not to be trusted in any public capacity'. Taylor conceded that it was 'difficult not to feel more lay behind. None of Beaverbrook's friends could discover what it was. Something about Mountbatten touched Beaverbrook on a raw nerve.'[5] Some of those who worked for Beaverbrook felt that it was a culmination of his wartime mistrust of Mountbatten's actions coupled with a serious questioning of the judgment of a man whose life had been beset by scandal of one sort or another in the twenties and thirties, about which Beaverbrook had a better knowledge than most. He was kept well informed of the 'social misdemeanours' of Lord and Lady Mountbatten by his two star infiltrators of the socialite scene, Tom Driberg, who was William Hickey of the *Daily Express*, and Sir Robert Bruce Lockhart, whom he hired in 1928 as 'Londoner' on the *Evening Standard*.

It was perhaps inevitable that Prince Philip should be caught in the backlash, and not just by Beaverbrook. Cecil King at the *Mirror* – then the *Daily Express*'s main circulation rival – was one who was seriously to question Prince Philip's actions even to the point, as we will discover, of complaining about him in a 'confidential letter' to Harold Wilson.

One man who worked for both, Robert Edwards, twice editor of the *Daily Express*, recalls a classic Beaverbrook–Prince Philip story:

We were walking in Green Park one day (around 1960) when a helicopter came over flying low. In those days, before too many of them were about, most people would assume it was Prince Philip. Beaverbrook instinctively ducked and said, 'Bow down, Bob, bow down, bow down before your lord and master.' That was Beaverbrook and the Mountbattens. At Buckingham Palace once, I talked to Prince Philip about Beaverbrook. Philip said they could never persuade him to visit the Palace.[6]

Over at the *Mirror* camp, there were moans that the Crown was spending too much money and the paper pleaded with them to cut costs; five months' holiday a year at the family retreats of Windsor, Sandringham and Balmoral more than counterbalanced their workload. Writer B. A. Young complained that thirty public appearances in the space of ninety days was hardly a backbreaking programme 'for a company whose principal *raison d'être* is the making of public appearances.'

On it went. Even the *Church of England Newspaper* joined in with a controversial piece bemoaning the fact that the monarchy seemed to have become some sort of substitute religion. And, horror of horrors, it even challenged the right of accession, comparing the monarchy with a family business of which 'no man would be allowed to take over effective direction with no qualifications other than being the son of a particular father.'[7]

This was all a minor skirmish compared with the trouble that arose in August when Lord Altrincham,* though a Monarchist and genuine supporter of the Queen, wrote a critical piece in his own obscure monthly magazine, *National and English Review*. He said there were many faults in the way the monarchy was working and most of them could be blamed upon the tweedy set who still formed a tight little enclave of English ladies and gentlemen around the Queen. He blamed them for the poor impression Her Majesty was making in her general appearance and more especially in having to deliver the speeches they had prepared for her: 'The personality conveyed by the utterances which are put into her mouth is that of a priggish schoolgirl, captain of the hockey team, a prefect and a recent candidate for confirmation!'

Altrincham should be hung, drawn and quartered, said an outraged defender of the Queen's entourage, the Duke of Argyll, Master of her Scottish Household. Altrincham received threats through the mail, an attack from the Empire Loyalists, and was challenged to a duel. That opinion was not shared by some of the younger members of Her Majesty's staff, however, and some years later Sir Martin Charteris – at the time of Altrincham's article deputy to the Queen's Private Secretary Sir

* Later to revert to John Grigg after dispensing with his title in 1963.

Michael Adeane – congratulated Grigg on the 'great service' he had done to the monarchy.[8] The *Daily Mail* ran a poll and discovered its younger readers wholeheartedly supported Altrincham.

More was to follow. John Osborne, still youngish and angry, had just returned to the theatrical limelight with the opening of his new play, *The Entertainer*. He wrote in the magazine *Encounter* that Queen-worship sickened him; the whole panoply of Royalty was symptomatic of a deeply sick society and overwhelming evidence of bankruptcy in the nation's culture – picking up Beaverbrook's theme. Then he added a very pertinent sentence, which could well have been written again three decades later:

> It bores me, it distresses me that there should be so many empty minds, so many empty lives in Britain to sustain this fatuous industry; that no one should have the wit to laugh it into extinction or the honesty to resist it.[9]

By now, the family was getting a little punch drunk, for apart from these asides there was the general day-to-day reporting to contend with. The next encounter arrived in another bout of large-headline type, heralding a major furore and again emanating from the *Express* building. Malcolm Muggeridge, whose piece for the *New Statesmen* a year earlier on 'The Royal Soap Opera' had not gone down too well, was back in the fray with a fairly innocuous article for the New York *Saturday Evening Post* about the strange power of the British monarchy with its ability to whip up such a frenzy of interest. As is the usual way, in castigating Muggeridge for his attack on the Queen, whom he said duchesses found 'dowdy, frumpish and banal', the *Express* ran most of the article and edited out only the less critical and contentious sentences.

Uproar! Muggeridge was suspended from the BBC and the Press Council refused complaints against the newspaper's misinterpretation of his original article – all of this in 1957, long before the *Sun* came into existence, long before the strident members of our popular press took on Royalty face to face and ditched the cap-doffing for good. It was, even by today's standards, a relentless pursuit of our young Queen and her husband. And this kind of irreverence for the monarch could only be published with the approval of proprietors like Beaverbrook and Cecil King. Only the ever-loving *Times* and the BBC were equally dogged in support.

As Philip's cousin ex-Queen Alexandra wrote, that summer saw him going through a phase of 'fundamental if not critical' readjustment which would also reflect itself in major changes to the system.[10] If the phrase 'No more Mr Nice Guy' had been in use then, it would have been around this point that Prince Philip would have used it. He was boiling with rage and showed it. Yet the enigma of the man was never more apparent than in that year, as he flashed on his devastating charm one minute and an ice-cold dismissiveness the next. On the one hand he seemed worried by the criticism of the monarchy, while on the other he seemed uncaring that he actually might contribute to it. That summer, for instance, he 'let off some steam' by playing polo often, sailed at Cowes and elsewhere at every opportunity, and even took his first solo flight in Peter Scott's glider. Yet it seemed he had still not taken account of the adverse publicity that could result from his own activities, as was proved one day when he flew from the royal yacht *Britannia* by helicopter to pilot a glider during the National Gliding Championships, then left by helicopter to play polo at Cowdray Park. Some of his apologists have described that episode amusingly as 'pure Philip'.

He had taken notice in other directions, however. He was the instigator of a number of rapid changes that would at least spike the guns of some of the Royal Family's critics – although to give Philip his due, some of the changes were already in place or in the pipeline by the time these critical articles had begun to appear.

Even before he went on his world tour, he had suggested holding occasional informal lunches at Buckingham Palace for a good cross-section of the community, with churchmen, industrialists, union leaders, artists, authors, scientists and so on being invited to attend, although establishment figures were certainly not excluded. It was noticeable that the first one was attended by Sir William Haley, editor of *The Times*. In July it was announced that these were to be put on a more regular footing to give the Queen and Prince Philip the chance of keeping in touch with a continuous and representative flow of her subjects.

Future guest-lists made it look as if the Prince had just discovered that quotation of Edward VIII that 'class can no longer stand apart from class'. Actors, actresses, footballers, athletes and cricketers were soon finding themselves ushered in through the side-entrance of Buckingham Palace. Guests like Christopher Brasher, Donald Campbell, Alec Guinness, Flora Robson, Mike Hawthorn, Billy Wright and even Osbert Lancaster were among them. It was social revolution! An unheard-of air of informality was introduced to the lunches. 'What a difference from the old days', one of the old courtiers recalled:

> when there was a stiff rule that no one spoke to the Sovereign until he had spoken to them first. I remember all too well those ghastly silences at Buckingham Palace meals – one in particular when there was a deathly hush, interrupted only by the sound of George V spitting cherry stones on to his plate.

Philip had embarked upon a personal fact-finding exercise to familiarize himself with every aspect of monarchy, public and private. He gave special thought to the unwieldy staffing arrangements in Buckingham Palace and in this he followed almost to the letter the early initiatives of Prince Albert when he first arrived at the Palace. Albert called them his 'investigations' which he undertook through lack of employment elsewhere; Victoria kept him well away from her royal prerogatives in the early years of their married life. And Albert, coming as he did from a small economical Court, often ridden with financial problems, was acutely aware of over-spending and inefficiency:

> It always seems to me, as if an infinitude of small trivialities hung about me like an ever present weight. We shall never be in a position to occupy ourselves with higher and graver things, so long as we have to deal with these mere nothings.[11]

So he began his complete review of the royal household, its functions and its people. Among the things he discovered was the following:

> The Lord Steward finds the fuel and lays the fire; the Lord Chamberlain lights it and provides the lamps but the Lord Steward must trim and light them. The inside cleaning of windows belongs to the Lord Steward's department; the outside must be attended by the Office of Woods and Forests.

The Palace staff hated Albert and his own imported German staff, whom they labelled 'spies', especially for his insistence that some of the housemaids take a pay cut. He ended a lot of the perks and invisible earnings, like 'supper with wine'. He uncovered the candle scandal – the practice of renewing every single candle in the Palace every day even if it had not been lit, including those in servants' rooms. Naturally, a cottage industry had sprung up in 'Palace ends', with footmen dashing up to the West End with their bags of candles and other 'perks' to sell to shopkeepers. Albert discovered, for example, that a single order for a particular coloured candle that had been required for one of Victoria's State balls had resulted in the same order being delivered to the Palace every week for some years.[12]

A hundred years later, when Philip moved in, the revolution that Prince Albert had brought was still in place, tinkered with briefly by Edward VIII, and had itself become archaic; 'quaint practices' of which Albert complained were still enveloped in the hazy aura of 'tradition'. Philip studied Prince Albert's previous findings and began his own investigations almost from the day he arrived and his process of dragging the organization of monarchy into the twentieth century spanned the next ten years and beyond. He strove to keep up with new technology; a huge card-index system he installed, for example, on which they meticulously recorded everyone with whom the Palace had contact, was seen as an incredible innovation at the time, though twenty years later the system itself looked quaint and outdated in the face of computerization.

During the first year of the Queen's reign Philip and Mike Parker inspected every single room in the Palace. It is said that when two people set off to count them, neither would come back with the same answer. The same could almost be said about the staff! There were around 230 in Buckingham Palace and about 120 at Windsor. He examined the work procedures, stopped people in corridors and asked them what they did, who they worked for and what they thought of their job. One of his first tasks was to end the practice of uniformed flunkies delivering messages from one member of the family to the other, or between staff, by hand and on silver plates. If he was working in his office and wanted a sandwich, it took four different people to convey the message and deliver the food. So he introduced internal telephones, intercoms and was, of course, among the first in London to have his cars installed with telephones. He was puzzled by some of the customs, like the fresh bottle of Scotch whisky that appeared in the Queen's bedroom every night, even though she did not drink. The staff could not enlighten him, so he dug into the archives and discovered that it had begun when Queen Victoria, plagued with a cold, asked for a bottle of whisky to be brought to her room. The next day, it was replaced by a fresh one and the custom continued through four reigns.

He inspected the kitchens and the laundries and brought in such new-fangled appliances as dishwashers and automatic washing machines. On the vast royal estates, which became his responsibility as Chief Ranger, he discovered that things had not changed much in 200 years; a top-to-toe overhaul of pretty well every aspect of estate management and farming was needed and Philip began setting up the machinery to achieve it over the coming ten years. He called for regular reports from each of the farms, and those who felt he might lose interest were soon to be disappointed. If any paperwork was late, the offending employee would receive a personal telephone call: 'Where are your reports?'

Back at Buckingham Palace, there were other annoying inbuilt traditions in staffing that were set in a dusty age and were choking the system – a strange mixture of titles, sinecures, necessary duties and others, many of which were performed simply because they had always been performed. The holders of these positions were formidable adversaries and held titles like the Gold Sticks, the Ladies of the Bedchamber, the Extra Ladies of the Bedchamber, Women of the Bedchamber, the Extra Women of the Bedchamber, the Groom of the Robes, the Gentlemen of the Corps, the Gentlemen Ushers, the Bargemaster, the Clerk of the Closet, and so on. Most still exist.

Even after five years of the Elizabethan rule, an 'old guard' was still in place, commanding a younger element of staff who in the main sided with Philip. As one of them said, 'He had to beat them or bow to them.' The more senior and élitist of the courtiers were horrified, for instance, when he suggested that the débutante system should be abolished. The Queen agreed and announced that the 1958 season would be the last at which the debs were presented at Court.

'But the girls so enjoyed it,' said the Queen Mother when the news was broken to her.

'So did all the people who were getting a rake-off on the side,' Philip retorted.

Next on the cancellation list were some of the more antiquated and often boring activities, such as the formal Courts, State balls, levees and audiences. With some, Philip needed to draw upon all his powers of persuasion to talk the Queen into ending these traditions, revered by her father and grandfather. But eventually, like the débutante presentations, they were largely stopped.

Speeches came next in Philip's streamlining. He had already shown that he intended to write his own and seldom took advice on content. Lieutenant General Sir Frederick Browning, first Comptroller to the Prince, recalled how it happened. He had prepared a speech for a particular occasion, but when Philip got up to deliver it, he discovered that he had altered everything. 'There was not a bit of my stuff in it and I was never asked to write another speech after that.'[13]

Inroads were being made towards humanizing the Queen's speeches. That year was to be her first on live television, with a broadcast to the Canadians in conjunction with her important autumn tour, followed by her traditional Christmas broadcast to the Nation and the Commonwealth. Normally left in the hands of more senior figures, this time the task was handed to 45-year-old Lieutenant Colonel the Honourable Martin Charteris, Adeane's deputy and one of the Palace 'modernists'. Though still one of the old school, he was at least relatively young and his brother-in-law Ian Fleming, creator of James Bond, might well have been able to offer some advice. The Queen stressed that she wanted her speeches to be more personal and direct, and that is what she achieved, helped by television personality Sylvia Peters, who made a ten-minute film of useful tips for Her Majesty to follow. Philip added his advice; he had already made a couple of television appearances, notably a programme on his tour which he called *Around the World in 40 Minutes*. He advised the Queen to take off her shoes before she began because it would relax her and no one would notice. 'Forget about protocol, darling,' Philip is supposed to have told her. 'What people want to see is you smile – the rest can go hang.' She was relaxed, but the smile didn't get through. Someone described her as looking as 'miserable as Anne Boleyn at the scaffold' in the Canadian broadcast, although she looked better in the Christmas one.

Another notch in the modernization process came with the appointment of Philip's new Private Secretary, in which once again he ignored the tradition of choosing from within a family of courtiers. He sought advice from Mountbatten over the appointment and apparently wrote to say he looked forward to discussing possible candidates – though added that they had to be 'a bit careful . . . because I'm sure you realize what fun some people would have if they thought you were "choosing" my staff.'[14] The man selected was ex-Gordonstoun pupil James Orr, who had been head boy a year or two before Philip. They had met briefly when Philip called at Mombasa and discovered Orr, then a chief inspector in the Kenyan police, among the welcoming party. He was as surprised as anyone to receive a letter inviting him to become Private Secretary to the Queen's husband.

More changes were on display when the royal couple took off for Canada and America in the autumn of 1957 for what was the most elaborate North American tour ever arranged. The scale of it can be judged from one statistic alone: 3,000 reporters and photographers were granted official accreditation. Their first task after stepping off the plane was to attend a press reception at which they shook hands with no less than 600 of the people who would be observing their every move for the next ten days and giving an instant replay on live television to an audience of millions – a task made all the more crucial from the media point of view by the recent publicity.

It had become a fact of life that if a monarch's popularity once depended upon great displays of pomp and circumstance, now it was very definitely in the hands of newspapers and television. They approached this greatest change of all with apprehension, again through mixed ambitions. Philip, like his uncle, wanted to bring the Queen closer to her people, but not too close. They wanted to retain firm control of their television exposure to make sure that the cameras were kept out of earshot and away from private moments. This was an aspect of their relationship with television people that they maintained for years, though their children and other royal offspring were less inhibited.

The dangers of this new exposure were to become very evident on the North American visit in 1957, more so than at any previous time: it would lead to the presentation of Royalty as media people. The royal party managers totally misunderstood 'those awfully brash' American journalists who liked to write headlines and banners saying 'HIYA, LIZ AND PHIL', yet meant no disrespect. The *Chicago Daily News* described her as a 'Doll, a living doll'.

Whoever called the Queen a doll?

Commander Colville, the Press Secretary, well remembering that it had been an American reporter who broke the Princess Margaret love story and an American who wrote nasty rumours about the state of his employers' marriage, kept the newspapermen fastidiously away from the Queen. All other members of the entourage were naturally prohibited from speaking to the press and, as *Time* magazine pointed out, the puzzled journalists ended up interviewing each other. The *Washington Post* remarked balefully, 'As far as we can tell she is human.'

The reluctance of Philip himself to allow the party to receive the kind of treatment given to film stars was perhaps best summed up on the steps of the White House where they had all posed for pictures. The Queen turned away to go inside and moved Philip to join her.

'Just one more,' shouted a cameraman in the crowd.

Philip glared back, his eyes searching for the culprit. 'What do you mean – one more?' and he turned his back on them and walked inside.

Some things simply would not change. By the end of the year, however, they had 'taken account' of a great deal of the criticism. They even moved towards answering Beaverbrook's complaints about the philistine views of the Royals. The Queen and Philip decided to open an art gallery at Buckingham Palace in the bombed ruins of the old chapel, thus allowing the public the opportunity of viewing the world's greatest collection of art treasures at long last.

It was an excellent idea, of course, and it was passed to the hands of the Surveyor of the Queen's Pictures, Professor Anthony Blunt. How were they to know he was a Russian spy?

PART FOUR

Chapter Eighteen
Images and Auras

The comedian Spike Milligan fell foul of his royal friends by commenting on how well Prince Philip had done for himself: 'When he married the Queen, his arse was hanging out of his trousers.'[1] Spike spoke the truth. Philip's change of lifestyle had been dramatic and the pleasurable interludes he was able to indulge in between engagements were on display through his very public pursuit of fulfilment. He acquired a vivid image as a trendsetter during the fifties and sixties, typically philistine in his attitudes and possibly the first yuppie of Great Britain, his upward mobility assured by his status. He was to be seen driving a Lagonda or an Alvis or a Scimitar, speaking on his car telephone, dashing down to Cowdray Park, galloping around on one of his polo ponies, swigging liquid direct from the bottle at half-time and then flying off somewhere in a helicopter, perhaps to deliver another of his urgings on industrial reform or mercantile greatness.

The image of philistinism has continued to rankle and it is still a relevant discussion point thirty years after Lord Beaverbrook first complained of it. The family's palaces are fortresses laden with treasures and works of art almost beyond description or value; yet Buckingham Palace has hardly become the hub of British cultural life in the twentieth century. Philip has fathered and moulded, by his own example, an outgoing, free-spending family, who can be miserly about certain things (for example, Palace staff salaries, recycling clothes, making do and mending curtains with moth-holes in them, and many other instances of penny-pinching) but who seem to have no inhibitions whatsoever about their sporting pleasures; that is a common denominator in all their lives. Their inspiration in terms of artistic and cultural endeavour has been rather limited.

From the days of Edward VII, they have all liked show people. Some of Mountbatten's best friends were in showbusiness and Philip also turned to them when he wanted to raise money, as indeed Prince

Charles turned to the pop-music world. So attention paid by the Royal Family to the popular categories of entertainment and the Richard Attenborough division of the performing arts has been grossly out of proportion to their patronage of the theatre, art, opera, ballet or classical music. They also seem to be happy wallowing in publicity about their admitted 'ordinariness', such as the Queen and Queen Mother watching *Coronation Street* just like any other middle-class family – which they most definitely are not!

The Queen's personal contribution to the cultural scene has been in building up her own art collection. Philip paints and has become an accomplished photographer, yet there remains of him the impression of a colourful, handsome figure who for twenty years unashamedly followed his two great passions, polo and sailing. He was never happier than when scrambling aboard one of his string of horses or on to one of his yachts with his friends down at Cowes. The pictures of him, from the time Mountbatten introduced him to polo in Malta, were endless and whenever he had a fall or a collision, as often happened, the newspapers were quick to remind him that, as husband of the Queen, he had a certain duty and responsibility not to put his life at risk. He could be 'damned inconsiderate' with those who tried to prevent him from breaking his neck. Once when he was being trained as a pilot, a warning light showed the engine on fire. He looked out, saw no smoke and diagnosed a fault which did not need immediate attention. He carried on flying. His trainer co-pilot promptly took over, stopped the engine, filled it with foam and left His Royal Highness to limp home on one engine. Philip, it is said, behaved 'like a bloodshot bull, stubbornly refusing to understand the worries of those charged with protecting him.'[2] The *Daily Mirror* became so concerned about his adventurous pursuits that it asked him to reflect for a moment on 'what would the Queen do without Philip?'[3] Audrey Whiting, one of the advance guard of modern-day royal correspondents, whom Mountbatten trusted enough to speak and give interviews to, produced quotes from an unnamed 'lifelong friend' of Philip and the Queen to inform the world that life without Philip was unimaginable for her. He was the pillar of her life, she was more in love with him now than she had ever been and without him she would 'retire to the country for a very long time'.[4]

Philip did not moderate his activities one little bit, however, and strove to become one of the top ten polo players in Britain. His Sunday afternoon games attracted most attention: Sundays are slow news days and the sight of Philip dashing about with his polo stick swirling around his head and the Queen on the sidelines shouting, 'Go on, go on!' made good photographs.

What did the Archbishop of Canterbury think of it all? Dr Robert Runcie, the present Archbishop, did not want to discuss it when the author approached him. But successive primates can not have enjoyed the sight of the head of the Church getting all excited about a reckless husband swerving around Cowdray Park on the Sabbath. The whole scenario has been repeated over and over again throughout his polo career, and was promptly taken up by his eldest son, who at his peak was spending more than £80,000 a year on polo. The Lord's Day Observance Society and many others deplored this image and example; yet the crowds thronged to see Britain's first family at play. Philip's appearances were so frequent that sometimes as many as 10,000 people jammed the nearby town of Midhurst on their way to catch a glimpse of the Royals.

It was a Philip invention, this Sunday sport for the Royal Family. George VI was a deeply religious man to whom Sunday was Sunday, a quiet, reflective, family day. His example was jettisoned and the protesters branded as out of date. The modern monarchy that the Queen and her husband were creating allowed for these changes, which were excused by Philip's apologists as a 'safety valve' through which he could release the forceful head of steam built up during the frustrations of his life as consort. The phrase 'letting off steam' is applied by the Royals themselves to their menfolk whenever they seek to get away from their official duties. It crops up often in the descriptive recollections of various courtiers of their masters' sporting exploits. Philip was an extravagant user of the safety valve, and under the ever-increasing glare of public interest he led the newspapers down yet another avenue of much-documented royal activity which had been largely untapped until now: the royal male at play.

Next, Philip's 'toys' became a matter of some comment. His pride and joy: the brand new, sparkling Lagonda waiting for him when he returned from the first Commonwealth tour. He had made the choice after trying out that and a Bentley and it long remained his favourite car, although his private usage was limited; in the first three years it clocked only 12,000 miles. He liked to play 'ordinary people' in it, personally driving the Queen away from the Palace for Windsor whenever they managed a weekend off.

He was able to supervise the final construction of the royal yacht *Britannia* and actually had the bridge adapted to his own suggestions, at extra cost, providing their own personal ocean-going liner to replace the *Albert and Victoria*. At the same time, by coincidence, British Railways was constructing a new royal dining car to be added to the already extensive royal rolling stock. Philip also introduced greater use of the helicopter and always made a study of the day's diary and routes so that he could carve in a few extras by using the chopper. He would talk in terms of military precision: 'I can chopper from Goodwood. Should be quite easy. An hour? Start the thing [an official opening], lunch and chop back.'[5]

When Churchill first heard about the helicopter, he summoned Philip's then Private Secretary Michael Parker to Downing Street. 'Is it your intention to wipe out the entire Royal Family in the shortest possible time?' he growled, knowing full well that his words would be passed on to Philip, for whom they were really intended. It was the third or fourth time that Churchill had voiced his objections to royal air travel. Philip's answer was that it had already proved its worth in saving hours of time and enabling him to get to more places. Soon they had two of the latest airliners attached to the Queen's Flight, which he piloted himself on most flights.

These were Philip's playthings, his critics said – especially when he used the new royal yacht as a base for Cowes week in its first year, 1954, while he was racing *Bluebottle*. Uffa Fox and friends came aboard and had a few drinks. So was it Philip's floating gin palace?

Although he didn't have much luck at Cowes that year – he won only 50 shillings and a lot of distracting spectator attention – the Queen was doing better with her racehorses. On 17 July her horse Aureole won the richest prize in British racing, bringing her personal winnings so far that season to £35,799 – rather more than Philip's take-home pay after tax.

Critics began some murmurings about the pleasant, privileged playtimes of the new management at Buck House, and the newspapers had their say. Philip did not seem to bother about it in terms of his personal habits and, in spite of a period of intense criticism of the monarchy in general, he continued with his acquisitions, some of which came courtesy of the State, others from the family's private finance. By 1966 the inventory of boats, planes and trains, Prince Philip for the use of, was impressive.[6]

Financed by the Treasury were: one royal yacht, *Britannia*, on permanent duty and on which he found 'absolute joy' in sailing; two aircraft of the Queen's Flight which he used and flew regularly; two Westland helicopters which were given constant royal useage; extensive royal railway rolling stock; four Rolls-Royces.

Items financed by himself, or the Queen, included: seven polo ponies, stabling, transport and feeding of same, later to be replaced by a collection of carriage-driving teams; eight family horses kept at various homes for periodic use; a collection of sporting weaponry, such as his pair of James Purdey hammerless ejector double-triggered game guns; a Swift catamaran for family use and racing, bought by the Prince and kept at Balmoral; *Bluebottle*, the Dragon class yacht he had as a wedding present from the Island Sailing Club (later went on permanent loan to Dartmouth College); the Flying Fifteen yacht *Coweslip*, received as a wedding present from the people of Cowes and rebuilt in 1962; a Sanders Cup racing dinghy presented to him in Australia in 1956 (later went on loan to Dartmouth); *Fairey Fox*, the racing yacht he had built in 1959; *Bloodhound*, the yacht bought by the Queen in 1962 for £10,000; the

Lagonda bought in 1956 was replaced in 1961 by an Alvis Convertible costing £3,110.14s.6d with shortwave radio and green glass in the rearview mirror; added to his car collection in 1963 was a Triplex Reliant Scimitar special version, designed to boost safety class, which he bought at that year's Motor Show for £2,000. There were other assorted objects of automation and mechanization which he introduced to streamline the working of monarchy and for his own enjoyment.

Philip was equipped for the best and he received plenty of accolades as he demonstrated his expertise. Uffa Fox said, 'He is a wonderful sailor. I've never known anyone take a boat across the tide as skilfully as he does. All the hours I've spent with him have been filled with joy and happiness. He's got all the qualities a man ought to have.'[7] It was during these years, from the late fifties and throughout the sixties that he picked up his 'playboy' image: with all his new accessories, he looked as if he had suddenly come into money and had gone out and spent it.

The *Daily Mirror* seemed to have adopted Philip as their number-one whipping boy – as opposed to Mountbatten at the *Express* – and criticized his spending and patronage of the top people's stores. A major leading article headlined 'THE DUKE'S LAUNDRY' (of all things!) strongly attacked the fact that traders who supplied Philip with his clothes and other requirements could now label themselves 'By Royal Appointment'. A list of twenty-nine of these people appeared in the *London Gazette*, which, the *Mirror* complained, was like a published guide to Philip's shopping, naming as it did those who supplied him with his suits, kilts, boots, shoes, hats, jewellery, guns, cars and even the man who gave him his short back and sides, a hairdresser named Mr Charles Topper.

> Are the working men of Britain now expected to be topped by Mr Topper, to choose their jewellery at Boucheron and order their guns from James Purdey and Sons? Are working women likely to send their bras and scanties to the White Heather Laundry in the hope that they will pass through the same mangle as the ducal underpants? . . . What utter nonsense . . . it is Royal Patronage at its most undignified.[8]

A noticeable 'edge' to any matters relating to the coverage of Prince Philip was becoming apparent in the newspapers. It was no accident. For several years, there had been this undercurrent of gossip – 'an aura', as Hugh Cudlipp at the *Mirror* once described it – and if they thought that 1957 was bad enough, 1959 proved to be another year of continued attack from pretty well all quarters: the press, churchmen, politicians all had their say. It was in many respects inexplicable that the monarchy as a whole should come in for a renewed round of such critical attack; the family's performance on the international stage had been spectacular.

But if there was a 'rumbling' of anything untoward, no one was spilling the beans.

The major role stories were, first, the Queen's pregnancy with Prince Andrew after a ten-year gap since Princess Anne's birth – this long pause had itself been used as further evidence of the strained relationship between the Queen and her husband. Then there was the engagement of Princess Margaret to Antony Armstrong-Jones, which was known to the family in December – a few days after Peter Townsend married Marie Luce Jamagne, a 27-year-old Belgian tobacco heiress – but not formally announced until February 1960 to avoid upstaging the birth of Prince Andrew.

Thirty years later, on 1 January 1990, the Cabinet papers of the Macmillan government released for the year 1959 did not provide a clue to the reasons for the new criticism. Files released at the Public Record Office did indeed confirm that the Royal Family was discussed in Cabinet on three separate occasions that year, but the subject matter was sufficiently sensitive for the government to order that it be kept secret for a much longer period than normal. One of the items was stamped with a 50-year embargo – as opposed to the usual 30 years – and two items were locked away for 100 years, not to be revealed until the year 2059.

What could possibly be serious enough to warrant this kind of secrecy? It was virtually without precedent in times of normality. From recent times only the Cabinet documents relating to the Abdication remain precluded. In 1959 there were no wars, political upsets or Constitutional crises. The Profumo Affair was still a long way from exposure. Sir Anthony Blunt is unlikely to have been a topic of discussion, since Macmillan had only just cleared the Third Man, Kim Philby, of spying for Russia, never mind discussing the prospect of a Fourth Man. Even if he were brought up at Cabinet meetings, it seems unlikely that he would fall under the heading of 'Royal Family'.

The year of 1959 was also the one in which the Queen agreed to change her family name to Mountbatten-Windsor after continued pressure from Philip and his uncle, though again the news was withheld from the public to coincide with the birth of Andrew. There was some lively Cabinet discussion on the change, and since it is not recorded among the documents made public in 1990 we must assume that it is among the three items which have been retained from public view. So let us examine this as one of the 'secret' mysteries.

Back in 1952, when the issue first arose, Churchill and Eden opposed changing the name of the royal house. Churchill himself, as we have seen, acted swiftly and with 'great pressure' to correct the accidental removal of the House of Windsor created by the 'Battenberg marriage' of which Queen Mary spoke so bitterly. The name reverted to Windsor only after Churchill had told the Queen that 'the feeling of the government reinforced by public opinion was that Her Majesty should drop the Mountbatten name and reign under her father's name of Windsor.[9] This she did, much to Mountbatten's disappointment, though he continued to lobby for the next seven years, by which time he had come up with the compromise suggestion of Mountbatten-Windsor to fall in with the arrival of Prince Andrew.

In 1959 the Queen informed Macmillan that 'it was the wish of all the family' that their name should be changed and he took her request to his ministers for a reappraisal – well aware of the heated exchanges it was likely to provoke. At least two Cabinet ministers were known still to be deeply opposed to attaching the Mountbatten name to the British royal house, and they were not alone. Scathing criticism came from all quarters – not least, of course, from the press.

At the *Mirror*, the view of Cecil King was made known with a leader article decrying the move as unnecessary:

> only fifteen years after the second world war against Germany we are abruptly informed that the name of Mountbatten, formerly Battenberg, is to be joined willy-nilly with the name of Windsor. Were the Prime Minister and Cabinet merely informed or did they agree? Earl Mountbatten was fully aware of what was going on.[10]

Which was the *Mirror*'s way of saying that they thought he had pressurized the Queen into it.

Lord Beaverbrook was in no doubt that he had. He wrote in more pointedly vitriolic fashion with the emphasis directed as usual at the Earl himself:

> While he sat in his office in Whitehall and pondered the problems of defence or the Navy or whatever high position he happened to be holding, one spectre has always confronted Earl Mountbatten of Burma; that his family name should die out. . . . he has a nephew who is the Marquess of Milford Haven and another who holds perhaps a greater honour and responsibility than any other member of this ancient family. Prince Philip. Small wonder that Lord Mountbatten, whose devotion to his heritage is little short of fanatical, has for many years nursed a secret ambition that one day, the name of the ruling house of Britain might be Mountbatten. Within the conclave of the family he has raised the matter more than once, suggested that even if the name of Windsor be retained, the name of Mountbatten might be included. Prince Philip was less concerned than his uncle . . . though he took pains to see that the Prince of Wales should know of his heritage. He sent over to German genealogists to secure a complete family tree for Prince Charles to see. Through all this, the Queen remained steadfast in

one respect. She could never see the name of Windsor, chosen by her grandfather, abandoned by the royal house. On the other hand she sympathizes with her husband's feelings and more particularly with the overtures of his uncle. So the compromise. . . .[11]

The Macmillan government did not, however, give straightforward approval. They handed down an agreement for a name change which was so complicated that it raises legal interest even today; so complicated it could only have been drawn up by an expert in civil service gobbledegook.

Eleven days before the birth of her third child, the Queen announced her decision – or, more correctly, the one which the government had bestowed upon her:

> While I and my children will continue to be styled and known as the House and Family of Windsor, my descendants, other than descendants enjoying the style, title or attributes of Royal Highness and the titular dignity of Prince or Princess and the female descendants who marry, and their descendants shall bear the name Mountbatten-Windsor.[12]

Legal brains have toyed with this over the years and the consensus is that the prospect of Mountbatten-Windsor ever being adopted as the name of the ruling house seems extremely unlikely. It is left in the realms of third generations and the female descendants – like Princess Anne, who became the first to use it when she married Captain Mark Phillips, describing herself as Anne Elizabeth Alice Louise Mountbatten-Windsor. Buckingham Palace made it plain that this had been done 'as Her Majesty wished her husband's name to appear on the Marriage Register of their daughter.'

What were the remaining two royal 'secrets' that we will not be allowed to see until the next century? The marriage of Princess Margaret to Antony Armstrong-Jones might well have been another topic to have been raised in Cabinet; almost certainly, in fact, after the last débâcle. Though previously unmarried himself, Mr Armstrong-Jones's parents were divorced and slightly colourful in their remarriages: his mother was now the Countess of Rosse; his divorced stepmother was the former actress Carol Coombe and his second stepmother, his father's third wife, was Jennifer Unite, an air hostess who was barely a year older than her stepson. With this small but attractive collection of mothers on the groom's side, an eyebrow or two might well have been raised and was surely enough to warrant a Cabinet discussion about keeping up with the Joneses? Even if it was, there seems little in it to merit a longer delay than normal before the documents are declassified. Even the groom's selection of a best man who turned out to have a conviction for a homosexual offence is unlikely to have tipped the scales.

Incidentally, wasn't it probable this time, now that divorce-once-removed had become an acceptable if barely palatable fact of life, and if Nazi connections were no longer to be held against one, that the Duke and Duchess of Windsor should receive an invitation to the wedding of their second niece? No, again. The Lord Chamberlain to the Queen Mother was instructed not to invite . . . you know who.

'Ah well, perhaps there'll be a funeral soon,' said Wallis, pointedly. Unfortunately there was – but they would not be welcome at that either. Lady Edwina Mountbatten's suicidal workload as President of the worldwide Save the Children Fund and the St John Ambulance Brigade finally took its toll. On the last day of February 1960, she collapsed on a Far Eastern tour, soon after landing at Singapore. From those scandalous beginnings, she had turned her life from worthless pleasure-seeking to unqualified dedication and service to others; she died a heroine, one of the most astonishing women of this century, if for nought else but for her life story, which has been honestly told by Richard Hough.

One secret remains from the 1959 Cabinet papers, assuming that the name change and Margaret's wedding plans account for the other two. It might have been a scene at an official dinner in Paris where the British Embassy staff walked out on the specific instructions of the Ambassador, Sir Gladwyn Jebb, because the Duke and Duchess of Windsor turned up with Sir Oswald and Lady Diana Mosley.* But that seems an unlikely Cabinet matter. Some have suggested that it could have been conjecture over the state of the marriage of the Queen and Philip that attracted discussion; again, that is unlikely, so the third mystery remains.

As the decade turned, however, there were developments in two personal matters which were consistently to return to haunt Philip.

The first really began with the publication of the autobiography of his friend Hélène Cordet, who had by then achieved fame as star of the popular television variety show *Café Continental*. Commonly described as a 'nightclub queen', her rise to success was due in part to her royal connections, in particular Philip's contacts through his membership of the showbusiness charity groups.

Her relationship with Philip would not have merited much comment at all but for the fact that he was who he was. The continental media had been attempting to make a good deal out of their friendship.

* The ruling that British Embassy staff should not remain in the presence of Mosley was rigidly pursued during Sir Gladwyn's tenure, from 1952 to 1960.

Unfortunately, far from quelling the innuendo, Miss Cordet's autobiography merely fanned it; that way her book sold more copies. She meticulously took her readers through her recent contacts with the British Royal Family, yet left blurred and incomplete the details surrounding her two marriages and two divorces in the forties when her children were born. Marcel Boisot, readers will recall, had been posted to Cairo almost immediately after their marriage. When he returned, Hélène discovered that he was involved with another woman and she was left alone with the task of raising her two children, Max and Louise. She took them back to London to live with her mother while she began her nightclub career to earn their keep.

She next cropped up in links with Philip before his wedding, when – in her own words – she was being classed as 'the mystery blonde' in his pre-marriage life. This theme was taken up again when only Madame Foufounis was invited to Philip's wedding, bringing suggestions that the Queen mother had 'banned him from inviting Hélène Cordet' because of their past relationship.

At the Coronation, Madame Foufounis and Hélène's two children were all invited to the Palace to watch the historic procession set off and return. Everyone went except Hélène. She has since said that she 'overslept', having returned home from a nightclub engagement only a couple of hours before they were due at the Palace. In 1954 Madame Foufounis, writing in *Look* magazine, revealed that Philip had acted as godfather to the two Cordet children when they were christened and had continued to take an interest in them.

Hélène has said she has been invited to the Palace with the children on numerous occasions and once took them to see Philip playing polo on a Sunday. She added in her innocently revelatory style, 'I suddenly noticed that cameras were focused on our group and we were followed around by journalists. . . . we said goodbye to Philip . . . and decided not to watch polo again.' Her recollections were written in a way that invited the reader to scent an air of mystery – even if none existed. For example: 'As I was writing this my television set was switched on to a circus performance . . . one of the spectators was Philip himself. For one moment I went back years and got quite hot under the collar.'

Well, that was all quite enough to spark off a story of major proportions which has since led to a rather greater interest than normal in the parentage of the Cordet offspring. It was discovered that Hélène's former husband Marcel Boisot, from whom she parted in 1946, did not declare himself to be their father until shortly before her book was published. When the elder, Max, was discovered as a pupil at Gordonstoun the rumours started that he was in truth Prince Philip's own son.

The contacts between the two men have not been secret. When Philip went to China in October 1986 he made a special detour to see Max Boisot, by then Professor of Economics at the Euro-Chinese Business

Centre on the outskirts of Beijing. Max insists that the Frenchman Marcel Boisot is his father: 'I have heard these rumours all my life but they are ridiculous. My father – my real father – lives in Paris and it is silly to say otherwise. This all goes back to their childhood friendship and there is nothing more to it than that.'[13] Though vague and mysterious in her book, in 1988 Hélène herself eventually denied that Philip was Max's father; he had merely helped her at a time when she was virtually destitute.

Their friendship has continued and she even met the Queen, once.

The second case history that contributed to the unfortunate 'aura' around Philip has been rather more difficult to shake off. It relates, of course, to Dr Stephen Ward and the Profumo scandal, to which Philip became linked for two reasons. First, Ward, who committed suicide in 1963 during his trial for living off the immoral earnings of prostitutes, was brought in the forties by Baron to the Thursday Club meetings, as Larry Adler has recalled. Ward liked to boast that he knew Prince Philip. And indeed, Ward, who was an accomplished artist, obtained permission to sketch eight members of the Royal Family between March and July of 1961; the drawings were to be published in the *Illustrated London News*.* It was distinctly odd that this agreement should be forthcoming; that an unknown artist should have the most prominent members of the British Royal Family posing while he went to work with his sketchpad and charcoal was unprecedented. Other, more prominent, artists had been rejected. Buckingham Palace said later that the commission was achieved through Sir Bruce Ingram, the magazine's editor, who was a friend of the Queen's late grandfather. Ward also sketched many other famous names, including Macmillan and Churchill. There was nothing untoward about that, except that it was all terribly embarrassing when the scandal broke. At the time the sketches were being displayed in an exhibition of Ward's work at a London gallery. A smart-suited gentleman promptly arrived, took several thousand pounds in cash from his briefcase and bought every one of the royal likenesses. They have never been seen since.

The more hair-raising side of this highly contagious scandal concerned allegations about some photographs from Ward's private collection, dating back over a number of years, which had found their way into a safe at the offices of Odhams Press, publishers of the *Daily Herald* and the *People* and part of the Cecil King empire. The photographs were subsequently handed over to the police and were mentioned by Labour politician Richard Crossman in his diary for June 1963: 'I said to Hugh [Cudlipp] "How are those pictures that the Secret Service took?" Everyone of Hugh's staff around the room was uneasily aware that I was on to something.'

* Prince Philip, Princess Marina, the Duke and Duchess of Kent, the Duke and Duchess of Gloucester, Princess Margaret and Antony Armstrong-Jones all sat for Ward.

At the time, Mirror porprietor Cecil King was well aware of the subject matter of the photographs and discussed the implications of running a story with senior executives. Another of his newspapers, the *Sunday Pictorial*, had after all been among the first to get hold of the central figures in the case and since then the whole of the British press had been consumed by its investigations and, as Macmillan wrote in his diary, had produced 'one mass of the life of spies and prostitutes; day after day the attacks developed.' King was excessively strident in his wish to expose any matters of corruption or other alleged wrongdoings among people in high places. His judgment was also often open to question, as was his discretion. It was certainly not unknown for him to personally dictate a story to one of his newspapers purely on the basis of what he had gleaned from one of his famous VIP lunches at which he picked brains of national figures in politics and industry and listened to gossip.* The press had virtually run out of names to become involved with the Profumo affair until 23 June when Cecil King gave approval for the devotion of the entire front page of the following day's *Daily Mirror* for a story which ran: 'The foulest rumour being circulated about the Profumo Scandal has involved a member of the royal family. The name mentioned is Prince Philip.' The report did not actually state what the rumour was but merely added that it was 'utterly unfounded.' Thus Philip was dragged into the scandal of the day.

The decision to run the story was not taken lightly. King would have been shown the words and those of us who worked for him were ever thankful for the buffer of caution from his editorial director Hugh Cudlipp, one of the author's of modern popular journalism, who incidentally doesn't' much like what it has become. At the time, he was a mainstay of the *Mirror*, was the instigator of some of its finest campaigns and generally fought to ensure that the *Mirror* should be regarded as a respectable, responsible newspaper which indeed it largely was. On this occasion, however, the Press Council adjudicated the *Mirror*'s treatment of the story was in bad taste though the Council felt unable to judge whether the *Mirror* was justified as being in the public interest in repudiating the rumour, thus giving it greater publicity.

The story and the rumours have refused to go away. When the book *Honeytrap* was published in 1987 on the Profumo Affair, one of its authors, former *Panorama* reporter Anthony Summers, said in an interview on Radio Ulster that among the photographs found in Stephen Ward's flat was one in which two girls were shown with Prince Philip, the photographer Baron and another man. The girls were naked, the men were not and Summers later added he was not claiming they were

---

* In the end, his dangerous abuse of his position became an embarrassment to the Mirror Group, when in May 1968 he tried to persuade Mountbatten to join him in the formation of a government of national unity to oust Harold Wilson and he himself was sacked as chairman of IPC, the Mirror parent company.

doing anything sexual. The pictures came into the possession of a man called Warwick Charlton, who worked at the time for Odhams Press. The BBC subsequently apologized for the reference. Buckingham Palace merely commented that it was 'old hat'.

The whole, however, demonstrated once again how easy it has become for the glistening British crown to gather tarnish. Moreover, it boosted yet further the 'aura' around Philip, which continues to this day. At least two gossip columnists known to the author relate how – on two separate occasions – they have seen Philip in a wine shop buying a couple of bottles to take away. Now that, of course, may well have been a perfectly innocent situation, but a single fact like that can be sufficient for speculation. Why was he buying wine when the Palace has cellars full? Where was he taking it? Whom was he meeting?

Certain actresses and ladies in the royal circle have found their names linked to his and there is an oft-repeated tale that first his Secretary Mike Parker and later his equerry Lord Rupert Nevill were the carriers of invitations to female company for dinner engagements. It is a fact that well-known female personalities have only had to be placed next to him at a Variety Club luncheon or some other function for rumours of affairs to be up and running.

The aura remains; the causes, the rumours, the coincidences are easy to pinpoint. The gossip in high society – as opposed to that which appears in the newspaper columns – is rife and it has been for years. The élite do not like Philip and never have, so they chatter away about any morsel they can lay their hands on. It eventually reaches the continental press, which has long delighted in making allegations that he has a penchant for pretty ladies, has long continued various associations and has led no more than a nominal married life for years.

Proof – if such exists – is rather more difficult to come by, as most British newspaper reporters charged with such a story have discovered. The old chestnut that Philip and the Queen have not – in blunt terms – slept together in years is based upon gossip emanating from Palace servants and is no foundation for rumours of a troubled marriage; they have always had not just separate bedrooms, but separate suites, as do most couples of their social standing and breeding. It is a traditional, habitual situation that has always existed in the royal households: the Duke of Windsor's butler Georges Sanegre revelled in the story that some mornings when the staff went in to serve tea to their master they actually found him and the Duchess in bed together!

However, that said, it has been and still is true that Philip spends so much time away from his family on his worldwide travels that observers might be forgiven for drawing the wrong conclusions – 'he's never there' is a well-worn quotation. That the Queen was deeply in love with her husband when they married was obvious to all. What a pity that the loving, romantic image portrayed at the time has been cruelly dented.

Chapter Nineteen
A Job of Work

It is probably true to say that the pattern of the new Elizabethan monarchy, and Philip's part in it, was largely established after those early traumatic years when they were given a taste – through death, life, politics, religion, war and scandal – of pretty well everything that would confront them in the second half of the twentieth century. It was as if some hidden hand had painted a picture for them of all human life, especially their own, and run it past their eyes with the caption 'Be prepared'.

Lessons might have been learned, but not necessarily remembered. Philip has said:

> One of the things about the monarchy and its place, and one of its great weaknesses, is that it has to be all things to all people and of course it cannot do this when it comes to being all things to people who are traditionalists and all things to people who are iconoclasts. We therefore find ourselves in a position of compromise and we might be kicked from both sides. The only thing is that if you are very cunning you can get as far away from the extremists as you possibly can because they kick harder.[1]

Philip is cunning. However, he has seldom managed to avoid the kicks of the extremists or those of many other non-extreme critics.

Republican MP Willie Hamilton, whose attacks were to become a constant reminder that not everyone in Britain bows to Royalty, was certainly an extremist but, like others of the same view, spoilt his cause by going over the top too often with comments which otherwise would have found sympathy at popular level. There was often a measure of support for his words. He struck a nerve in America, for example, during a television interview when he said: 'Prince Philip should be told to go and do a job of work.'[2]

A job of work? Either there is a monarch or there isn't. And while there is, there is also a consort. And that was Philip. His only route was towards a career as a professional prince, away from his wife's apron strings and out on his own. To use one of his own most frequent adjectives, he worked bloody hard and in this it is interesting to observe just how closely Princess Anne has followed his example, almost to the letter.

There are two or three avenues to explore, and a suitable starting-point is Philip's 'good works' programme – a hefty catalogue of many examples of his determination to make his mark. Other, more controversial, ways of leaving his initials on contemporary events will be examined in later chapters.

In this one outstanding respect, Philip set a standard for which there had been no royal precedent either among consorts or kings: that is in the amount of extra-monarchial duties he took on and the hundreds of organizations which either had his name in patronage or were associated in another way. His sense of royal duty became, after a sluggish start through thoughts of a naval career, as strong as Prince Albert's and was pursued along a more useful, community-minded course.

Only the Duke of Windsor, when he was Prince of Wales and before he got bored 'with all this princing', comes close in the royal book of 'good works', though in recent years even Philip has been overtaken by the Palace workhouse, his daughter Anne, the Princess Royal.

In his day, Philip had something to prove and a role to manufacture, otherwise he would have died of boredom. Mike Parker, who remained the closest of all to Philip with a friendship that endured long beyond his resignation, reckoned the Prince had few helpers, apart from King George VI, Lord Mountbatten and literally two or three personal friends who joined him on the way. Starting from the very beginning, when there was nothing at all, he had to build it up brick by brick: 'There wasn't a collection of great men who had suggestions to make. He had to think it out alone. I know that his prime object from the word go was to be one of service.'

Service. It is rammed home to them all. Philip spat out the word purposefully and deliberately, knowing full well that it was all he seriously had to offer, apart from holding his wife's hand and making his famous rallying speeches to British industry to which only the newspapers paid much attention.

He went about it in the same tough, pedantic manner that he tackled everything; he got people's hackles up, upset a few with his frankness and moved largely volunteer forces along at a pace that amazed themselves and which was certainly too quick for some of those with a less active brain. Volunteers argue among themselves more than any other group; they tested his patience and he responded in the only way he knew how. Often he was too rude; sometimes he apologized but more often he did not. Fools are fools and everybody knows he could never suffer them gladly – or otherwise – and it didn't matter anyway, because invariably, regardless of any abuse he may have handed them, they all turned round and said what a nice chap he was.

Recording this aspect of his life is beyond the scope of a few hundred words; it would take a volume of its own, and then some, to log and record the number of organizations with which he has been connected; then another to examine and detail his work with any one of the groups with which he became deeply involved. In the end, it becomes as monotonous to describe his diary as it must be to live it. His patronages, trusteeships, presidencies, chairmanships, committee memberships and military ranks cover sixty-six close typed pages in his Patronage Book at Buckingham Palace. All have at some time or other received his attentions – some more than others, but the total adds up to very considerable demands on his time because he made a rule at the outset that he would never take on any duty as a mere uninvolved figurehead.

Unlike the Queen, whose engagements are carefully weighed against her leisure time, he has been out and about from the word go and kept no set hours. Handshakes, speeches, lunches, dinners, banquets, buffets, committee meetings, informal talks. Here, there and everywhere. Home one day, abroad the next. Week in, week out. His life was never mundane but, like a miner's or a bank clerk's, each year would be relentlessly similar in its format, in perpetuity. His work also took him abroad often and for fairly extensive visits, which he enjoyed for the sheer joy of getting away from the Palace and out on his own. It also brought its problems on the domestic front.

Those who come into contact with him in the course of this side of his work have, by and large, only good things to say about him. Even the vociferous critics who have preferred to take the view that that, after all, is why he is being paid fairly hefty operating expenses, with an office car, train, boat, plane and four large houses thrown in, cannot help a modicum of admiration for his contribution to British life, particularly through the fifties and the sixties when he was at his most energetic. Philip was honest enough constantly to challenge his role, and in one speech he posed the very pertinent question: 'You might ask whether all this rushing about is to any purpose. Am I just doing it to make it look as if I am earning my keep?' Indeed, one might well ask that question.

Those who worked with him would testify that he could have spent far less time and energy on his projects if he just wanted to bolster his work record. They called him a workaholic, and the description did not come from those who fell into the category of sycophants in an era when royal patronage was still believed to be the highest honour that could be bestowed upon the lowly. He may well have had his own reasons for packing his schedule, but his contribution can be seen to have been very worthwhile.

The beneficiaries in the early days were predominantly organizations working for young people and underprivileged young adults – an area which had been especially decimated by the war and needed a lot of rebuilding and innovation. The social consequences of the early days of Thatcherism, coincidentally, recreated the problems and, next time around, it was to be taken up by Prince Charles with his Prince's Trust.

But when Philip was going down the same road, back in the early fifties, it needed someone with his strength of character to get things moving and the National Playing Fields Association was, among others, selected as his first foray into the good-works programme. Captain Roy Harry, the appeal's Secretary at the time, remembered:

> Anyone expecting the position would be honorary was due for a big shock. He took over an office in our headquarters for three months and during that time he worked as just another official, only harder. Turning up at his desk each morning he got through whatever problems were piled up for him – and took his morning coffee from the communal coffee pot just like anyone else. Philip wanted to find out how we operated. Once he knew that, he set out to liven things up all round. He earned money through sheer personality; he turned up at a fruit auction in Covent Garden and it raised £3,900. Then he went away with a Wyatt Earp stetson which he bought for £50.[3]

The much-publicized 'familiarity' with Frank Sinatra and Ava Gardner, as we have seen, provided an early boost to the funds; and, following Mountbatten's tip, he continued with the showbiz theme. Bob Hope was dragooned into helping with a film shot in Malta which made £16,000 – enough for several playing fields in those days – and Billy Butlin had a reunion of his campers at the Royal Albert Hall which raised £7,000. Philip played cricket with Bill Edrich and Denis Compton to raise cash and rewarded boxing promoter Jack Solomons with an invite to the Palace to present the proceeds of a fight tournament. Within five years or so, the appeals target for the National Playing Fields Association was exceeded and about 4,000 new playing fields were built throughout the United Kingdom, though their dream – and Philip's campaigning stance – that there should be 6 acres of open space per thousand head of population and a playground for children every quarter of a mile in all urban areas, would never be achieved.

He was in the thick of it and, in spite of the changing needs of each new decade, he continued to inspire work for young people. Just one example of many came in 1973 when he opened a £2 million sports centre in Holloway, London, built with money raised by the Variety

Club of Great Britain and a hefty donation from Sir Michael Sobell, the electronics tycoon. The centre was another landmark; it was one of the first of its kind in Britain and was reckoned to be one of the finest in Europe. A regular source of income for this and several other of his pet projects was the Variety Club of Great Britain, of which he and Mike Parker followed Mountbatten as members. He was made a Life Clown soon after the club was formed in 1949.

A few courtiers protested when he allowed himself and the Queen to be quite so closely associated with some rather common show people; they tried to stop the public showing of a film clip shot at a Variety Club luncheon in which Philip became Tommy Cooper's stooge in a comedy–magic routine. It angered him that the film had been banned without his knowledge and he promptly gave his permission to release it. (Eyebrows were still being raised in 1990 when he became the first royal to appear in a TV commercial for charity, along with Warren Mitchell and Dennis Waterman.) They helped him, he helped them. In their first ten years, they gave him £400,000 to spend on his various projects and in return he became an unofficial fund-raiser. In 1966, when he was touring specifically to raise money for the Variety Club, a Miami businessman offered him $100,000 if he would swim in his private pool. Philip stripped off and dived in. There are countless stories and a thousand and one people with no axe to grind who are prepared to bear witness to his enthusiasm, zest and continued patronage. One, who was at his side on that eleven-day tour of America, said:

All right, so he has his moments. We had a few run-ins with the press and he bollocked a few people but in the end, he did what we came to do: raise a million dollars for the Variety Club charities and spread the word about England. He was actually a bit upset by British firms in New York who claimed he didn't bang the drum enough. He said he wasn't going to be a bloody commercial traveller and that was that; I think the Americans actually liked him better for it.

Overlapping with his other work, he became involved in similar fund-raising for the Federation of Boys' Clubs, which was also a desperately needed facility in any town or city in those deprived days. Few had premises, equipment or money and they needed lots of local groups and organizers to begin the creation of a nationwide movement from virtually nothing. Similar recollections emanate from this quarter: lots of attendance, plenty of hard work and always speaking his mind. Once when a committee was arguing over finances, he banged the table with his gavel so hard that a glass ashtray smashed. But the meeting came to order and Philip got his way; he scared them into action.

The area of his youth work which will be longest remembered was his own idea for sponsoring young people in the concept of challenge. He went to see Kurt Hahn to put the finishing touches to a plan he had devised as an initiative and endurance test. National Service would soon end* and Philip wanted to initiate national, if not global, encouragement for the youth of the late fifties who were rocking and rolling to Elvis Presley and Bill Haley and mimicking the leathers-and-jeans slouch of James Dean and Marlon Brando. The result was the Duke of Edinburgh's Award Scheme. He launched his award in 1956 with a statement from Buckingham Palace:

> This scheme is intended to help both the young and those people who take an interest in their welfare. It is designed as an introduction to leisure-time activities, a challenge to the individual to personal achievement and as a guide to those people and organizations who are concerned about the development of our future citizens. I hope that all who take part in this scheme will find an added purpose and pleasure in their lives. I am quite sure that all who enter and all those who help run it will gain that special sense of satisfaction which comes from the discovery of hidden abilities and from helping others to overcome a challenge.

The Duke of Edinburgh's Award received a nationwide fanfare and went on to be adopted all around the world under various titles, since many countries did not wish to give him the credit. It became the Head of State Award in Ghana, the National Youth Award in Nigeria, the Prince Mohato Award in Lesotho and, in a final accolade, the Congressional Award – based on the D. of E. scheme – introduced in America in 1978, although they did bring him over for advice and the launch.

The award has certainly attracted critics for its élitism and competiveness at a time when competition was becoming increasingly taboo in our learning systems; in many respects the principles of the award harp back to those Kurt Hahn had used at Gordonstoun. In spite of the deprecations, however, it cannot be regarded as anything other than a success. On 13 December 1989 the 2 millionth teenager joined a rigorous programme of commitment, which, most who go through it agree, does them some good. It was also adopted as a demanding kind of mission for the underprivileged and disabled, whose participants have grown substantially each year.

Lord Hunt, formerly John Hunt the Everest climber, recalled for the author:

> My association with him was during those early years when I was the first director of his award scheme. It was planned and launched . . . at a time when he was already actively involved in many other

---

* National Service ended in the United Kingdom in 1962.

organizations concerned with sport and youth but the award was something new and unique. That initiative backed by his spirit of enterprise and youthful vigour acted as an inspiration to the nation at a crucial period of time. One of his outstanding skills has been to bring together organizations and individual people who have tended to compete in rivalry for resources and opportunities.[4]

The Central Council for Physical Recreation, of which Philip became President in 1951, also received his divided but regular attention. This was a volatile body of people involved in establishing and organizing some of the amenities the nation badly lacked. Similarly, through his constant worldwide travelling, he brought a forceful and at times controversial contribution to the Council for Volunteers Overseas (now the British Volunteer Programme). These bodies formed a minuscule section of his involvements, but as the list grew he became an important link between many organizations all pulling in different directions for what was basically a single cause.

He once said that he wandered about storing knowledge in what was a vast mine of 'useless information'. In fact, he became a roving know-all whose personal store of information was passed on from one organization to another, often inspiring competition between the groups, sometimes bringing about a merging of interests; he was able to make sure that two or three groups in a similar area who were trying to divide the same small portion of a particular cake did so effectively. Conversely, they could speak as one on major national issues.

It is impossible to do justice to Prince Philip's contribution to many, many organizations whose very being was for the welfare and interest of ordinary people, young and old. Few really appreciated the volume of his work, nor its importance, especially through the decade of the sixties. It has continued, understandably with less vigour, into the eighties, when those in the know talk of him as being an 'institution'. No one, without examining his list of 'credits', can truly appreciate the wide cross-section of organizations, ranging from the Automobile Association to the restoration of the *Cutty Sark*, that have devoured hours of his time and energy. It is a pity that some of his other high-profile characteristics have tended to put his 'good works' in the shade. Just as he has achieved some kind of public accolade, he has tended to spoil it with another thoughtless, careless deed or saying. For example, presenting some of his awards in Edinburgh in 1984, he told a joke to a blind girl – the old one about the blind man who walked into a pub, swung his guide dog around his head by the tail and said to the barman, 'I'm just having a look around.' The blind girl laughed politely. Others did not.

These days the Prince devotes more and more of his time to conservation and matters green, in which he has become one of the world leaders.

The paradox of Philip, the gunman whose annual bag of pheasants continues to be collected and whose sporting activities have downed countless fowl and assorted other varieties of game birds, and who refuses, still, to condemn hunting, is well known. He refuses to admit to a paradox. The two, he says, are distinctly different topics, the latter being no different from a butcher slaughtering animals for daily food. Big game is a different matter. He has not shot a tiger since 1960, as far as is known, though other species of a more prolific nature continue to fall under his sights. Pheasants and stags are not endangered species!

It is also undoubtedly true that his interest in nature and wildlife was born out of his enjoyment of blood sports as a young man; he has hardly become the poacher-turned-gamekeeper, but at least his recognition of other people's difficulty in understanding the conflict is sincere. The jacket notes to his last book, *Down to Earth*, published in 1988, do admit

it is oddly paradoxical that, so often, visionaries become conservationists. . . . the Prince was one of the first openly to voice the unpopular view that man was exploiting his privileged position of power, that he had become a primitive predator with no thought for the future survival of the human species.[5]

He was able to exploit his own privileged position to get the World Wildlife Fund moving – 'a title always looks good as head of a charity.' He did more than just provide his name. He made the cause his own and he has travelled the world speaking on its behalf – sometimes at Civil List expenses but often at the cost of the WWF.

In the preface to his book, he explains that during his twelve years in the Navy he became fascinated with birdlife when he came ashore and this was heightened on his world tour in 1957, when he took hundreds of photographs of many species in their natural habitat. It occurred to him that their 'conservation depends on international co-operation'. He became involved in a diverse range of countryside protection initiatives; he organized the first conference in 1963 to predict difficulties in the countryside of 1970; and he became a prominent member of European Conservation Year.

Philip became a founder of the World Wildlife Fund in 1961, at the instigation of his old friend Sir Peter Scott. Scott, who had already established the Wildfowl Trust at Slimbridge, Gloucestershire, had along with other interested conservationists outlined a plan for an international fund. In July 1961, Scott took the proposals to Buckingham Palace and asked Philip if he would become President of the British National Appeal for the World Wildlife Fund. They also wanted an international figure for the post of President of the World Wildlife Fund International, which was to be based in a country of traditional neutrality, Switzerland, at the town of Morges on the banks of Lake Geneva. Prince Bernhard of The Netherlands was suggested and Philip contacted him immediately; thus the WWF was launched. Britain was the first country to run an appeal and there it all began.* In its first twenty years the WWF was able to fund 2,800 conservation projects worldwide costing $55 million.

Philip was immediately in the headlines with admonishing lectures about people killing things and the wildlife of the world being in crisis. In 1962 he said:

> The basic and most urgent purpose of this fund is to help those species of animals which face extinction. It is not setting out to protect all animals from everything. It has no intention of campaigning against mousetraps or fly-paper. . . . I freely confess that I had no idea whatsoever that all sorts of wild animal species are dying out. . . . man is the crux of the situation . . . we should be able to control our own even involuntary actions. [6]

Well, of course, in the early days it was fairly basic stuff; the serious business of the WWF came later when the true green revolution began to gather pace. Philip's early commitment might well have been questioned. While touring India with his wife in the very year that he had been asked to become British President of the WWF, he and the Queen were photographed with the magnificent tiger he had felled in one shot lying before them ready to be made into a rug. The British nation was even more incensed than the time he had had six handbags made out of an Australian crocodile! Ten years later, the tiger population of India had dropped to such alarming levels that the WWF had to invest $100,000 in Mrs Ghandi's scheme to help save it from extinction – a very real threat, since the tiger population had dropped from 100,000 at the turn of the century to a mere 1,800 in 1972.†

Philip's involvement did not, apparently, give him any pangs of conscience; nor did it the rest of the Royal Family, which has long treated Britain as its country estate. And before leaving this brief accolade of his extensive efforts on behalf of the animal population of the world, and the vast and pressing problems of our polluted planet, it is interesting to take a similarly brief look at the 'paradox' that isn't: the complex and unresolved question of the conflicts that he and his entire family have managed to excuse while supporting the ideal of conservation.

George V, Edward VIII, George VI and Elizabeth II have all been excellent shots. George VI kept meticulous records of the number of woodcock that he shot, from his first in 1911 to the last at Sandringham

---

* Philip became President of World Wildlife International in 1981.

† When King George V went on a tiger shoot arranged during the Delhi Durbar, he and his party killed thirty-seven tigers in one day.

shortly before he died – it was number 1,055. Wildfowling has been another popular royal pastime. George V never managed to shoot any in flight – they were always on the water. George VI, however, sent them up from the haunt at Sandringham and took 526 duck in flight. His game book records the first shoots on which Philip joined him in 1946. One day's entry notes that they secured a mixed bag of 'five hares, 188 rabbits, 2 woodcock, 2 snipe, 1 black game, 30 grouse and a capercailzie.'[7]

When the royal game reserves came under new management upon the death of George VI, the sport was continued with equal, if not greater, vigour. Philip kept personal checks on the restocking of the estates and the conservation of habitats, and still does. This programme of continuous supply of pheasants and the like goes on everywhere, of course, and at Sandringham, for example, it ensures the royal sportsmen and women daily averages of 300–400 birds to start the season. At Balmoral, Philip used forty or fifty soldiers from the Balmoral guard as beaters. The Balmoral gillies tell the tale of his returning after a hard day's shooting on Lochnagar and betting among themselves on whether he would decline the planned pigeon shoot after tea. Most were not surprised when he came striding out an hour later to begin again.

The *diversion par excellence* at Balmoral, however, is deerstalking, which the Queen herself loved to join. She and Philip would be seen crawling on hands and knees up and down the slopes to get close to their quarry. Edward VII held the record for a deerstalking: he shot seven stags in one day. The Queen was no mean shot. Her best was twelve stags from three stalks. Her own game book records that she shot one of the five best deer taken by women in Scotland and on the walls of Balmoral Castle was hung the mounted head of a stag with massive twelve-point antlers, felled by Philip.

All their children learned to shoot from an early age. One of Prince Charles's earliest encounters was with Philip when they went shooting on Hickling Water; Charles held the angler's net ready to collect his father's shot birds, which included coots, tufted duck, mallard and pochard. Since then, of course, we have seen them all develop into excellent marksmen and January would not be January without the now regular photographs of one or other of them firing away to their heart's content at the well-fed pheasants of Sandringham. The unfortunate part of it is that the grandchildren seem similarly inclined. Witness in January 1990 Zara Phillips killing off a wounded bird by stamping on it with the heel of her shoe.

More 'exciting' were Philip's private visits to Germany to the Schloss of one of his German relatives, whose vast acreages harboured wild boar which fell to his gun with ease.

But that's different. Game shooting, deerstalking, wildfowling, duck shooting, wild-boar chasing, foxhunting, rabbit disposal have nothing at

all to do with Wildlife with a capital 'W'. Paradox? There is none, Philip continued to insist in the year this book was being researched, when once again, and for the umpteenth time, he was being challenged over double standards. One of his more spectacular skirmishes was with Richard Course, Chairman of the League Against Cruel Sports, an organization which has long been critical of the Prince. Mr Course wrote with anger: 'A man who involves himself in the slaughtering of wildlife and the fieldsports lobby cannot be regarded as a conservationist.'[8] His colourful invective indicted Philip as a clown prince, who was capable of high hypocrisy.

Philip is prevented by protocol from replying direct. He can defend himself through the many speeches and lectures he gives every year, but he seldom does. In his book *Down to Earth*, he makes a veiled mention of the critics. He says he has enjoyed the family and country practice of game pursuits since he was a boy:

> This interest in wild animals and plants combined with a love of countryside sports has never ceased to cause problems for rational thinkers who convince themselves that the two characteristics are incompatable. Hunters, shooters and falconers take great care of their horses, dogs and birds and become very attached to them but that does not inhibit their love for country sports.[9]

He says it is also worth bearing in mind that the hunters have pressed for game laws to protect the game and forests in their own countries.

He remains sincerely convinced that his attitude is an acceptable one and, in any event, since the WWF was founded, the conservation of wildlife in itself has become just one element of the Fund's international concerns, which now cover the spectrum of the ecological order in general: intensive farming, pollution, trade in wild species, commercial fishing, the human population explosion, captive breeding and tropical rainforests.

However much he may be criticized for his own activities, Philip's knowledge is great and he has earned the international reputation as one of the original drum-beaters; his lectures are self-prepared and display an experience over a wide range of topics that few can match. In this respect, as in the field of aiding the youth of three decades, he has carved himself a notch of which, one way or another, future historians must take account.

Chapter Twenty
Shut Up, Philip!

If achievement is the measure of success, Prince Philip has gloomily concluded that he is unlikely to have made much impact. Unfortunately, this prediction might well prove to be correct. He has actually achieved many things in vastly different spheres, as we have seen, and ought to be credited, at least, for his service and his dedication to any one of a dozen chosen causes, including the institution of monarchy itself. His speeches have covered an enormous range of subjects.

History might be kinder in its assessment of his work than current commentators; in the future, for example, his pleadings on behalf of the planet might be seen retrospectively as an incisive knowledge of environmental problems. Contemporary politics continue pretty well to ignore him.

Whereas Prince Albert, for instance, figured strongly in the political memoirs and biographies of his age, Philip barely rates a mention in those of latter-day political leaders. His name is not even in the index in the volumes of Anthony Eden's recollections dealing with his premiership. He receives the scantest of mentions in the two volumes of Alistair Horne's biography of Macmillan. Macmillan's own references to him are negligible, as are those of other memoir-writing evacuees from Downing Street, Alec Douglas-Home, Harold Wilson (who gave him a single passing mention), and James Callaghan (who remembered a trip to Yugoslavia for Tito's funeral). Prince Albert, on the other hand, eventually became deeply involved with his wife's political advisers. Before the first year of their marriage was out, Lord Melbourne gave Victoria's consort the keys to the red boxes containing Cabinet and confidential papers. But then again, more recently they had to give security clearance to the documents that went into Edward VIII's boxes because he kept showing them to Mrs Simpson! A certain nervousness has remained.

But going back to Albert, Cecil Woodham-Smith tells us:

It was a piece of good fortune for the Queen that the Prince not only possessed an excellent mind, patience and capacity for taking pains, but that his philosophy was to 'sink his own individual existence in that of his wife', to aim at no power for himself . . . but making his position entirely part of the Queen's continually and anxiously to watch every part of the public business in order to advise and assist her at any moment of the multifarious and difficult questions brought before her.[1]

Victoria came to depend on Albert in every way. They had a double desk – he sat at one side and she at the other (it is still on display at Osborne). He read State papers and drafted her replies, which she copied. Disraeli said he had much political influence and perhaps even power. When Albert died, the effect was felt by Her Majesty's government almost as much as it was by Queen Victoria herself and, again according to Disraeli, his death robbed the nation of 'the blessing of an absolute monarchy'.[2]

Lytton Strachey provided another view, similar in some respects to Disraeli's, with a prediction of Albert's involvement had he lived beyond his forty-two years: 'It is easy to imagine how under such a ruler an attempt might have been made to convert England into a state exactly organized, as elaborately trained and as autocratically controlled as Prussia herself.'[3]

Philip is Prussianly autocratic, as his co-workers and his children will bear witness. But has he secretly been ruling over us? In many ways, he has. Dermot Morrah, the approved royal author who worked with the support and guidance of the Queen's closest advisers, declared that, though officially he was scarcely known to the constitution, Philip had become perhaps 'the most influential unofficial voice in the land.'[4] This was especially apparent in the first decade of the Queen's reign, when the nation listened with loyal attention to whatever he had to say on the variety of topics to which he applied his mind and tongue with vigour and enthusiasm. Things would change. Public acceptability of his words would lessen as the years advanced.

The Queen herself stuck rigidly to her own principles and her father's teachings and Philip was to find that his influence on Constitutional and political matters was frustratingly nil. She could not help listening to his thoughts, ideas and observations. At the breakfast table, he would provide a running commentary on world events as he read the morning papers. The Queen's remark when the Suez Crisis broke out was very telling: 'Thank goodness Philip isn't here . . .' Like his uncle, he might make a suggestion about what the Queen 'should say to the Prime Minister', or propose that she might refuse to see some politically unpleasant person. He must have advised the Queen, quietly and shrewdly, on certain problems that have arisen during her long reign, and must also have become privy to – though it could never be admitted – many of the nation's inner secrets. In spite of her own firmness against external interference, the joint persuasive forces of Philip and his uncle – complicated by their own polarization of political thinking – must have presented her with some trying moments.

As Lady Longford has told us through a quotation from one of the Queen's closest friends, the Royal Family understands that 'party politics cannot enter in any way the thoughts or activities of the Royal Family. Her Majesty never even thinks in these terms.'[5] If, as Lady Longford indicates, it was against everything she had been taught so that it had been completely 'bred out of her', the same could not be said for Philip.

Whilst not apparently lending public support to any one particular party – and in spite of his continual denial of any political thoughts or motives – many of his speeches have been well within the realms of sensitive political and social issues, cutting right through controversial topics. It would be difficult for him not to be drawn into controversy unless he had religiously followed his father-in-law's advice about never saying anything controversial, because one way or another most of the organizations with which he has become involved have been on the periphery of politics; any comment can therefore be taken as a political statement, though he has seldom been allowed to get away with it scot free. On those occasions when he has put his head above the parapet with some statement or other affecting our lives and his, he has been immediately advised to shut up. He has not done so.

Fury! A good, short tabloid word that fits nicely into a confined headline space. It has been used at the top of Philip stories so often that it has lost its impact. The headline begins 'FURY OVER . . . PHILIP, and with MPs readily on hand for a quote to express their anger over his views on matters political, the story might start 'Fury erupted last night over Prince Philip's comments on . . .'

As a controversialist whose hectoring, interfering delivery of his thoughts can be guaranteed to spark a row, Prince Philip is without a rival in this age. Headlines like 'HE ISN'T A RACIALIST . . . HE'LL INSULT ANYBODY' or 'HE'S GONE TOO FAR THIS TIME' became so common that, whereas once they made whole front pages, they have since been demoted to single-column tops and occasional leader articles. In the early days he was actually taken seriously and some of his more outlandish comments caused considerable embarrassment to Her Majesty's government and Her Majesty alike. The *Daily Telegraph* ran a poll in 1969 on who would make the best dictator for Britain. Philip won. His extrovert pronouncements on everything from coloured condoms to the shape of a Chinaman's eyes are sayings that will go down in history and 'The Thoughts of Chairman Philip' look likely to outlive all other remembrances of him.

In perspective, if one considers that he makes around 80 major speeches a year – some years it has been as high as 130 – it works out that Philip's utterances in forty years amount to several hundred thousand words, because he never uses the same speech twice. On the law of averages, he has had a greater opportunity than any comparable public figure to put his foot in it, and inevitably this has become his trade-mark.

He naturally became a very good public speaker, never profound but always well researched and intelligent. Unlike Albert, who was an intellectual with a background of philosophy, literature and science at Bonn University, Philip had no academic well to draw on. He kept telling us that he was a non-university bum, which he said never did him any harm. He gained his knowledge by meticulous preparation, making science and technology in industry his target in the early days of his speechmaking. He took advice and guidance from two of his mentors, Sir Harold Hartley and Sir Solly (later Lord) Zuckerman, both of whom pushed him towards the view that Britain was filled with an unrealized inventive potential.

Philip proceeded to tell us so and to ask what we were doing about it. America invented the term 'yes-men' while Britain is full of 'no-men', he said early in his speaking career. He asked the Coal Board how much longer they were going to exploit every feature of this land purely for gain, and he told British airline experts that our safety standards were lower than most. His more intense speeches and essays were heavy discussions of life in Britain and the social consequences of the pattern of its development. Increasingly his views veered from a fairly liberal stance to right wing.

The trade unions were suspicious of him from the outset, when, in 1956, he launched the Duke of Edinburgh Conference on 'The Social Responsibilities of Industry'. But actually it was a total success, bringing 600 people from Britain and the Commonwealth to talk about their respective lives and their hopes for the future. There was no place for wafflers, as one of Britain's own captains of industry discovered. He made a three-minute speech that clearly indicated he had done no homework whatsoever; when he had finished, Philip said, 'I'm afraid I didn't quite get the sense of that, would you mind repeating it?' The man could not. (Philip's own important speech also did not work in its first draft and when he showed it to his advisers they suggested he scrapped it and wrote another. He did.)

He seemed to enjoy public speaking and, according to Willie Hamilton, the sound of his own voice. He obviously feels that what he has to say is of some relevance; others would disagree, but several volumes of his selected speeches have been published – though it was upsetting and disconcerting to discover that a children's book written by his son outsold his own publications in exceedingly large numbers. This situation was repeated again in the late eighties when his conservation book *Down To Earth* was published, only to be eclipsed in sales by Prince Charles's *Vision of Britain*. And he was far outsold by the Duchess of York's children's book.

When Prince Philip confined himself to his prepared text, he actually never sounded especially pompous; just a good after-dinner speaker who, if he had not been royal, might have been found in the debating societies of various seats of learning – coherent, sensible and sometimes boring. The trouble arose in those lapses into arrogance – and there is no other word to describe them – in which he was, and still is, prone to spit out some exceedingly tactless remark or venomous statement capable of causing extreme offence. On other occasions, his fault has been plain rudeness, which his defenders have put down to the pressure of work and nervousness.

In every newspaper office in what was once Fleet Street there is a file of Philip's sayings that can be drawn on and published now and again to remind us of some of his appalling gaffes. His 'Get your finger out' speech to British industry, for example, was splashed across the front pages of every national newspaper in the land in 1961 and rapid-fire condemnation followed. Not because there was outright disagreement with his sentiments; quite the reverse. His disparaging remarks about bosses and unions were exactly in line with the view of many, and no doubt he had been put up to it in the first place by either his uncle or one of his friends. But Parliament does not like members of its royal house to say such things and newspapers concur – or say they do. In fact, he has always made good copy.

Sometimes he has been silly and irresponsible. Throughout the sixties, Philip was a supporter of a closer relationship with West Germany; he wanted the Queen to make a State visit and he had been an advocate of inviting German President Heuss to Britain in 1956. The cool reception Heuss received from the public was as good an indication as any that the bitterness had not died away completely and it was certainly too early for the Queen to make a return visit. However, Philip's ambition for such a trip was eventually achieved in 1965 and it was to his delight that, at last, his wife and family could then visit his own relations in their own homes – a prospect denied the Queen by protocol until she had made a State visit to the country. In a private part of their trip which was kept from the press pack, Philip took the Queen to Wolfsgarten, the old Hesse–Darmstadt family home where treasures of a past age were stored and memories of Queen Victoria's many visits recalled by pictures and mementoes. The Hesse clan and other relatives gathered to welcome their English kinsfolk for their long-awaited party in Germany. They were no strangers to each other, of course, because the German relatives had long been frequent visitors to Britain and to the Queen's homes, but it was the symbolic nature of the Queen's presence for the first time that was important to them all.

Philip was full of his visit when he came back to London and told everyone what a great success it had been. Whatever discussions took place around the dining tables of Wolfsgarten had also made their mark, and his enthusiasm caused eyebrows to be raised. When in July he spoke about white rule in Rhodesia and Ian Smith's threatened illegal Unilateral Declaration of Independence, the *Daily Mirror* responded with a full frontal attack. But the newspaper was not concerned with Rhodesia so much as with the possibility that Philip might be about to pronounce publicly on another delicate topic well to the fore in his thoughts: Germany.

This fear was expressed by Cecil King, chairman of the Mirror Group, in a self-explanatory letter he wrote to Prime Minister Harold Wilson on 13 July 1965:

CONFIDENTIAL

Dear Harold,

I much enjoyed our talk yesterday and was glad to find you in such good heart.

There is one point I forgot to mention and I don't know if Hugh Cudlipp did when he saw you on Friday.

Our attack on Prince Philip was not really caused by his pretty innocuous remarks about Rhodesia. But a few days earlier he had been a guest at a lunch of Denis Hamilton [of the *Sunday Times*] at which various newspaper men were present including our Edward Pickering. At this lunch Prince Philip's main theme – following the Queen's visit to Germany – was the urgent importance of the reunification of Germany. Hugh Cudlipp thought that we cannot have Prince Philip saying in public anything like what he had said in private at this lunch. Hence the decision to seize on his remarks about Rhodesia as an opportunity to fire a shot across his bows. We are informed from the palace that the point has been taken.[6]

It is an interesting letter, showing the manner in which the popular newspapers dealt with such situations a mere twenty-five years ago; such warning shots would not happen in the eighties. There would just be a straightforward report with no suppression because the event was private, and the *Mirror*, or any other newspaper for that matter, would have given Philip's comments the prominence they deserved.

Either way, the views on the reunification of Germany which he had brought back from his tour of the Fatherland were at least a quarter of a century too soon. The spectre of a Fourth Reich was even proffered by the Mirror Group – by then in the control of Robert Maxwell – when the Berlin Wall was breached in the dying days of the eighties, let alone in 1965.

The Palace said the point had been taken. Did it stop him? Hardly.

The following year's classic that he was 'fed up with making excuses for Britain' and, a couple of years later, his suggestion that there should be a tax on babies were followed with a list now so long and familiar that it does not bear further repetition. He has been attacked from both sides of the political spectrum for his meddling but his chief critics have been within the Labour Party and more especially its left-wing MPs, who in their time have attacked him for making Margaret Thatcher look like a Marxist. Other jibes have been rather more hurtful, such as that of MP Tom Littlewood who called him a 'useless reactionary parasite'.

The point is that his usefulness as a controversialist or even a benevolent busybody – as John Grigg warmly described him[8] – suddenly became blurred. He saw it himself. In 1968 he said, 'As so often happens, I discover that it would have been better to have kept my trap shut.' The interesting question which will probably never be answered is how much, consciously or subconsciously, he has deliberately set out to make headline news, thus drawing attention to himself or to a particular cause or theme he wished to promote, or even to the monarchy itself when he used himself as the devil's advocate to get across a particular point on behalf of the Queen – like money. Ninety per cent of his speeches were, and still are, totally ignored and unreported by the media. It must have been incredibly disappointing for him that – especially after the initial novelty of having a royal personage who actually said something quotable had worn off – he would spend hours writing a speech on some important issue, make a long journey to deliver it, endure for several hours the company of people who might not interest him and then discover that not a single word of it had appeared in the national press – 'and when it did, they changed it around and took paragraphs out of context to make it unintelligible. I tried writing speeches in a way that they couldn't change around but it did not work.' The regional papers and some specialist magazines have been kinder, but by and large the only time he has become headline news has been when he has spoken controversially or insultingly; on those occasions there have been copious notetakers all anxious to file their story home.

Philip could become seriously depressed about his work, that it was persistently being trivialized by the coverage it received. Mountbatten recognized this in 1974 – when his nephew was twenty-seven years into the job, incidentally – when he thought that Philip was 'disappointed, perhaps frustrated would be a better word.' The uncle attempted some consolation: 'I feel you underestimate your effect on the UK and especially the Commonwealth. I hear more and more praise and appreciation from people in all walks of life.'[9]

Politicians and the press have remained his most constant critics.

Since the early skirmishes, dating from the years of sustained attack by Beaverbrook on the Mountbattens, Philip's relationship with the press deteriorated through his legendary rudeness and was not helped when in one single year, 1962, he described the *Mirror* as 'not quite respectable', *The Times* as too stodgy and the *Daily Express* as a bloody awful newspaper again.

After that, he never looked back. He told an American film crew what they could do with their microphone and called some Swedish photographers a bunch of amateurs. Then while on a Caribbean tour, when the patron of a hospital spoke of the trouble they had with mosquitoes, he said, 'I know what you mean. You have mosquitoes, I have the press.' Vincent Mulchrone, who was there, recalled that the press corps demanded – and received – an apology. 'Some pompous ass of a reporter stirred things up and we were all asked to gather under a tree. Prince Philip took time out to come over and apologize humbly, almost humiliatingly.'[10]

Philip could probably have lived with the British press; it was the continental newspapers and magazines that broke the camel's back. Whereas in the eighties it is Charles and Diana or Anne and Mark on the front pages, in the sixties it was the Queen and Philip. An analysis of continental press cuttings from 1960 to 1972 reveals that the Queen had been on the verge of abdicating on sixty-three occasions, was about to divorce Philip in seventy-three stories and was pregnant ninety-three times.

In 1973 he made his tenuous attempt at peace with the press, with whom his relationship had developed into a running battle involving frequent exchanges of four-lettered adjectives. He chose a meeting of the Newspaper Press Fund in Glasgow to discuss the subject:

> I have it on no better authority than *Time* magazine [9 July 1973] that I am no friend of the press. That's the trouble with reputations – they cling much more tenuously than the truth. Incidentally, if anyone can offer me any advice about how I can improve this reputation or even offer any reason why I have it, I shall be more than grateful.

Naturally, with such an invitation, several of the brethren rushed into print with some pertinent suggestions!

The continuing enigma of the man is apparent even in this thorny topic. On that same day there were tributes, one of them from a totally unexpected source. Jack Campbell, then managing editor of the *Scottish Daily Express*, described Philip as a 'warm human being at ease as much with the road sweeper as high dignatory, fulfilling a difficult role with infinite good humour and inventive positive thought. He is above all courageously outspoken and frank when needed.'

Frankness is a virtue which has earned him consistent rebukes. Occasionally a prime minister has been drawn into the debate. During the difficult days of discontent leading up to the last nightmare days of a Labour government, Philip made some pointed remarks about the dependence of a certain section of the British populace on State aid. He sounded like the advance party for Thatcherism when he wrote:

> People are slowly coming round to feeling that we have been driven too far along one road; that we have got to come back a little and not concentrate quite so heavily on the unfortunate, the underprivileged but try to create a situation whereby the enterprising can make their contribution. . . .[11]

As one who was extremely fortunate and very, very privileged indeed, Prince Philip must have fully realized that he was asking for trouble; of course he knew. It was a considered essay, not some off-the-cuff remark, and was surely a deliberate piece of bull baiting. With all his experience, he could not have imagined any reaction other than a furore in its wake. The response was not long in arriving.

Impudent and ill-advised, said Mr James Lamond, MP. Arrogant, said Mr Dennis Skinner. And the most incisive of all: 'As one of the best-kept social security claimants in the country, he ought to have spoken with a better sense of responsibility,' said Tom Litterick. The Speaker interjected and reminded members that it was normal to speak with respect of the Royal Family. Prime Minister James Callaghan cautiously dismissed Philip's words. He did not think that such speeches would have any impact at all, whoever made them, and he had no intention of assuming any ministerial responsibility for Philip's speeches.[12] This was a good enough cue for Keith Waterhouse to write in the following day's *Mirror*:

> What I find refreshing about the Duke of Edinburgh's outspoken views is that no one any longer takes much notice of them. There will always be a few left-wing MPs and phone-in freaks snapping at royal heels like Pavlov corgis. But as a theme for serious (even frivolous) national debate, the Duke's latest outburst was a nonstarter.[13]

All good knock-about stuff that has helped make the British monarchy what it is today!

The Philip 'season' wafts in and out of fashion, because on the royal merry-go-round everybody gets a turn in the headlines. When things get dull, he can be relied upon to roust them up; the daily cut and thrust that he established led the Royal Family and the press down a new road of accessibility. He and his uncle always wanted plenty of media coverage for the family, and got it. Without publicity the Royals would drift off into the same kind of obscurity that enveloped most of his European relations. The trouble is, he has found, Buckingham Palace cannot control the publicity as much as they would have liked and this became especially apparent as his children and their respective spouses moved into the limelight. To a very large extent, he drew the pack – like a hunted fox – down that cul-de-sac and then did not much care to have them snapping constantly at his heels.

There is one area about which he has been especially low key over the years – and one must assume it is quite deliberate – and that is on race relations. Searches through Philip's speeches have uncovered very few mentions of race, and since the number of black employees in royal service can be counted on the left hand of a man who has lost two fingers, one must further assume that the Prince is not as fussed about the underprivileged coloured population of this country as his son Charles obviously is. Mountbatten once criticized him for having no black employees. He merely answered in stammering fashion, 'I really don't know. I mean . . . it is a dreadfully difficult problem. Racialism is peculiar isn't it?'[14] It is, and his attitude to that problem doubtless explains the dislike that several Commonwealth leaders have of Prince Philip.

But before leaving this aspect of the Prince's public-speaking image, there is an area of his personality, a weakness, which cannot be blamed on any desire for controversiality, publicity or even benevolent meddling. Nor has it anything to do with his battles with the press. It stems entirely from his own sheer rudeness to people who least suspect it; and not just to individuals, but to whole communities.

Again there are many reported examples, most of which occur when he has no prepared words in front of him. Some of his more notorious sayings, it must be pointed out, are the result of misconstrued attempts at humour, such as the time in 1963 when he was handing over Kenya to Mr Jomo Kenyatta, lately the Burning Spear of the Mau Mau. A few moments before midnight, they stood in front of 50,000 chanting Kenyans and, with a galaxy of would-be Eastern and Western political sponsors waiting for the chimes that would signify independence, Philip turned to the new leader and asked, 'Are you sure you want to go through with this?'

A few of his best one-liners were not meant in the same jocular fashion. Of a Chilean representative who turned up in an ordinary lounge suit for a reception that the Queen was attending, Philip asked, 'Why are you dressed like that?'

The Chilean replied, 'We are poor; I could not afford a dinner suit so my party told me to wear a lounge suit.'

Philip retorted, 'I suppose if they'd have said wear a bathing suit, you would have done that too.'

Of a photographer who fell from a pole while trying to get a better view, 'I hope he breaks his bloody neck.' To American newsgirl Jan Phillips, who politely asked him at a San Diego equestrian event, 'What do you think of the British team's chances?' he snapped, 'Look at the scoreboard and work it out for yourself.' To a Canadian official while on a visit with the Queen, 'If at any stage people feel the monarchy has no further part to play then for goodness sake let us end the thing on amicable terms without having a row about it.' And then he went and ruined it all by adding, 'We don't come here for our health, you know.' To the Sultan of Oman, he said, 'I'm not one of the corgis.' To singer Tom Jones, 'What do you gargle with, pebbles?' To reporter David Leith, standing in front of him at a Moroccan beauty spot, 'Get that bloody man out of my way. Hey you, didn't you hear what I said? You're blocking my bloody view.' And to another Canadian, who greeted their arrival in Toronto by asking what sort of flight the Queen and Philip had just had, he replied, 'Have you ever flown in a plane? Yes? Well, it was just like that.' Finally, to the managing director of a Manchester knitting firm to whom he had just been introduced: 'I suppose you are the head nit.' But perhaps the greatest uproars have occurred over a couple of his more recent utterances. First, while in China in 1986 he made his much-maligned comment to a British student: 'If you stay much longer, you'll get slitty eyes.' Then on his return he told an appalling joke which the Chinese present regarded as an insult: 'If it's got four legs and it's not a chair, if it's got two wings and it's not an aeroplane, if it swims and is not a submarine, what is it? Answer, a Cantonese dinner – they'll eat anything that moves.' *Daily Mirror* editor Richard Stott christened him the Great Wally of China in 3-inch black type on the front page.

The statement that brought Philip greatest criticism was his insult to wives in December 1988. During yet another discussion on the paradox of hunting animals while supporting conservation, he made his usual analogy that it was no different to a butcher killing animals and selling meat for money. Then he made an even more ridiculous comparison, that it was the same as wives and prostitutes – 'I don't think doing it for money makes it any more moral. I don't think a prostitute is more moral than a wife but they are doing the same thing.' More fury!

He once actually tried to explain the reason for his *faux pas*: 'You make it sound as if I were deliberately plotting to upset everyone. This happens quite by chance. In fact, most things I get kicked in the teeth about happen by chance.'

After forty years of wit, wisdom, platitudes and acid, we have become too accustomed to Philip and it is an unfortunate fact that even his important, sensible and well-prepared speeches on the future of mankind can now evoke serious interest only among a minority audience of like-minded conservationists, or those fixed to their seats by the fact that they are attending a conference or function at which he is speaking.

Unlike politicians and other figureheads whose timespan of very public utterances is far less lengthy, Philip is now more likely to get the response, 'Oh, not him again!' Which is a pity.

Chapter Twenty-one
Dominant Force

The Royal Family which brought the nation through the hardships of the Second World War was a warm and cosy, typically British group of unremarkable individuals. The little Princesses called their parents Mummy and Papa, and the image in the post-war movie newsreels of a pleasant, homely family remains with all those who can remember the era. They had a magic and a mystique which – unlike previous reigns – was allied more to ordinariness than to glamour. The King was a traditionalist who did not care much for change, a view which was shared by his daughter. But it was a bland, unexciting style of monarchy that simply had to change to keep pace with the times, and especially the demands that came with the sixties when Philip observed, 'If we are not careful, we shall all become museumpieces.' He was deeply concerned that this 'image' was not the right one for the age and he wanted to display a more human face to make sure the Royals never fell from public gaze, while at the same time trying to walk the fine line between adequate exposure and sheer trivialization.

But before examining more closely the influence he has brought to bear on the family in this direction, it is interesting to look back to 1967 for a mid-term report on his work, because it was at this point, with Prince Charles's emergence into public life, that Philip earnestly began to relaunch the monarchy and the entire Royal Family.

It was during the celebrations of the Queen's twentieth wedding anniversary that historian A. J. P. Taylor gave Philip a jolting reminder that he existed as he did only because he had married whom he did when he did. Left to his own resources, he would in all probability have become a retired naval officer who had passed gay and undistinguished years and was now seeking part-time employment as secretary of a golf club or home bursar at an Oxford college. His only worry might have been an occasional shortage of money. Instead, he had performed with 'admirable patience a subordinate task as consort' in which he had been

231

expected to behave like a dutiful Victorian wife whose position would have provoked outcry from the suffragettes.[1]

Now, more than twenty years further still, Taylor might wish to revise his assessment. Philip, if he read the original words, would certainly argue that he had shown more resourcefulness than merely aspiring to the running of a golf club. Some republicans might disagree.

Rather more questionable is the thought of his having subordinated himself to anyone! True, he has kept out of matters of State in which the Queen, on the other hand, has become so devastatingly experienced. Her prerogatives have been, and still are, as unassailable as ever. In all else, however, Prince Philip has dominated the British monarchy – not perhaps as the power behind the throne but certainly as the power behind the family, the toughest royal male since George V. No one, with the possible exceptions of the Queen Mother and Mountbatten, has seen fit to challenge him.

It is a domination that has run through almost every facet of life at the palace, and more especially in the wider family circle in which the Windsors were substantially outnumbered by offspring from Philip's multi-branched family tree whenever there was a gathering of the clans – a situation which nature has latterly begun to rectify. Among these relatives were lessons for Britain's own monarchy; it is therefore relevant to divert for a moment to look at the fate of some of the other European royal houses and how their example – and even non-existence – affects the magic of the British version and provides a warning.

Philip was the last prominent survivor of his family and in many respects became a benevolent father-figure to the dispossessed. Years ago, he made Buckingham Palace the unofficial hub of the remnants of scattered Royalty who have roamed the Continent without purpose since the war, while the Queen became the formal link with the remaining crowned heads who have managed to stay in position, though with their status diminished. The deposed came and went with regularity, enviously catching an insight of what might have been had they remained in power; the British monarchy, meanwhile, looked dubiously at where they could so easily end up.

The German faction's visits to London were once frequent, though they have become less so in the eighties. Conversely, Prince Charles discovered the full extent of this relationship when he first went to Germany in 1962 and found that his father's relatives had provided him with no less than sixteen first cousins of German birth alone; they were powerless, disinherited throwbacks from an unwanted age. As Beaverbrook once pointed out, Philip was anxious for Charles to get to know his German family and be aware of the complete family tree.

When the Greeks, Yugoslavs, Swedes and Danes were added, the gathering of Philip-connected relatives – as shown in Mountbatten's book of lineage – provided a formidable list of so-called European princes and princesses; regardless of their current position, they continue to call each other by the royal prefix. On the occasion of the wedding of Princess Marina's daughter Princess Alexandra to Angus Ogilvy in 1963, for example, the guest-list included three reigning Queens – of the Hellenes, Denmark and Sweden – all more closely connected to the Mountbattens than to the Windsors.

On that night, Prince Charles danced vigorously with his cousin Princess Clarissa of Hesse, daughter of Prince Christopher who died in the war. These family get-togethers pleased Philip. He loved to play uncle to his nieces and nephews, and helped any of them who came to England to study. Princess Beatrice, eldest daughter of Philip's sister Princess Margarita of Hohenlohe-Langenburg first came in Coronation year and returned later with Princess Christina of Hesse – Princess Sophie's eldest daughter – to enter the Royal College of Art, where Christina studied art restoration. The two cousins discovered that their generous uncle had rented and furnished an apartment for them in Dolphin Square. By all and sundry, whether they were the Hesses, the Hanovers, the Hohenlohe-Langenburgs or the Badens, the Queen was addressed as Aunt Elizabeth. Past political sensitivities, forced upon King George VI by his daughter's choice of husband, had drifted away.

The link to the remaining European Royals was strengthened by the marriages of two of the children of Philip's cousin King Paul of Greece and Queen Frederika. Their first child, Sophie, born in 1938, married Prince Juan Carlos of Spain in 1962, thus becoming Queen Sofia when Franco restored the Spanish monarchy in 1975. Paul I's second child and heir, Constantine II of Greece, succeeded his father in 1964 and in the same year married Princess Anne-Marie of Denmark, who is a second cousin of both Philip and the Queen. They were unlucky in their recaptured tenure of the Greek throne; reinstated in 1964, they were rejected again in 1967 and have spent most of their married life living quietly in exile in North London.

Another poignant reminder of the past came in 1979 at the funeral of Lord Mountbatten, where six deposed Kings and Queens gathered forlornly. Constantine II and Queen Anne-Marie were joined by King Simeon of Bulgaria, King Umberto of Italy, King Michael and Queen Anne of Romania (whose aspirations – even with the wave of anti-Communist revolution that swept Eastern Europe in 1989 – remains in the basement of hope). Oddly, none ever appears to be hard up.

In the Romanians' case, the ten trainloads of loot that King Carol took with him to Switzerland in 1940 from some of his 153 palaces doubtless stood them in good stead, though in 1980 'King' Michael claimed he was not a wealthy man. All are firm friends and supporters of each other. As ex-Queen Helen of Romania said:

My brothers became kings, my husband Carol was a king and my
son Michael was a king. Well, it's all gone now and we went through
some awful things. But we do keep a sense of humour. That's why
I'm glad Prince Philip has such a sense of humour. He has talent,
charm, wit and authority and has made a success of his job. Who
else could have done it so well? Certainly not some chinless
wonder![2]

She was probably right.

But there must have been times when Philip and the Queen worried
that their great heritage might go the same way. They could not have sat
side by side on their thrones for forty years or more without giving the
possibility a passing thought. Critical times, like the scandalous affair of
Princess Margaret and Roddy Llewellyn which preceded her divorce from
Lord Snowdon,* was surely one moment when their hearts skipped a beat.
It needed only some adjacent Constitutional crisis or some statesman or
other poking about amongst the Queen's rights seriously to damage their
future aspirations. Perhaps that is why the British Royal Family has become such a very tight-knit and almost introspective group within the
wider family circle. Will the monarchy survive? Can it survive?

Private lives and preparation for their calling have always been important
to the roles the Royals perform. They are human, after all. The privileges
are great; the pressures are at times unbearable – though as Philip once
said, 'You get immune to it after the first twenty-five years.'[3]

How attentively has he played the role of husband and father?

Life at the Palace evolved and revolved around two key elements: the
Queen's official duties and, after that, whatever Philip might be doing
professionally or privately. This was the pattern until the children grew
up and began to branch out on their own, acquiring their own duties
and spouses. Their private life has been a decidedly odd one, and again
it was more to do with Philip than with his wife. Apart from holiday
times, few months during the past three decades have been free of his
extended travel and, far from his being cast in the role of A. J. P. Taylor's
'dutiful Victorian wife' waiting at home for his spouse to perform the
duties of State from which he was precluded, a rather opposite picture
has been drawn by those close enough to observe the family. More often
than not, it was the Queen who would be left at home to study the
raceform books while Philip went off on his travels, either on duty or in
seach of sporting adventure. A facetious headline writer once proclaimed:
'PHILIP VISITS BRITAIN'.

The foreign visits have increased rather than decreased over the past
few years. Since 1980 alone, he has completed eighty-three official

---

* Antony Armstrong-Jones was created Earl of Snowdon in 1961.

overseas trips – excluding those on which he has accompanied the Queen – visiting sixty-eight separate countries, many of them twice or more. He has made five official visits to Australia in those ten years, while the United States and Canada have received fifteen visits, again not counting the tours he made with the Queen. And his travel calendar, issued by the Central Office of Information, carries the preamble:

> The Duke has also made unofficial visits and many private visits to friends and relatives in a number of European countries; he has frequently visited units of the British armed forces in the Federal Republic of Germany and carried out engagements abroad in connection with the many associations of which he is patron.

If we analyse further the content of a typical year, it will be seen that, though on paper it appears a heavy workload, it is not perhaps as punishing as, say, Princess Anne's. Take 1982 as a random choice: February/March visited Federal Republic of Germany, Austria, Italy, Egypt, Oman, Pakistan, India, Sri Lanka, Sudan, Tunisia, Spain and Switzerland in connection with the World Wildlife Fund and while in India attended a Commonwealth Study Conference; April visited United States and briefly, France; May attended Rome Horse Show; July visited Switzerland for World Wildlife Fund; August visited The Netherlands for World Driving Championships; August on holiday at Balmoral; September/October, Australia for Commonwealth Games; October/November went to Japan, United States (Houston, Washington, Chicago) and Canada for the World Wildlife Fund; November, Switzerland for the World Wildlife Fund; November/December, Federal Republic of Germany to Army and RAF units and private visits.[4] Added to that are the engagements Philip performed during the year on home territory. It reveals a daunting workload, but carefully measured. Not one of his overseas engagements was traumatically demanding, though of course by then he was over sixty.

When similar pressures were applied to the marriage of Princess Anne and Captain Mark Phillips, it cracked. Like Anne and Mark, who eventually reached the stage – partly by design – of passing each other like ships in the night, the Queen has seen rather less of her husband over the years than might be expected, even of a high-powered couple with separate careers.

They are said always to have possessed a perfect understanding of each other, and the Queen especially has been able to make allowances for her husband's nomadic needs – which could have been resolved quite easily by accepting fewer commitments. This he steadfastly refused to do and it was left to other defenders – including Lord Fisher, former Archbishop of Canterbury – to rebuke the gossips who seemed to imagine 'that Philip had a lady discreetly stowed in some remote German Schloss and the Queen was neglected.'[5]

Almost throughout his married life, Philip's workload has taken a heavy toll on family relationships and very few personal, intimate joint friendships have been built up between himself and the Queen and other couples; weekends with friends usually meant staying with one of the Mountbatten daughters or with Sir Harold and Lady Zia Wernher at Luton Hoo.

Philip has always insisted the children did not suffer unduly. Nanny Mabel Anderson recalled that Philip was a 'marvellous father when the children were young' and when he was around, although Prince Charles has said that one of his saddest recollections of childhood was that his father was seldom present for his birthdays; he missed the first five and 'sent notes instead.'

Yet in childhood and early teens, Charles idolized his father. He copied him in his actions, his stance and walk, especially in that famous emulation of strolling along with his hands behind his back, one cupped in the other. Philip pushed his son towards all the manly, toughing-up sports that he himself loved; he was duck shooting at ten; on the pheasant shoots with his own shotgun a year later; hunting in his teens; then soon taking up polo with verve and daring, though never with quite the same ferocity as his father. (Nor, incidentally, has Charles been noted for any other major sporting achievements.) Just before he went to Gordonstoun, he was taken by his father to visit one of his old friends from the Thursday Club days, James Robertson Justice, who had a small estate in Scotland; the three of them swam in the ice-cold Scottish waters and went on long walks, cooking their own food over campfires.

In Philip's view the children were not to be mollycoddled – he once took some of their toys away because they had too many. He was strict and stern and the children generally feared his awesome temper, inherited by Princess Anne but not by Prince Charles. Nor was Princess Anne – and perhaps especially not Anne – shown any favours. The world has watched as they matured into adults of quite different characters and temperaments, though all inheriting Philip's stern and rigid defence of their birthright and position, which they protect – even in times of calamity – as if there were an ever-lingering threat to make the monarchy extinct and evict their mother from the Palace. Only the middle two, Anne and Andrew, seem to have inherited their father's total toughness, untempered by the caring streak that is apparent in Charles or the softness – masked by arrogance – in Prince Edward.

Yet throughout, Philip's theme for his family has continued to be that of ordinariness. He and the Queen, when Charles first went to Cheam, had Richard Colville contact all national newspaper editors to remind them that they wanted Charles treated just like any other pupil and that his school life should not be hampered by the press's constant intrusions.

When he went to Gordonstoun, one of the principal reasons given was that the Queen and Prince Philip wanted him to taste the experiences of his contemporaries in unrestricted surroundings, thus becoming the first future monarch in British history not to have private tutors – just like any other 'ordinary student'. Princess Anne was sent to Benenden, to become lost in a sea of blue uniforms like any other 'ordinary' middle-class girl, and so the theme has been perpetuated through to Prince Charles's own children – both attending 'ordinary' schools. 'Ordinariness' is of course a total fallacy; they use the word themselves as if it has been drummed into them from birth, though how it can honestly be applied to the Royal Family remains defiantly unobvious. Princess Anne attempted this definition:

> What some people don't appreciate is that one thing you want to do is to live what they laughingly call an ordinary life. And the older you get, of course, the more you realize that all lives are ordinary – it's just what other people choose to think on the basis of their own knowledge which makes them unordinary. I don't believe Royals are so very peculiar. I don't think we live a particularly different life – in so far as there is an average life, a common denominator of life, we see a great deal of it. We meet a very large number of people.[6]

Anyway, ordinary children they were supposed to become.

And certainly, to have the Royals, and especially two future Kings, educated outside the old Palace tutorial system was a great and significant departure from tradition, again spearheaded by Philip and with the Queen's full support, though they did argue over the place. Philip decided that the three boys would follow him to Gordonstoun. In the case of Prince Charles, he was challenged over this choice by both the Queen – who sought additional advice from senior courtiers – and the Queen Mother, who firmly believed he should take a more conventional education, such as Eton. Philip's wishes prevailed.

When asked once how his son was taking to the school, he replied, 'Well, he hasn't run away yet.' Charles said later that he was glad to have had the experience – well, perhaps he would, wouldn't he? – and the test will come when he selects schools for his own sons. At the time it undoubtedly brought him closer to his father, whom he saw often but so fleetingly. With the passing of years, however, it has become obvious to all that Philip's attempts to mould Charles into a clone of himself – isn't that what all strong-minded fathers unconsciously attempt? – was in vain.

His eldest son's character is as different from his own as chalk from cheese. That is what has caused antipathy in later life, though Princess Margaret, never backward in supporting her own apologists – and

Charles has been one of the staunchest – says, 'We don't row in our family; we discuss.' In which case, there have been some fairly loud discussions in the Mountbatten-Windsor household as Charles, almost from his coming of age, began to become closer to his mother both in temperament and views.

Whereas Charles once saw his father as a rather godlike, heavy-duty, all-action figure whom he wanted to imitate, his new vision was more of a demanding, strict and heavy-handed man, who, as the son grew older, treated him with increasing degrees of Navy-style discipline. For example: one must stand up during lessons and learn to remain on one's two feet without wavering or fidgeting. Or Philip would give Charles an exact time in which to get dressed and arrive at the foot of the stairs to join his parents; father would be there with watch and chide, 'Fifteen seconds late!'

These were minor moments in the process of moulding a son into kingly material. No further weaklings could be permitted in this century; Philip was going to make damn sure that his son could face the pressures. Charles cried sometimes, and his best friend was his grandmother, the Queen Mother, who acted as both mother and father (she taught him how to fly-fish at Balmoral) during his parents' long absences; she also found herself acting as peacemaker and psychologist.

Then Mountbatten took over as Charles's mentor, which did not please the old Queen, still suspicious of him even after all these years. Mountbatten was the key to the Prince's next major step in life: his education after Gordonstoun. Philip did not entirely agree with the way it transpired. The Queen threw a dinner for 'interested parties' to discuss Charles's future. Philip was there, of course, along with Prime Minister Harold Wilson, Lord Mountbatten as Admiral of the Fleet, the Archbishop of Canterbury Dr Michael Ramsey, the Dean of Windsor, and the Queen's Private Secretary Sir Michael Adeane. To-ing and fro-ing between what everyone thought was the right course for a future king, Wilson suddenly asked Mountbatten for a frank view. The Prince's great-uncle said straight away: 'Trinity College like his grandfather; Dartmouth like his father and grandfather and then to sea, ending up with his own command.' There were no dissenters, though Philip – perhaps recalling his own lack of academic prowess – cautioned that they should avoid the test of severe examinations; there should be no 'absolute need for him to take a degree'.[7]

Charles's course was set and when Mountbatten retired from the Admiralty to become what Philip Ziegler has described as the 'shop steward' of Royalty, he began to devote himself to the cause of Prince Charles, which merely aggravated the 'growing apart' – the much-talked-of 'rift' is far too strong a word – between Philip and Charles. And whereas Mountbatten had found his own nephew increasingly distant to his advice in the latter stages of his life, Prince Charles sought and accepted it with the willingness of a student in awe of his tutor, as he did the counsel of others like the Conservative politician Rab Butler. This kind of relationship never existed between father and son, and Philip's workload was as much to blame as anything. Mountbatten himself admitted:

> You know, the friendship between us is odd. We are separated by half a century in age and yet we can sit for hours in each other's company and never get bored – we're deep and affectionate friends. When we don't see each other, we still write to each other constantly.[8]

Mountbatten's private secretary John Barratt has claimed that if his employer had lived, he would have pushed Prince Charles into marrying his granddaughter Lady Amanda Knatchbull; that in itself was a demonstration of the influence Mountbatten held over Charles. The IRA put paid to it in August 1979, but by then the great-uncle had managed to pass on a good deal of advice to his 'honorary grandson'.

Charles went his own way, and the route he chose was consistent with the difference between his own temperament and that of his father, though his circumstances were similarly difficult: lacking the ultimate authority of the Crown, floundering between public service and attempts at controversiality.

Princess Anne, largely cast in the mould of her father, carved out her own career in the same forceful manner and using the same four-letter vocabulary; if anyone was following in her father's footsteps, it was she – she was and is his double in so many ways. Andrew has followed the Battenberg tradition of naval service and seems more likely to be the one who might fulfil A. J. P. Taylor's prediction by ending up as the secretary of a local golf club, having passed gay and undistinguished years. Edward, who felt his father's wrath for having the nerve to quit the Marines, remains for the moment in his odd vacuum on the periphery of both showbusiness and Royalty – or are they now one and the same? – showing no sign of greater ambitions. The children of lesser Royals show no interest whatsoever in the royal life.

In fact, the mystique of the British monarchy was fading long before the timely intervention of Lady Diana Spencer and has at times required specialist public relations to jack up flagging attention or overcome a damaging scandal. Even so, the convulsions of unprecedented fawning followed by outright voyeurism through the columns of the popular press in the eighties has given the family a hard knock and the spell is still in danger of being broken, in spite of Diana.

Were Philip and his showbiz uncle to blame? Partly, in as much as they gave an inch and the newspapers greedily took a mile. Philip could not have foreseen that the changes he had initiated to alter public perception of his family were being made at the very time that the media itself was becoming embroiled in its own competitive battles. In the late sixties Hugh Cudlipp gave Rupert Murdoch the *Sun* newspaper for a rather small consideration and changed the tone of popular journalism in Britain. This event was unfortunately to follow immediately upon the heels of Philip's clandestine relaunching of the British monarchy, which began in 1967.

The moment at which he inadvertently lowered their pedestals is quite easy to pinpoint. It was surrounded by a number of apparently unconnected events which were in fact wrapped up in each other.

First, Philip believed the Royal Family had become dowdy and distant, and was worried that their overall image had been dented by increasingly daring sniper attacks in the press, dating almost from the Margaret–Townsend affair, Philip's round-the-world tour, the Hélène Cordet autobiography and innuendo over the Profumo scandal.

Second, Commander Richard Colville, the poe-faced Press Secretary who had been stolidly fielding unwanted media attention for too long, was given a knighthood for services beyond the call of duty and retired at the beginning of 1968, to a collective sigh of relief from Fleet Street.

An enthusiastic new broom swept in an era of more change. Colville's successor was a vigorous Australian named William Heseltine, who at thirty-three had a good track record as former Private Secretary to Australian premier Sir Robert Menzies. There was an air of simultaneous anticipation and foreboding among the experienced press hands. The latter was brought on by two rare analytical statements from Sir Richard Colville about the monarchy in general. Before he retired, he gave this warning: 'If there comes a time when the British monarchy ever needs a real public relations officer, the institution of monarchy in this country will be in serious danger.' His next pronouncement had serious underlying implications: 'Royal lives have been progressively more exposed to public scrutiny and there is now constant conflict of what may be termed in the public interest and what is private.'[9]

He was doubtless aware of secret – the word is carefully chosen because even today it is not generally known – moves in the background: first, to use professional public relations men to help massage Philip's image on an American tour and to launch Prince Charles into public life; and, second, they were planning to go public with their private lives with the making of a television film called *Royal Family*, in complete and utter disregard of Colville's despairing words of warning.

Philip hired one of America's most famous public relations men, Henry Rogers, to arrange part of his 1969 US tour and do something about his jaded image. He thus joined the long list of Rogers's celebrity clients, who included Rita Hayworth and Brigitte Bardot. Next, Prince Charles's first personal equerry, David Checketts, was quietly enlisted to co-opt the aid of public relations executive Nigel Neilson, whom he had known in the war, to handle the launch of the new Prince of Wales prior to the formal Investiture in 1969 – a move which involved Philip and of which the Queen was surely informed.

Neilson, a fast-talking New Zealander, moved in high circles and had direct contact with those who mattered. One of his most satisfied clients of the day was Aristotle Onassis, by whom he was employed specifically to improve his image, recently scarred by Bobby Kennedy's references: 'The Greek . . . is a complete rogue on a grand scale'.[10] Suitably spring-cleaned, Onassis emerged as the next husband of Jacqueline Kennedy soon after her brother-in-law was shot.

The route to Neilson's involvement with Charles was opened through the appointment of David Checketts as a part-time director of Neilson's company, Neilson McCarthy, in 1968. The appointment received quiet approval from Buckingham Palace through William Heseltine, who was doubtless told of one of Neilson's first observations, that he considered Prince Charles to be 'a first-class product being criminally undersold'.[11] The strategy employed was for Checketts to sit in on the PR firm's meetings and relay their thoughts back to the Palace; thus Neilson McCarthy became PR consultants to Prince Charles without any formal connection.

Neilson made himself available for constant advice and quietly guided the Palace towards a new approach in handling journalists, especially the more imaginative members of foreign newspapers. Australia was targeted for special attention, because it was in that country that Charles was to spend some time after schooling. Discussions in which expressions like 'managing' the press were used became commonplace. They were totally new to Palace thinking on media coverage, which was really still set in the days when royal writers followed the family around the country and abroad to report as one 'how the people cheered . . . smiling, gleeful faces welcomed them wherever they went . . . the Queen spoke of the . . .' But by now the mass-market papers were straining at the leash to get at their private moments. Journalists who sent back reports of 'Oh, how they cheered . . .' had long since found themselves assigned to the gardening page.

As any good PR man knows – and the Palace presumably did not – journalists like to be fêted and treated with some degree of intelligent co-operation. They are actually quite easily manipulated and in the mid-sixties were still a comparatively responsible bunch. It was the Palace press office's own suggestion, for instance, that newspapers might like to consider appointing specialist royal reporters. This was a Neilson-inspired idea for the launch of Charles and the effect was quickly evident. It was a complete reversal of the bland wall of silence that had emanated from the Colville camp; royal writers were surprised to find themselves being ushered into the royal halls for interviews, not just with Charles but with Philip and later with Princess Anne.

Neilson put Charles through some gruelling rehearsals, making him speak into a tape-recorder and then playing it back with his corrective comments. Next, Neilson began placing Charles in front of a small, intimate but high-pressure audience of businessmen and bankers at his London apartment. Few people outside the Palace were aware of what was happening, but in the space of two years Charles's outward appearance, his whole stance and attitude, changed dramatically. The techniques, once learned, would be reapplied, over and over again. When Princess Anne went through a bad time with her public image in 1981, she was relaunched into her Mother Theresa role.

One of the hallmarks of success in this field is that the changes should take place without anyone realizing they are deliberate. Certainly, the newspapers seemed to feel they had been responsible for changing the perception of Princess Anne. *Daily Mirror* writer James Whitaker claimed credit for starting the 'let's be nice to Anne' movement. He may well have written the first story in such a vein; but really the Palace – under Philip's guidance – started it. Similarly, when the Princess of Wales became too 'pop' in 1985, they redesigned her workload to present her in a new and caring light. At the time of writing, a relaunch of the Duchess of York was apparently still on the drawing board. Such PR techniques have been applied to more serious topics, too. The separation of Princess Anne and Captain Mark Phillips had all the hallmarks of a controlled leak rather than a direct public statement, though this has been denied.

But in the chronology of Philip's dramatic move towards what he hoped might be a more controlled relationship with the press, whom he truthfully hated, the next major step back in 1968 was the production of a royal film. The reason for it was not to do so much with press relations as with the presentation of the monarchy in a better light to the public. As so often happens, however, the one led directly to the other.

The original idea came from Neilson via Heseltine, that there should be a filmed biography of Charles to coincide with the Investiture. Philip liked the idea but thought there was insufficient material – as Dermot Morrah indeed discovered when he wrote the first official biography of Charles, commissioned and published simultaneously with the Investiture: six rather innocuous chapters about the Prince's schooldays.

Philip had another thought. They had all seen – several times – a film made some months earlier on the life of Lord Mountbatten by his film-producer son-in-law Lord Brabourne, and the prospect of something similar on the Royal Family was thrown into the melting pot. There were immediate objectors in Court who felt strongly that the monarchy could not take much more of this attack upon its mystique; once the television cameras were brought through the front doors and unguarded moments of nose-picking or bottom-scratching observed, the masses might begin to realize that the growing family of Mountbatten-Windsors were, in truth, just like themselves only richer. Much richer.

That, of course, is exactly what happened. The BBC camera team, which was allowed to follow the family for almost a year, was so skilful and treated the project with such seriousness that the end result was a classic documentary of its age. Until then, the voices of members of the royal house were never recorded unless on officially scripted occasions, and that rule still applies more than twenty years later. The Queen had never been observed on camera in any kind of informal speech, conversation or aside. The BBC production team faced the delicate problem of recording members of the family in their casual home surroundings without crossing the dangerous line of invading their private lives.

The film itself achieved this aim quite successfully; in the aftermath the taboos were completely ignored in the welter of press attention. The Royal Family was really shown for the very first time in a new, human light. Prince Philip saw it as a great success; the whole family enjoyed the film and certainly to see him barbecuing a steak and the Queen mixing salad was a novel piece of keyholing.

But that was exactly the point made by the wary courtiers who were against the film in the first place. It is true that few people who have attempted to use television for popularization have escaped being trivialized by it. More importantly, perhaps, it signalled the next phase of press attention.

The whole blame cannot be laid upon Philip, Mountbatten or the PR advisers. There were too many other forces at work at exactly the same time. How could they have foreseen the emergence of the daring new stridency among the tabloids, vying with each other for royal scoops, which by the mid-seventies had become an established part of daily newspaper coverage? Where once stories criticizing any member of the Royal Family or showing them in an uncomplimentary light had required the permission or instigation of the proprietor, it suddenly became a creative free-for-all, a self-feeding, self-perpetuating and self-deluding scenario long ago warned against by those who said that once the traditions of monarchy are banished, then the whole will fall like a deck of cards. As the author can well testify, the stage was reached where no issue of a Sunday popular newspaper was complete without its 'royal' element, and nothing sold daily newspapers like a smashingly attractive picture of the Princess of Wales on the front page. At the height of her popularity, it was Di-mania; nothing less.

The family members themselves added to the excitement with their usual sense of the spectacular by providing a succession of highly extravagant and eminently newsworthy events: births, marriages and deaths, plus that unheard-of word 'divorce', a touch of scandal here and there, with the odd four-lettered word from Anne or her father thrown in for good measure.

The discretion of the edited television film was quickly replaced by the feverish activities of the *paparazzi* with their long-tom lenses that could catch the Princess of Wales in her bikini from half a mile away. From that moment in the mid-sixties when Philip was heard to say that he feared they would all become museumpieces if they were not careful, the British Royal family has exploded into a massive, dispassionate industry: a circulation-building, TV-ratings grabbing, book-writing, charity-promoting, export-supporting, tourist-enticing, sports-sponsoring extravaganza on a scale that no one could either have imagined or desired.

Within two decades the family firm to which King George VI had referred as 'the four of us . . . with additions of course at suitable moments' had expanded into an ongoing saga involving eleven major players and a supporting cast of hundreds.

Museumpieces they did not become, but that fear is now renewed for a reason very different from public apathy . . .

Chapter Twenty-two

The Price

In Jubilee Year, 1977, Prince Philip wrote a more profound assessment of Britain's ills than normal and said there were 'many worms in the fruit'.[1] Poor output and productivity and industrial unrest were the origins of many of the nation's present troubles. He went on to say that high unemployment, falling living standards, falling exports and frightening increases in government spending gave hardly the most auspicious start to the Queen's Silver Jubilee – 'yet it may well be that this experience is needed to bring us all back to a greater sense of reality.'

He explained that Buckingham Palace had recognized the need for savings and reducing costs. They had to distinguish between those things which were traditions and customs worth preserving and those which – like the débutantes – were out of touch with modern attitudes. While trying to adapt to these changes, Philip said that 'we' – i.e. he and the Queen – had remained conscious of the need to retain known and familiar things to give a feeling of continuity to people who were grappling with constantly changing conditions. The nation continued to have emotions of pride and attachment to its homeland.

Next came his explanation of the paradox:

> People still respond more easily to symbolism than to reason; the idea of chieftainship in its representative rather than its governing function is still just as clearly and even instinctively understood. From the point of view of national identity, this function is perhaps more important than ever.

Monarchy is the symbol, Philip was saying, and the Queen's people understand that there is a difference between themselves and the 'chiefs'. It is a moot point, particularly when argued by one so privileged. And does the symbol have to be adorned with such obvious displays of wealth and opulence?

The monarch's money – too little or too much, depending on your view of the nation's first family – became an open issue in 1969. Until that time it was seldom mentioned publicly; jibes rather than debate had been the norm. Philip used himself as the devil's advocate and brought the subject into what would turn into a much wider discussion when he revealed that the monarchy was about to go into the red.

By that, he did not mean the Royal Family was going broke; merely that the amount allotted them by the government annually was no longer sufficient to meet the expenses incurred in their public duties and in the upkeep of the House of Windsor, which in turn – as his critics soon pointed out – meant that the Queen would have to start spending her own money on public duties. Unfortunately, Philip made two basic errors of judgement in revealing this information: he chose to do it on American television and be provided the opportunity for personal expenditure – and consequently the personal wealth of the Queen – to cloud the issue.

Asked about the rumours that the Royal Family was spending more than the £475,000 allowance made by the government, he replied:

> We go into the red next year, which is not bad housekeeping if you come to think of it. We've in fact kept the thing going on a budget which was based on costs of eighteen years ago. So there have been considerable corners that have had to be cut and it is beginning to have its effect.[2]

Fair enough. It was a valid point. His next statement, however, was pounced upon by headliners and cartoonists the world over:

> Now inevitably if nothing happens we shall have to – I don't know, we may have to move to smaller premises, who knows? We've closed down, well, for instance, we had a small yacht which we've had to sell and I shall probably have to give up polo fairly soon . . .

The Palace tried to get the words edited out before the film arrived for transmission in Britain but they failed. The consequence was the beginning of a damaging eighteen-month discussion over the wealth and spending of the Queen, Philip and the monarchy as a whole. It has never been satisfactorily resolved.

The two distinct and separate concerns of private income and State spending suddenly became blurred by wild speculations of the Queen's personal wealth, which she could draw upon instead of using the donations of the British taxpayers. The figures were as meaningless then as they are today. No one knows the true value of the Queen's possessions; and anyway the whole question disintegrates into the murky categories of what she and her family can regard as their own and what should truly be regarded as part of the breathtaking collection of national heritage in her care.

At the time, the Lord Chamberlain, Lord Cobbold, said, 'In no practical sense does the Queen regard these items [the Crown Jewels, etc.] as being at her free personal disposal.' There was, however, a considerable amount of property – furniture, art, jewellery – obtained by inheritance, gift or purchase which the Queen and Prince Philip considered to be their own private property.

After Philip's warning of imminent poverty in the royal household, Prime Minister Harold Wilson found the subject so complex and politically fraught that he opted for a thorough investigation by a select committee – a promise which was inherited by Edward Heath's Conservative government when it came to power in 1970. The committee began its task in January 1971 and met from time to time for six months. The outcome was a triumph for the monarchy in terms of achieving an increase in their Civil List allowances while keeping their true worth and wealth an absolute secret.

In examining their riches, it is a fatuous exercise to try to separate out what they personally own and what is the rightful property of the nation. The most obvious area of confusion is in the family's collection of jewels, art and precious metals. If the monarchy were abolished tomorrow, there is no one on earth who could say with any certainty what she would be allowed to take with her into exile.

Even the Lord Chancellor has refused to show just how it could or would be resolved that the Royal Family actually owned one particular item but not another, except to state ambiguously that the royal collection not alienable covers all property and works of art purchased by all sovereigns up to the death of Queen Victoria and also includes certain property acquired by sovereigns and their consorts since then.

The differential between ownership or custodianship of treasures like the Crown Jewels is clear cut. Equally, the Queen's ownership can be established of much of the exquisite and substantial collection of jewellery amassed and bequeathed by Queen Mary. It was bought with her own money and includes a large number of the Romanov treasures brought to England after the massacre and acquired by Queen Mary through ruthless bargaining at knock-down prices from the penniless survivors of the Russian Royal Family; it is now worth millions.

But who owns the Queen Mary jewellery which came flooding in in 1893 as public wedding gifts from the boroughs and shires of England? There was a diamond tiara from the county of Surrey, a diamond and platinum bow with a tremulous pendant pearl from the inhabitants of Kensington, a diamond bow from the county of Dorset, a diamond ring from the people of Windsor. These were all displayed alongside the family presents such as a diamond necklace from the Duke of Westminster, a sapphire and diamond bracelet from Nicholas II of Russia, a sapphire and diamond brooch from his Empress.

Also debatable is the ownership of 'gifts' made personally to the monarchy, such as those legendary handfuls of priceless emeralds, diamonds and rubies bestowed upon them by Indian princes and maharajas. At the Delhi Durbar for the Coronation of the King–Emporer George V, 135 ruling princes all came bearing gifts. First was Prince Nizam, who gave the King a ruby necklace in which each ruby was the size of a pigeon's egg. His Highness of Panna brought an umbrella for George's throne which was at least 12 inches in diameter and was carved out of a single piece of emerald from his emerald mine. When Edward VIII came to the throne he clearly believed they were his own because he gave a large number of the Indian stones to Wallis Simpson; some were found scattered on Sunningdale Golf course in 1946, dropped by a thief who had just stolen her jewellery pouch from the country house she was visiting.

This somewhat ambivalent attitude towards royal gems is perhaps no better demonstrated than in their ownership of the famous Cullinan diamond. The stone, named after the owner of the South African mine, was an unimaginable 3,025 carats when it was found and weighed 1½ pounds. It was presented to Edward VII by the government of South Africa as a peace offering at the end of the Boer War and 'proudly accepted on behalf of myself and my successors', in spite of Lord Esher's advice to the King not to take the gift. It was cut into two principal stones: the first, Cullinan One, was named the Greater Star of Africa and was set in the head of the Sceptre and the Cross. The second, Cullinan Two, was set in the Imperial State Crown. Both form part of the Crown Jewels displayed in the Tower of London.

Nine 'chips' from the Cullinan diamond remained in the hands of the Dutch firm of jewellers as their fee for cutting the original stone.* Edward VII bought one of the chips, the Marquise Stone, and presented it to his Queen the year before he died; it was subsequently inherited by Queen Mary. The Transvaal government purchased the remainder and presented them to Queen Mary in 1910. Thus the entire Cullinan diamond came into the possession of the British Royal Family and they would doubtless claim direct ownership of all but the first two parts which form part of the Crown Jewels. The fourth and fifth cleavings were formed into a brooch and this single item of jewellery, made from just two of the chips, is alone now conservatively valued at between £8 million and £10 million, not counting royal prestige value.

Valuations are virtually impossible because no one can really assess historical worth or appeal. The Duchess of Windsor's jewels, for instance,

---

* It was so magnificent and valuable that Mr J. Asscher, the diamond cutter at I. J. Asscher, fainted as he performed the first stroke and the first two stones fell away.

were expected by the experts to make £5 million at the most, but ended up fetching almost £32 million – and her's was a tiny, paltry collection compared with those of the real House of Windsor. The Buckingham Palace vaults are filled with tiaras, necklaces, brooches, rings and pendants dating back to Victoria and beyond. Some have not been taken out for years.

As can be seen from the case of the Cullinan diamond, royal stewardship of the collections of national treasure hides the family's own personal mountain of trinkets, the value of which, on the basis of Wallis's sale, must run to between £300 and £500 million. When the assessment is extended to their personal ownership and custodianship of art, porcelain, furniture and precious-metal treasures – like the solid silver Georgian soup tureens which it takes two men to lift even when empty – that abound in their palaces, the result is a mind-boggling confusion. The complete list of their collections of antique furniture runs to seventy-five leather-bound volumes stored at Windsor Castle.

Their art collections run side by side with the paintings inherited down centuries of British monarchy. The Queen Mother has built up a small collection of French Impressionists; the Queen's own art collection is substantial and includes many fine works individually valued at millions of pounds. Between them they possess well in excess of 35,000 paintings and drawings, representing works by virtually all the Masters.

It would be an amusing, revealing and complicated exercise for the Prime Minister one day to wander through the royal treasure houses and ask the Queen and Prince Philip to point out 'what's ours and what's yours'. The ensuing arguments might well be heard in Trafalgar Square. 'Hang on a minute,' Philip might say as the Prime Minister picked up the Williamson 23-carat pink diamond brooch. 'That was given to the Queen in our wedding year by a Tanzanian diamond-mine owner. Value now? Oh, about £3 million. And that's definitely my bloody gold and platinum wristwatch. An Arab sheik gave it to me.'

The Arabs have been exceedingly generous to British Royalty. When the Queen and Philip last went there, they brought back gifts of jewellery worth over £1 million, including an 18-inch gold palm tree decorated with rubies, a golden horse encrusted with diamonds, a pearl and diamond necklace from the Emir of Qatar and a golden sword with mother-of-pearl scabbard for Philip.

Importantly, what these gifts do show is that royal wealth is not just a matter of property, landed estates and investment portfolios. It is based on personal and public gifts received as marks of esteem and respect for the British monarchy – gifts which, if accepted by an American president or his First Lady, would be taxable. And the wealth has been built up in less than 150 years: when Victoria came to the throne she actually inherited an overdraft and so the real wealth of the House of Windsor has been built up in the twentieth century.

And who owns the bricks and mortar? That would be another minefield for anyone trying to get to the bottom of the royal financial position.

The family has always regarded the country estates of Sandringham and Balmoral as its own property, as opposed to the other properties like Buckingham Palace, Windsor Castle, Kensington Palace and Clarence House, which are unequivocably owned – and maintained – by the State. But *do* they own them?

Balmoral, a 50,000-acre estate in Grampian Scotland, was bought and heavily refurbished by Queen Victoria from money Prince Albert managed to save from her Civil List allowance of £365,000 a year. Confusion over the ownership of this property, however, became apparent when Edward VIII abdicated and began arguing over how much George VI was going to give him for it. Edward said in their suggested agreement: 'If Balmoral does not pass to the Crown under Scottish law, His Majesty [Edward VIII] agrees to sell and His Royal Highness [George VI] agrees to buy the estate at fair value . . .'3 So it seems that Edward was not even sure if he owned it or not.

Sandringham, a 20,000-acre farming estate which Prince Philip has helped turn into a profitable business rather than the white elephant it had been for years, was bought with tax-free revenue from the Duchy of Lancaster and the Duchy of Cornwall.

In spite of these facts, which are a matter of public record, the Civil List Select Committee accepted that 'the Sandringham and Balmoral estates are the personal property of the Queen' and that some contribution towards staffing should be made since when in residence she continued official duties and required the necessary staff around her.

Both of these properties, because of the Queen's extremely beneficial tax privileges, have been relieved of the threat of death duties. The two estates provide the Queen with valuable revenue, but her main source of funds comes from the Duchy of Lancaster, a 50,000-acre estate with holdings in Yorkshire, Cheshire, Lancashire, Staffordshire and Northamptonshire. The Duchy earned £2,270,000 in the year ending 31 December 1988. This tax-free revenue goes into the Queen's personal bank accounts.

The foregoing brief excursion into the complicated and very secret world of royal treasure and finances barely scrapes the surface of the wealth in the hands of the House of Windsor, which in 1989 was estimated to be worth £7.5 billion; other financial writers have put it higher. This excludes the personal fortunes of Prince Charles, derived from the Duchy of Cornwall which owns 126,000 acres of land in twenty counties and at the end of 1989 was estimated to be worth £250,000,000.

Apart from these publicly available facts, the true details of the Queen's wealth remain known only to herself, Philip and a small team of advisers all sworn to confidentiality. Many have tried to deduce her worth and have failed, including the Civil List investigators of the last two decades. Neither could such figures be imagined back in 1969.

Prince Philip correctly perceived, after the furore that surrounded his opening salvo in the royal-finance row, that the formal request for an increase would cause considerable press comment and speculation. And it is interesting to note the chronology of events, from information now available, which occurred during the first half of 1971.

On 19 May the Queen sent a 'most gracious message' to the House of Commons formally requesting an increase in her Civil List Allowance because of developments since 1952. On 28 May an unsigned article (but rumoured to be the work of Richard Crossman, MP) appeared on the front page of the *New Statesman*. It began:

> What is the connection between the way in which we pay – and tax – Her Majesty the Queen and the Paris Commune which collapsed in bloody ruins a hundred years ago this week? The connection, one which Marx would instantly have perceived, is the effort established societies make to maintain the class structure. . . . A pay claim from a dustman is an attempt to 'hold the nation to ransom'. A pay claim from Her Majesty is termed as Her Majesty's 'most gracious message' . . .

The article went on to challenge her tax privileges:

> Anthony Barber [the Heath Chancellor] has said the Queen's resources in her private capacity do not come into this. But the Queen is not private; nor is she treated as such. The bulk of her wealth is not subject to death duties. She pays no income tax or surtax. She is getting it both ways. One has to admire her truly regal cheek.[4]

In the ensuing uproar, the republican MP Willie Hamilton, whom someone mischievously nominated for membership of the Civil List Select Committee, added his own invective: 'It is the most insensitive, brazen pay claim made in the last 200 years.' He proposed that the Civil List should be abolished and the Queen and Philip should just get the rate for the job. All those critics, of course, confused emotion with reality when they talked of 'pay rises'. As the Royals are ever ready to point out, they spend the Civil List money on salaries and expenses connected with their public duties. The polo ponies, the yachts and the rest come out of their own money.

All this talk of the Queen's money worried Mountbatten. As he viewed the tide of ill-feeling, he was, as always, ready to venture a considered opinion on his forte of public relations, and how public opinion, swinging once again away from them, might be massaged.

On 5 June he advised his nephew – after figures of between £50 million and £100 million began to appear, and this in 1971 – that unless they could get an informed reply published on the subject of their wealth, 'the image of monarchy will be gravely damaged.'[5] He suggested that they should try to get an authoritative article published in *The Times*; that would then be taken up by the popular press. 'So will you both please believe a loving old uncle and NOT your constitutional advisers and do it,' he wrote to Philip.[6]

Lo and behold, on 9 June Mr John Colville, former Private Secretary to the Queen and to Winston Churchill, and by then a bank director, appeared in *The Times* writing on the question of the Queen's wealth. He assessed that the true net worth of the Queen was 'probably not more than £2 million',[7] which in hindsight was something of an understatement, even for 1971.

It was not enough to quell the mood of resentment, which was merely heightened when the Select Committee discovered the 'hidden extras' to the monarchy – services provided by various ministries who also footed the bill and which went under the heading of 'Department Votes'. It seemed to come as something of a shock to some of them that the little private airline, the Queen's Flight, operated and paid for by the Ministry of Defence, was rather a costly item. By the end of 1989 the two BAe 146 planes attached to the Queen's Flight cost £5 million a year to run, regardless of the capital cost of £76 million. The royal yacht *Britannia* costs around £4.5 million a year to operate, in addition to the refits which cost £10 million in 1987 and £6 million in 1984.* Then there was the royal train operated by the Ministry of Transport and which was up for renewal in 1987 over a four-year period at a cost of £7.5 million; the post and telephone services (including the 6,500 telegrams sent annually to centenarians and other anniversary celebrants); maintenance of twelve royal homes, palaces and castles, plus a contribution to the running expenses such as staffing, gas, electricity and fuel; operation of other royal cars; remuneration and pension contributions to the Queen's staff while on State business . . . it went on and on.

In 1971, the year the Committee presented to Parliament the one and only investigation into royal expenses, the additional costs amounted to £3 million. Four years later, this had risen to £6.5 million, including the new Civil List payments. Harold Wilson, back at Number 10 in February 1974, agreed that the increase in expenses was in line with inflation and was especially needed to provide for pay rises for the 437 staff on the royal payroll. In the circumstances, said Wilson, no further investigation was required and this time the increase went ahead, though not without

---

* It has been regularly refitted in its thirty-four year history. By 1974 it had been refitted ten times – almost one refit for every two years of service.

a thought-provoking debate in the Commons on 26 February 1975. Even the most polite of speakers, Mr Michael Stewart, admitted that the

> example of a head of State who is immune from that part of the law which requires us to pay tax is unfortunate. . . . immunity exposes the monarchy to unnecessary criticism. . . . this way of paying for the monarchy . . . is slovenly and an undignified way of going about the matter.[8]

The increase was approved, though ninety MPs voted against. The Civil List is now reviewed annually. In 1989 the total Civil List payment to the monarchy was £5,602,000. Philip received £225,000 compared with the Queen Mother's £404,000, the Princess Royal's £140,400 and the Duke and Duchess of York's £155,000. ThePrince and Princess of Wales take their funds from the Duchy of Cornwall, estimated in 1989 to have paid them £2 million. He voluntarily pays twenty-five per cent tax. The hidden extras have continued to escalate to meet the demands of the eighties: higher transport costs; increased workloads involving more members of the Royal Family; the ever-mounting costs of maintaining the royal buildings; the advent of new technology and computerization; the security of property and the personal protection squad, the cost of which has risen by astronomical proportions; these are just some of the areas which cause those handling the budgets a few headaches. The total cost of monarchy was expected to reach £50 million a year by the end of 1990 and at least £80 million a year within five years.

Against that must be set the tax that the Queen does pay on portions of her estate income, the voluntary 'tax' that Prince Charles makes from the Duchy of Cornwall – though of course without knowledge of the personal income and wealth of the Queen and her heir, it is not possible to assess what tax is not being paid; a tidy sum, no doubt. There is also the income from the Crown Estates, the vast and valuable collection of property held in the Queen's name but which must certainly be viewed as belonging to the nation, although the Royals may not entirely agree.

Are they value for money? Has Philip earned his keep? Or are they too privileged by half? There are perhaps many other areas of national life less cost-effective and without such tangible advantages as the monarchy. The controversy rages on into the 1990s, when doubtless it will be re-examined with the close scrutiny of the 1971 Select Committee, that even so earned criticism for not delving deep enough; they won that one, but future inquirers, in a new age in which the Royal Family – and especially some of the minor Royals – will need to be seen to be earning their keep, might not be so understanding.

Philip continues to use the services of the Ministry of Defence at the drop of a hat. He has first call on the Queen's Flight, just as he has had since the early days when the newspapers tracked his movements to inform us of the number of times in a week that he had use of a helicopter for even shortish journeys into Kent, or to tell us that he used a destroyer and a helicopter to get him to a polo match. Nothing changes, except that he is not in so much of a rush these days and he no longer plays polo, of course.

The greatest demand on his time, apart from escorting the Queen, is the Worldwide Fund for Nature, as the former World Wildlife Fund is now called, which regularly benefits from the generous provision of its President's travel arrangement by the British government. He ignores criticism that on occasion he is the sole passenger on an aircraft; he has even used *Britannia* for solo trips – like the time he sailed to the Gambia in 1985 to boost his wildlife fund and arrived as the single Royal on the shores of a land of poverty looking like a remnant from a past imperial age.

Depending on his diary, he can still be found using the helicopter two or three times a week and, invariably, the RAF have to make the journey twice – once to make a reconnoitre of the area for landing and security facilities and once for the visit proper. This applies whether it is Philip, the Queen Mother or Princess Anne, who all use this facility as if it were the only way to travel. Perhaps it is, for busy and worthwhile members of the Royal Family.

One last unforgettable Philip moment. He was in Newcastle-upon-Tyne and turned up at the local airport dressed in full Field Marshal's uniform, expecting to find a BAe 146 airliner of the Queen's Flight waiting to take him back to London. He ordered his car to drive straight to the tarmac, where he got out and looked around.

'Where's my bloody plane?' he said to anyone who would listen, in a voice loud enough to be heard above the passing engines of a jet plane.

The control tower, not recognizing their VIP passenger, shouted back: 'Get that bloke in uniform off the apron. He shouldn't be there.'[9]

Philip was politely informed that he had arrived half an hour early. He grunted, refused coffee and continued to pace up and down until the plane landed, strode aboard, took over the controls and flew off.

He will undoubtedly be the last royal male from whom this kind of behaviour is both expected and tolerated.

Sources

Chapter One
For the immediate history of Prince Philip's family and its arrival in Greece, I viewed the Lord Mountbatten family tree and drew from the descriptions of a number of previous works on Greece and the European monarchies, notably Sir Charles Petrie's *Monarchy in the Twentieth Century*, HRH Prince Christopher of Greece's *Memoirs* and Alan Palmer's *Crowned Cousins*, which supplemented my examination of Greek State Archive material. Lord Lambton's recent history, *The Mountbattens: the Battenbergs and Young Mountbatten*, has injected another note of controversiality into an already colourful family tree; George Lichtheim's *Europe in the Twentieth Century* filled in some of my historical colour. Specific references are as follows:

1. *Ethnos* (Athens newspaper), editorial, 6 March 1963.
2. Sir Henry Channon, *Chips: the Diaries of Sir Henry Channon* (ed. Robert Rhodes James), Weidenfeld and Nicolson, London, 1967, p. 283.
3. Mountbatten Lineage, British Museum.
4. HRH Prince Christopher of Greece, *Memoirs*, The Right Book Club, London, 1938, p. 30.
5. Sir Charles Petrie, *Monarchy in the Twentieth Century*, Andrew Dakers, London, 1952, pp. 166–67.
6. Prince Christopher of Greece, p. 32. Little did he know he was producing a traceable blueprint for the family history of a future consort to the Queen of England!
7. Ibid., p. 34
8. Letters of Queen Victoria to her granddaughter, quoted in James Pope-Hennessy, *Queen Mary*, Allen and Unwin, London, 1959, p. 400.
9. Letters of Queen Victoria in Kronberg Archive, quoted in Pope-Hennessy, p. 154.

Chapter Two
Early contact between the House of the Hellenes and the British Royal Court is well documented in Cecil Woodham-Smith's *Life and Times of Queen Victoria* and James Pope-Hennessy's *Queen Mary*. Other clues were to be found in various works, including a rare book I discovered in a tiny second-hand bookshop in Eire entitled *A Royal Correspondence: Letters of King Edward VII to George V* by Admiral Sir Henry E. Stephenson, published in 1938. There are also many

checkable files at the Public Record Office at Kew. Specific references are as follows:

1. Anthony Lambton, *The Mountbattens: the Battenbergs and Young Mountbatten*, Constable, London, 1989, p. 42.
2. Lambton, p. 49, and discussed in Richard Hough, *Louis and Victoria*, Hutchinson, London, 1974, pp. 8 and 9.
3. Lambton, p. 52.
4. Sir Hubert Ponsonby (Private Secretary to Queen Victoria), Ponsonby Papers.
5. Interview, 1976.
6. Hough, *Louis and Victoria*, p. 206.
7. Ex-Queen Alexandra of Yugoslavia, *Prince Philip: a Family Portrait*, Hodder and Stoughton, London, 1969, pp. 21–23.
8. George V letters, quoted in Georgina Battiscombe, *Queen Alexandra*, Constable, London, 1969, p. 298.
9. Unpublished account by Lady Maud Warrender, quoted in Harold Nicolson, *King George V*. Constable, London, 1953, p. 309.
10. Public Record Office, Privy Council Papers for 17 July 1917.
11. George V's diary, quoted in James Pope-Hennessy, *Queen Mary*, Allen and Unwin, London 1959, p. 431.

Chapter Three

Richard Hough's most excellent trio of books on the Mountbatten family (*Louis and Victoria: the First Mountbattens; Edwina, Countess Mountbatten of Burma*; and *Mountbatten, Hero of Our Time*) are invaluable works to be read alongside the heavier volume of Philip Ziegler's unbeatable biography, *Mountbatten*. Lord Lambton takes issue with both in many ways and unkindly says that Mountbatten 'dictated' to Hough – a harsh description of tape-recorded interviews. However, it is interesting to note the varying tone of the three writers and there is a mine of information for the researcher, supplemented in this chapter by reference to Prince Andrew of Greece's own gloomy book, *Towards Disaster*, and by excursions to the Public Record Office, the British Museum Library and the British Museum Newspaper Library, Colindale, for accounts of contemporary events. Specific references are as follows:

1. HRH Prince Christopher of Greece, *Memoirs*, The Right Book Club, London, 1938, p. 62.
2. Victoria, Dowager Marchioness of Milford Haven, letter of 16 February 1919, quoted in Richard Hough, *Louis and Victoria*, Hutchinson, London, 1974, p. 69.
3. Prince Christopher of Greece, p. 152.
4. Princess Alice of Greece, introduction to Prince Andrew of Greece, *Towards Disaster*, John Murray, London, 1930.
5. Denis Judd, *The House of Windsor*, Macdonald and Jane, London, 1973, p. 49.
6. Agnes Blower, account published in the *Daily Mirror*, October 1962.
7. Ex-Queen Alexandra of Yugoslavia, *Prince Philip: a Family Portrait*, Hodder and Stoughton, London, 1969, p. 32.
8. Interview, October 1962.

9. *Daily Mail*, editorial, July 1922.
10. *The Times*, 15 September 1922.
11. Public Record Office Docs FO/16H22, Greece.
12. Prince Andrew of Greece, p. 34.

Chapter Four
1. Hélène Cordet, *Born Bewildered*, Peter Davies, London, 1961, p. 68.
2. Madame Anna Foufounis, article in *Look* magazine, June 1954.
3. Victoria, Dowager Marchioness of Milford Haven, letter of 20 June 1926, quoted in Richard Hough, *Louis and Victoria*, Hutchinson, London, 1974, p. 352.
4. Ibid., p. 355.
5. Interview, 1978.
6. Ex-Queen Alexandra of Yugoslavia, *Prince Philip: a Family Portrait*, Hodder and Stoughton, London, 1969, p. 44.
7. Interview, 1947.
8. Interview, 1977.
9. From ex-Queen Helen of Romania's own account, August 1964.

Chapter Five
1. A. J. P. Taylor, *The Course of German History*, Hamish Hamilton, London, 1985, p. 65.
2. Richard Hough, *Louis and Victoria*, Hutchinson, London, 1974, p. 362.
3. Quoted in Richard Hough, *Edwina, Countess Mountbatten of Burma*, Weidenfeld and Nicolson, London, 1983, p. 67.
4. The Beaverbrook Papers, January 1928, House of Lords c/255.
5. Articles alleging Mountbatten's homosexuality have now appeared in several quarters, notably in *Private Eye*, 12 October 1979 and 5 December 1980; Philip Ziegler discusses and quotes Mountbatten's denial in *Mountbatten*, Collins, London, 1985, p. 52.
6. John Costello, *The Mask of Treachery*, Collins, London, 1988, p. 216.
7. Confirmed to the author in interviews during earlier research for *King of Fools* and quoted in Charles Higham, *The Duchess of Windsor*, McGraw-Hill, New York, 1988, p. 80.
8. Ibid., p. 83.
9. Richard Hough, *Edwina, Countess Mountbatten of Burma*, p. 119.
10. *Sunday People*, 12 May 1932.
11. The gossip over Edwina and Robeson rattled on for months on both sides of the Atlantic and brought a devastating array of headlines. Even today there is still dispute over Edwina's claims not to have known him. Hough supports the theory that she did; Ziegler reports Edwina's denial in her diary; while writer Marie Seton has insisted she heard Robeson state categorically that he and Edwina did 'go to bed once' and at her instigation. He had 'graciously consented' to her bringing legal action against the *Sunday People*.
12. Sir Robert Bruce Lockhart, *The Diaries of Sir Robert Bruce Lockhart* (ed. Kenneth Young), Macmillan, London, 1959, p. 326.
13. Penelope Mortimer, *Queen Elizabeth: a Life of the Queen Mother*, Viking, London, 1986, p. 117.

14. Robert Sencourt, *The Reign of Edward VIII*, Gibbs and Phillips, London, 1962, p. 36.
15. The author's own research for *King of Fools*, following original quotation by Michael Thorton in *Royal Feud*, Michael Joseph, London, 1985, pp. 402–3.
16. Lockhart, p. 215.
17. Unnamed equerry to Edward VIII, quoted in J. Bryan and Charles Murphy, *The Windsor Story*, Granada, London, 1979, p. 101.
18. Public Record Office, Ramsay Macdonald Papers, 5 October 1934.
19. Quoting her father, Prince Nicholas of Greece, 1934.
20. Mensdorff Papers, 1No.1933, Austrian State Archive, Vienna.
21. HRH Prince Christopher of Greece, *Memoirs*, The Right Book Club, London, 1938, p. 162.
22. Dermot Morrah, *Princess Elizabeth, Duchess of Edinburgh*, Odhams, London, 1950.
23. Ex-Queen Alexandra of Yugoslavia, *Prince Philip: a Family Portrait*, Hodder and Stoughton, London, 1969, p. 48.

Chapter Six
1. Quoted in the foreword in tribute to Kurt Hahn.
2. Ibid.
3. HRH Prince Christopher of Greece, *Memoirs*, The Right Book Club, London, 1938, p. 244.
4. Sources on Philip, Prinz von Hessen, *Das Haus Hessen: Ein Europaïshes Fürstengeschecht*, Hans Philippi, Kassel, 1983, and Nuremberg Trial documents relating to his membership of the national Socialist Party from 1930, appointment as Oberpräsident of Hessen-Nassau province in 1933 and Gruppenführer in the SA; supplemented by detail of DeNazification Tribunal, 1945–47.
5. Albert Speer, *Inside the Third Reich*, Weidenfeld and Nicolson, London, 1970, p. 307.
6. Theo Aronson, *Countess of Athlone*, Cassell, London, 1981, p. 183.
7. Mensdorff Papers, 1No.1933, Austrian State Archive, Vienna.
8. General Sir Leslie Hollis, quoted 1961.
9. An assessment of Prince Philip by Kurt Hahn made for circulation by Reuters, 1947.
10. Ibid.

Chapter Seven
1. Sir Robert Bruce Lockhart first revealed the presence of Mrs Jones and she is mentioned in *The Diaries of Sir Robert Bruce Lockhart* (ed. Kenneth Young), Macmillan, London, 1959, p. 7.
2. Quoted in *The Times*, 25 November 1935.
3. Kurt Hahn's assessment of Prince Philip for Reuters, 1947.
4. King George V to Baldwin, recorded in the Boyle Papers and first quoted in Middlemas and Barnes, *Baldwin*, Weidenfeld and Nicolson, London, 1969, p. 576.
5. Public Record Office, Captured Documents on German Foreign Policy/Coburg files, in which is quoted Windsor's now famous comment to be

relayed to Hitler: 'Who is King here? Baldwin or I? I wish to talk to Hitler and will do so here or in Germany. Tell him that, please.'
6. Contemporary newspaper reports gave details of meetings between Windsor and Greek leaders.
7. HRH the Duke of Windsor, *A King's Story*, Cassell, London, 1951, p. 285.
8. Public Record Office, FO Doc. 371/20734.
9. Ibid.
10. Penelope Mortimer, *Queen Elizabeth: a Life of the Queen Mother*, Viking, London, 1986, p. 163.
11. Denis Judd, *The House of Windsor*, Macdonald and Jane, London, 1973, p. 80.
12. Ibid., p. 64.
13. Philip Ziegler, *Mountbatten*, Collins, London, 1985, p. 102.
14. Kurt Hahn's assessment of Prince Philip for Reuters, 1947.
15. Richard Hough, *Louis and Victoria*, Hutchinson, London, 1974, p. 365.
16. Interview, 1967.
17. Ex-Queen Alexandra of Yugoslavia, *Prince Philip: a Family Portrait*, Hodder and Stoughton, London, 1969, pp. 60–63.
18. Ibid.
19. Ziegler, p. 102.

Chapter Eight
1. In Frances Stevenson, *Lloyd George*, Hutchinson, London, 1971, p. 309.
2. Walter Schellenberg (external Gestapo chief), *Memoirs* (ed. Alan Bullock), André Deutsch, London, 1956. His recollections concern the moment in 1940 when Hitler instructed him to persuade the Duke of Windsor to take a villa in Switzerland and hold himself in readiness for return.
3. Biographical notes issued by the Central Office of Information.
4. HRH the Duke of Windsor, *A King's Story*, Cassell, London, 1951, p. 71.
5. Philip Ziegler, *Mountbatten*, Collins, London, 1985, p. 38.
6. Sir John Wheeler-Bennett, *King George VI, His Life and Reign*, Macmillan, London, 1958, p. 749.
7. Marion Crawford, *The Little Princesses*, Cassell, London, 1953, p. 59.
8. Chamberlain Papers NC/7-3-36.
9. Philip of Hesse's taped conversations, read at his DeNazification Tribunal hearings, 14 February 1946 and 19 December 1947.
10. Transcript of taped telephone conversation between Philip of Hesse and Goering, read at Goering's trial at Nuremberg, 29 November 1945.
11. History of the Luftwaffe Research Agency, source material from David Irving, *Göering*, Macmillan, London, 1989.
12. Ibid., p. 125.
13. Sir Henry Channon, *Chips: the Diaries of Sir Henry Channon* (ed. Robert Rhodes James), Weidenfeld and Nicolson, London, 1967, p. 238.
14. Public Record Office, FO 371/22445.
15. Ibid.
16. Public Record Office, Minute of 3 August 1940, PREM 4/100/3, ff. 129–32.
17. Public Record Office, PREM 4/100/3.
18. Alden Hatch, *The Mountbattens*, W. H. Allen, London, 1966, for which he received the assistance of Prince Bernhard of The Netherlands, p. 402.

19. Helen Cathcart, *The Married Life of the Queen*, W. H. Allen, London, 1970, p. 26. Mrs Cathcart's multitude of royal books are packed with intimate detail.
20. Judy Fallon (friend of Prince Philip), Australia, 9 January 1954.
21. Basil Boothroyd, *Philip: an Informal Biography*, Longman, London, 1971, p. 115.
22. Admiralty Log. S519, quoted in Boothroyd, p. 86.
23. Channon, p. 283.
24. Ibid.
25. Quoted in Boothroyd, p. 12.
26. Unity Hall, *The Man Behind the Monarchy*, Michael O'Mara, London, 1987, p. 34.
27. Helen Cathcart, writing in the *Daily Mirror*, 9 November 1970.
28. Mentioned in Martin Gilbert, *Finest Hour*, Heinemann, 1983, p. 1,043, and confirmed in Hugh Dalton, *The Political Diary of Hugh Dalton* (ed. Ben Pimlott), Jonathan Cape, 1986, p. 231.

Chapter Nine
1. Helen Cathcart, *The Married Life of the Queen*, W. H. Allen, London, 1970.
2. Queen Mary to Lady Airlie, in Mabel, Countess of Airlie, *Thatched With Gold*, Hutchinson, London, 1962, p. 223.
3. Hansard PD VO1. 3,874–1985.
4. Madame Anna Foufounis, writing in *Look* magazine, June 1954.
5. Unity Hall, *The Man Behind the Monarchy*, Michael O'Mara, London, 1987, p. 84, and Denis Judd, *The House of Windsor*, Macdonald and Jane, London, 1973, p. 165.
6. Peter Lane, *Prince Philip*, Robert Hale, London, 1980, p. 121.
7. *The Times*, 29 December 1943.
8. Ex-Queen Alexandra of Yugoslavia, *Prince Philip: a Family Portrait*, Hodder and Stoughton, London, 1969, p. 80.
9. Sir John Wheeler-Bennett, *King George VI, His Life and Reign*, Macmillan, London, 1958, p. 749.
10. Philip Ziegler, *Mountbatten*, Collins, London, 1985, p. 308.
11. Ibid.
12. Prince Christopher of Hesse death mystery: author can find no trace of documents relating to his death, or assassination as claimed by Lord Mountbatten; see Lambton's rejection of the claim in *The Mountbattens: the Battenbergs and Young Mountbatten*, Constable, London, 1989, p. 36.
13. Albert Speer, *Inside the Third Reich*, Weidenfeld and Nicolson, London, 1970, p. 307.
14. From Hitler's private notes, quoted in John Toland, *Adolf Hitler*, Doubleday, New York, 1976.
15. From Olga Franklin's scoop in the *Newcastle Journal*, April 1944.
16. Richard Hough, *Louis and Victoria*, Hutchinson, London, 1974, p. 322.
17. Judy Fallon, recollections of Prince Philip's wartime Australian visit.
18. Ziegler, p. 300.
19. Mountbatten in his diary, quoted in Ziegler, p. 303.
20. Judy Fallon, further recollections.

Chapter Ten
The bulk of the background material for this chapter is taken from documentary sources in Washington and Germany and reports of military tribunals concerning the main protagonists, notably the Military Court which heard the evidence against the Hesse castle plunderers between June 1946 and May 1947 (Military Court, Frankfurt, documents and reports in the New York Times, June 1946 onwards); plus the DeNazification Tribunal hearings against Philip of Hesse, October 1945 and 18 December 1947. To these I have added the quoted recollections of the leading authority on Nazi prisoners of that era, US Attorney John Loftus. Specific references are as follows:

1. Robert Lacey, *Majesty*, Hutchinson, London, 1977, p. 154.
2. Alden Hatch, *The Mountbattens*, W. H. Allen, London, 1966, p. 414.
3. Willi Frischauer, *Margaret, Princess Without a Cause*, Michael Joseph, London, 1977.
4. *The Times*, 5 September 1946.
5. Philip of Hesse's arrest and target number listed in Intelligence records of the Supreme Headquarters Allied Expeditionary Forces, April 1945, docs SHAEF G2, entries 254–80; see description of re-arrest in John Costello, *The Mask of Treachery*, Collins, London, 1988, p. 448.
6. In documents from US Attorney John Loftus, 1989.
7. First public intimation of the transfer of documents, confirmed by Prince Wolfgang of Hesse and reports in the *Sunday Times*, 25 November 1979.
8. Report of arrest of Durrant and Nash, the *New York Times*, 19 June 1946, and subsequent court martial.
9. Report of DeNazification Tribunal, Frankfurt, 19 December 1947.
10. Quoting Princess Victoria Louise, from *The Kaiser's Daughter*, London, 1977.
11. Quoting extract from the diary of Sir Alexander Cadogan, August–October 1945.
12. Copies of correspondence in Beaverbrook Collection, House of Lords, relating to captured Nazi documents, July 1953.
13. Public Record Office, Foreign Office Documents 371/59538.
14. Elizabeth Longford, *The Royal House of Windsor*, Weidenfeld and Nicolson, London, 1974, p. 196.
15. *Sunday Express*, 9 August 1959.
16. Brigadier Stanley Clark, *Palace Diary*, George Harrap, London, 1958, April–May 1947.
17. Ibid., p. 18.

Chapter Eleven
I have drawn on various sources for this chapter, notably the recollections of Prince Philip's valet John Dean, whose stories were serialized in newspapers as well as incorporated into the book *HRH Prince Philip, the Duke of Edinburgh*. I am also grateful to Larry Adler for his personal reminiscences of the Thursday Club, of which he believes himself and Prince Philip to be the last two surviving founder-members. I have gleaned other useful asides from a sweep of Hansard and contemporary coverage of the engagement of Princess Elizabeth to Prince

Philip which, as is often the case, was viewed in a totally different light by American newspapers such as the *New York Times*, who were able to give a less introspective account. Specific references are as follows:

1. John Dean, *HRH Prince Philip, the Duke of Edinburgh*, Robert Hale, London, 1954, p. 50.
2. Chuter Ede Papers.
3. Nationwide poll conducted by the *Daily Mirror*, July 1947.
4. Quoted in Sir John Wheeler-Bennett, *George VI, His Life and Reign*, Macmillan, London, 1956.
5. Hansard, 12 October 1947.
6. See Martin Gilbert, *Never Despair*, Heinemann, 1988, p. 341.
7. Hansard, various dates July 1947.
8. George VI, note to Queen Mary.
9. Interview with Larry Adler, October 1989.
10. Ibid.
11. Ibid.

Chapter Twelve
1. Lord Louis Mountbatten, 1968, reflective interview recalling the event.
2. Public Record Office, Attlee Papers PREM 8/652.
3. Attlee Papers Dep 51.
4. Quoted in Sir John Wheeler-Bennett, *King George VI, His Life and Reign*, Macmillan, London, 1956, p. 745.
5. Reported in *The Times*, 18 December 1947.
6. Public Record Office, PREM 8/652.
7. Sir Henry Channon, *Chips: the Diaries of Sir Henry Channon* (ed. Robert Rhodes James), Weidenfeld and Nicolson, London, 1967, p. 240.
8. Hansard, 17 December 1947.
9. Wheeler-Bennett, p. 736.
10. John Dean, *HRH Prince Philip, the Duke of Edinburgh*, Robert Hale, London, 1954, p. 101.
11. Eileen Parker, *Step Aside For Royalty*, Bachman and Turner, London, 1982.
12. Description of her father's feelings by Princess Anne in Kenneth Harris interview, *Observer*, 19 August 1980.
13. Ibid.
14. Foreign Office file, PRO 372/6683.

Chapter Thirteen
Detail in this chapter is drawn from interviews with Larry Adler, October 1989, allied to the recollections given to the author by others who were involved in certain aspects of the story at that time. I am also grateful to Brian McConnell, an investigative journalist of the era who filled in many gaps. Actress Patricia Kirkwood gave her version of events in an interview in December 1988, often corroborated by events outlined in *Honeytrap: the Secret Worlds of Stephen Ward* by Anthony Summers and Stephen Dorrill. Meanwhile, Brigadier Stanley Clark gave a colourful description of life at the Palace during the drama of the King's illness in *Palace Diary* from which I have drawn detail. Specific references are as follows:

SOURCES

1. Peter Townsend, *Time and Chance*, Collins, London, 1978, p. 182.
2. Cabinet Papers, PRO PREM 8/1–11.
3. Richard Sharples, personal recollections of Philip, *Daily Mirror*, 9 June 1971.
4. Generally quoting Eileen Parker, *Step Aside for Royalty*, Bachman and Turner, London, 1982, p. 66.
5. Patricia Kirkwood, interview with Terry O'Hanlon, December 1988.
6. Ibid.
7. Interview with Larry Adler, October 1989.
8. Ibid.
9. Anthony Summers and Stephen Dorrill, *Honeytrap: the Secret Worlds of Stephen Ward*, Weidenfeld and Nicolson, London, 1987, p. 27.
10. Ibid., p. 25.
11. Official bulletins, 23 and 29 December 1948.
12. Cabinet Papers, PRO PREM 8/1015.
13. Brigadier Stanley Clark, *Palace Diary*, George Harrap, London, 1958, p. 38.
14. Basil Boothroyd, *Philip: an Informal Biography*, Longman, London, 1971, p. 144.

Chapter Fourteen
1. Quoted from a speech.
2. Churchill Papers, PRO/PREM/8/826.
3. Truman Papers, quoted in Patrick Howarth, *George VI*, Hutchinson, London, 1987, p. 252.
4. Basil Boothroyd, *Philip: an Informal Biography*, Longman, London, 1971, p. 178.
5. Ibid., p. 165.
6. Philip Ziegler, *Mountbatten*, Collins, London, 1985, p. 302.
7. Ibid., pp. 51–53.
8. Ibid.
9. 'The Red aura', alleged in *Bulletin of Information Services*, USA, March 1952.
10. Quoted in Ziegler, p. 502.
11. L. G. Pine, in various newspaper articles, March 1952.
12. *London Gazette*, November 1948.
13. Elizabeth Longford, *The Queen: the Life of Elizabeth II*, Alfred A. Knopf, New York, 1983, p. 167.
14. Claims on the monarchy, recorded in Mountbatten Lineage, British Museum.
15. Interview, *Daily Express*, 2 June 1964.

Chapter Fifteen
Contemporary newspaper reports and interviews have provided the general of the source material for the chapter, supplemented by the Cabinet documents relating to the Princess Margaret proposal to marry Group Captain Peter Townsend; these documents were released at the Public Record Office under the thirty-year rule and relate to the political discussions surrounding Princess Margaret between April 1953 and October 1955. Specific references are as follows:

1. Peter Lane, *Prince Philip*, Robert Hale, London, 1980, p. 200.
2. Basil Boothroyd, *Philip: an Informal Biography*, Longman, London, 1971, p. 47.
3. Alden Hatch, *The Mountbattens*, W. H. Allen, London, 1966, confirms this aspect, p. 441.
4. Basil Boothroyd's comment made in *The Times*, 10 June 1981.
5. The Queen's worries are mentioned variously in Helen Cathcart, *The Married Life of the Queen*, W. H. Allen, London, 1970.
6. Quoted in John Pearson, *The Ultimate Family*, Michael Joseph, London, 1986, p. 52.
7. John Gordon, writing in the *Sunday Express*, 4 February 1953.
8. *Time*, 12 June 1953.
9. Churchill's initial reaction to Margaret's marriage plans quoted in Elizabeth Longford, *The Queen: the Life of Elizabeth II*, Alfred A. Knopf, New York, 1983, p. 164.
10. The *Sunday People*, 12 June 1953.
11. Nigel Dempster, *HRH The Princess Margaret: a Life Unfulfilled*, Quartet Books, London, 1981, p. 3.
12. Peter Townsend, *Time and Chance*, Collins, London, 1978, p. 182.
13. Willi Frischauer, *Margaret, Princess Without a Cause*, Michael Joseph, London, 1977, p. 34.
14. Townsend, p. 182.
15. Lady Selina Hastings, article in *You* magazine, 5 March 1989.
16. The Duchess of Windsor also called the Queen Mother 'Cookie', as revealed in an interview by the Countess Romanones, October 1986.

Chapter Fifteen

The massive press coverage of the divorce suit filed by Prince Philip's Private Secretary Michael Parker – coming as it did so soon after the first instalment of the Princess Margaret romantic sagas – gave rise the following year to further critical appraisal of the first few years of the new monarchy. I have drawn from these critiques and, of course, from the recollections of Eileen Parker, *Step Aside For Royalty*, another of the neglected wives of Palace aides who says life in the royal fast lane helped destroy her marriage and who earned some small compensation from her writing and newspaper serializations. Other first-hand interviews are drawn upon, along with the following specific references:

1. Unity Hall, *The Man Behind the Monarchy*, Michael O'Mara, London, 1987, p. 113.
2. *The Times*, 24 October 1955.
3. Ibid., 1 November 1955.
4. *Manchester Guardian*, 1 November 1955.
5. Prince Philip, *Selected Speeches 1948–55*, Oxford University Press, London, 1957.
6. Eileen Parker, *Step Aside For Royalty*, Bachman and Turner, London, 1982, p. 175.
7. *Daily Mirror*, October 1956.
8. Parker, p. 184.

9. *Baltimore Sun*, 13 February 1957.
10. Parker, p. 185.

Chapter Seventeen

The onset of a hostile press of unprecedented proportions, highly critical of the monarchy as a whole and, for the first time, attacking the monarch personally, had its beginnings from around the time of Prince Philip's return from his world tour. In preparing this chapter I have spoken to numerous journalists and editors who were involved at the time. I have also studied the modernization of the system of monarchy, which was instigated largely by Prince Philip, and have drawn from various bibliographic sources the detail of life and traditions at the Palace which he set about to change. Specific references are as follows:

1. John Pearson, *The Ultimate Family*, Michael Joseph, London, 1986, p. 131.
2. Prince Philip, *Selected Speeches 1956–59*, Collins, London, 1960.
3. Interview, 6 February 1959.
4. *Daily Express*, 25 February 1957.
5. A. J. P. Taylor, *Beaverbrook*, Hamish Hamilton, London, 1972.
6. Robert Edwards, CBE, letter to the author.
7. *Church of England Newspaper*, August 1957.
8. Quoted from speech by Sir Martin Charteris during a debate at Eton.
9. John Osborne, writing in *Encounter*, August 1957.
10. Ex-Queen Alexandra of Yugoslavia, *Prince Philip: a Family Portrait*, Hodder and Stoughton, London, 1969, p. 200.
11. Compton Mackenzie, *Buckingham Palace*, Hutchinson, London, 1953, p. 104.
12. Ibid., p. 113.
13. Lieutenant General Sir Frederick Browning, letter to General Sir Leslie Hollis, 1958.
14. Philip Ziegler, *Mountbatten*, Collins, London, 1985, p. 576.

Chapter Eighteen

1. Spike Milligan, *Daily Mirror*, 8 December 1987.
2. *World Times*, 14 August 1976.
3. *Daily Mirror*, 6 December 1962.
4. Ibid.
5. Burke's *Peerage*, 1973 edn, p. 68.
6. Survey of Prince Philip's accessories, *Sunday Times Magazine*, 6 November 1966.
7. Interview, October 1964.
8. *Daily Mirror*, 4 January 1956.
9. Professor Edward Iwi, writing in the *Law Journal*, March 1960, confirmed in Alden Hatch, *The Mountbattens*, W. H. Allen, London, 1966, p. 440.
10. *Daily Mirror*, leading article, 9 February 1960.
11. *Daily Express*, February 1960, and Beaverbrook Papers, House of Lords.
12. *London Gazette*, 8 February 1960.
13. Interview with Terry O'Hanlon, December 1988.

Chapter Nineteen

The author is grateful to a number of Prince Philip's charity organizers for their recollections, and especially to Lord Hunt (of Everest fame).

1. Statement for the Press Association, 1964.
2. Willie Hamilton MP, speaking on American television, 8 December 1975.
3. Interview, 20 June 1959.
4. Lord Hunt, to the author, October 1989.
5. From the jacket notes of Prince Philip's book *Down to Earth*, Collins, London, 1989.
6. Prince Philip, speech, 1962.
7. Helen Cathcart, *The Married Life of the Queen*, W. H. Allen, London, 1970, p. 119.
8. Comments made December 1988.
9. Prince Philip, *Down to Earth*, foreword.

Chapter Twenty

The wit, wisdom and *faux pas* of Prince Philip are so varied and so numerous that it was difficult to select the best for this illustrative guide to his thoughts. I have gleaned them from a variety of sources, including the British Museum Newspaper Library at Colindale, the Tasiemka Archive, which, like Fleet Street, keeps a special file, plus a scan of Philip's own volumes of selected speeches. Specific references are as follows:

1. Cecil Woodham-Smith, *Queen Victoria: Her Life and Times*, Vol. I, Hamish Hamilton, London, 1971, p. 218.
2. Ibid.
3. Lytton Strachey on Prince Albert.
4. Dermot Morrah, article in the *Daily Express*, 26 September 1958.
5. Elizabeth Longford, *The Queen: the Life of Elizabeth II*, Alfred A. Knopf, New York, 1983, p. 333.
6. Cecil King Papers, and *The Cecil King Diary, 1965–70*, Jonathan Cape, London, 1972, p. 20.
7. Hansard, May 1977.
8. John Grigg, writing in the *Observer*, 6 June 1971.
0. Mountbatten letter from Broadlands Archive, quoted in Philip Ziegler, *Mountbatten*, Collins, London, 1985, p. 683.
10. Vincent Mulchrone's recollections, *Daily Mail*, 11 July 1973.
11. From a signed article by Prince Philip, January 1977.
12. Hansard, 19 January 1977.
13. Keith Waterhouse, *Daily Mirror*, 20 January 1977.
14. John Grigg, writing in the *Observer*, 6 June 1971.

Chapter Twenty-one

Family matters and recent developments are drawn from the author's own interviews for this and two other recent royal biographies, *King of Fools* and *The Princess Royal*, and I am especially grateful to those who have contributed their thoughts, including Mr Edward Heath and Lord Hunt.

1. A. J. P. Taylor, writing in the *Sunday Express*, 19 January 1967.

2. Interview, 14 July 1968.
3. *Sunday Mirror*, 20 February 1977.
4. Résumé from References Service of the Central Office of Information, 1982.
5. Helen Cathcart, *The Married Life of the Queen*, W. H. Allen, London, 1970.
6. Interview, August 1980.
7. Alden Hatch, *The Mountbattens*, W. H. Allen, London, 1966, p. 136.
8. Private information, confirmed in Kingsley Martin, *The Crown and the Establishment*, Hutchinson, London, 1962, p. 131.
9. Quoting from his speech in December 1967.
10. Peter Evans, *Ari*, Penguin edn, London, 1987.
11. John Pearson, *The Ultimate Family*, Michael Joseph, London, 1986, p. 175.

Chapter Twenty-two
The bulk of the financial matter relating to the Queen's estates is taken first from the published proceedings of the Parliamentary Select Committee on the Civil List, 1971, and again in 1975, and much was revealed through detailed questioning by MP Willie Hamilton. These details are supplemented by the most recently available figures relating to the Duchies of Lancaster and Cornwall, and recent valuations of the Queen's assets. My research into the royal collections is from records available to the public and from recent works, notably Suzy Menkes's definitive, *The Royal Jewels*.

1. Prince Philip, special article written for the *Sunday Mirror*, 8 February 1977.
2. *U.S. Today*, interview 9 November 1969.
3. Quoted in Michael Bloch, *The Secret File of the Duke of Windsor*, Bantam Press, London, 1989.
4. *New Statesman*, 23 May 1971.
5. Philip Ziegler, *Mountbatten*, Collins, London, 1985, p. 684.
6. Ibid.
7. *The Times*, 9 June 1971.
8. Hansard, Vol. 887.
9. *Daily Express*, 3 September 1988.

Bibliography

Acland, Eric, *The Princess Elizabeth*, Winston, Canada, 1937.
Airlie, Mabel, Countess of, *Thatched With Gold*, Hutchinson, London, 1962.
Alexandra of Yugoslavia, ex-Queen, *Prince Philip: a Family Portrait*, Hodder and Stoughton, London, 1969.
Andrew of Greece, HRH Prince, *Towards Disaster*, John Murray, London, 1930.
Aronson, Theo, *Princess Alice, Countess of Athlone*, Cassell, London, 1981.
———, *Royal Family*, John Murray, London, 1983.
Asquith, Lady Cynthia, *The King's Daughters*, Hutchinson, London, 1937.
Avon, Earl of, *Memoirs of the Rt Hon. Sir Anthony Eden. Full Circle, Facing the Dictators, The Reckoning*, Cassell, London, 1960, 1962 and 1965.
Battiscombe, Georgina, *Queen Alexandra*, Constable, London, 1969.
Beaverbrook, Lord, *The Abdication of King Edward VIII*, Hamish Hamilton, London, 1966.
Bloch, Michael, *Operation Willi: the Plot to Kidnap the Duke of Windsor*, Weidenfeld and Nicolson, London, 1984.
———, *The Secret File of the Duke of Windsor*, Bantam Press, London, 1989.
Bolitho, Hector, *Albert, Prince Consort*, David Bruce and Watson, London, 1970.
Boothroyd, Basil, *Philip: an Informal Biography*, Longman, London, 1971.
Bryan, J., and Murphy, Charles J. V., *The Windsor Story*, Granada, London, 1979.
Butler, Peter (ed.), *The Wit of Prince Philip*, Frewin, London, 1965.
Campbell, Judith, *The Royal Partners*, Robert Hale, London, 1982.
Cathcart, Helen, *HRH Prince Philip, Sportsman*, Stanley Paul, London, 1961.
———, *The Married Life of the Queen*, W. H. Allen, London, 1970.
Channon, Sir Henry, *Chips: the Diaries of Sir Henry Channon* (ed. Robert Rhodes James), Weidenfeld and Nicolson, London, 1967.
Christopher of Greece, HRH Prince, *Memoirs*, The Right Book Club, London, 1938.
Churchill, Randolph, *The Rise and Fall of Sir Anthony Eden*, MacGibbon and Key, London, 1959.
Clark, Brigadier Stanley, *Palace Diary*, George Harrap, London, 1958.
Colville, John, *The New Elizabethans, 1952–1977*, Collins, London, 1977.
Cordet, Hélène, *Born Bewildered*, Peter Davies, London, 1961.

BIBLIOGRAPHY

Costello, John, *The Mask of Treachery*, Collins, London, 1988.
Crawford, Marion, *The Little Princesses*, Cassell, London, 1953.
Crossman, Richard, *The Diaries of a Cabinet Minister*, Jonathan Cape and Hamish Hamilton, London, 1975.
Dalton, Hugh, *The Political Diary of Hugh Dalton* (ed. Ben Pimlott), Jonathan Cape, London, 1986.
Dean, John, *HRH Prince Philip, the Duke of Edinburgh*, Robert Hale, London, 1954.
Dempster, Nigel, *HRH The Princess Margaret: A Life Unfulfilled*, Quartet Books, London, 1981.
Donaldson Frances, *Edward VIII*, Weidenfeld and Nicolson, London, 1974.
Duff, David, *Victoria Travels*, Frederick Müller, London, 1970.
Frischauer, Willi, *Margaret, Princess Without a Cause*, Michael Joseph, London, 1977.
Hall, Unity, *The Man Behind the Monarchy*, Michael O'Mara, London, 1987.
Hatch, Alden, *The Mountbattens*, W. H. Allen, London, 1966.
Hibbert, Christopher, *The Court at Windsor*, Longman, London, 1964.
Higham, Charles, *The Duchess of Windsor*, McGraw-Hill, New York, 1988.
Holden, Anthony, *Charles, Prince of Wales*, Weidenfeld and Nicolson, London, 1979.
Hollis, General Sir Leslie, *The Captain General*, Herbert Jenkins, London, 1961.
Horne, Alistair, *Macmillan*, Volumes I and II, Macmillan, London, 1088 and 1989.
Hough, Richard, *Louis and Victoria: The First Mountbattens*, Hutchinson, London, 1974.
——, (ed.), *Letters to a Granddaughter: Letters from Queen Victoria to Princess Victoria of Hesse*, Heinemann, London, 1975.
——, *Mountbatten, Hero of Our Time*, Weidenfeld and Nicolson, London, 1980.
——, *Edwina, Countess Mountbatten of Burma*, Weidenfeld and Nicolson, London, 1983.
Howarth, Patrick, *George VI*, Hutchinson, London, 1987.
Irving, David, *Göring: a Biography*, Macmillan, London, 1989.
Judd, Denis, *The House of Windsor*, Macdonald and Jane, London, 1973.
——, *Prince Philip: a Biography*, Atheneum, New York, 1981.
Lacey, Robert, *Majesty: Elizabeth II and the House of Windsor*, Hutchinson, London, 1977.
Lambton, Anthony, *The Mountbattens: the Battenbergs and Young Mountbatten*, Constable, London, 1989.
Lane, Peter, *Prince Philip*, Robert Hale, London, 1980.
Lichtheim, George, *Europe in the Twentieth Century*, Weidenfeld and Nicolson, London, 1972.
Liversidge, Douglas, *Prince Philip, First Gentleman of the Realm*, Arthur Barker, London, 1976.
Lockhart, Sir Robert Bruce, *The Diaries of Sir Robert Bruce Lockhart, 1915–1938* (ed. Kenneth Young), Macmillan, London, 1959.

Longford, Elizabeth, *The Queen: the Life of Elizabeth II*, Alfred A. Knopf, New York, 1983.

Marie Louise, HRH Princess, *My Memories of Six Reigns*, Evans Brothers, London, 1956.

Martin, Kingsley, *The Crown and the Establishment*, Hutchinson, London, 1962.

Martin, Ralph G., *Charles and Diana*, Grafton Books, London, 1986.

Menkes, Suzy, *The Royal Jewels*, Grafton Books, London, 1985.

Middlemas, Keith, and Barnes, John, *Baldwin*, Weidenfeld and Nicolson, London, 1969.

Morrah, Dermot, *Princess Elizabeth, Duchess of Edinburgh*, Odhams, London, 1950.

——, *To Be a King: the Early Life of Charles, Prince of Wales*, Hutchinson, London, 1968.

Mortimer, Penelope, *Queen Elizabeth: a Life of the Queen Mother*, Viking, London, 1986.

Morton, Andrew, *Theirs Is the Kingdom*, Michael Joseph, London, 1989.

Nicolson, Harold, *King George V, His Life and Reign*, Constable, London, 1952.

——, *Diaries and Letters, 1930–39* (ed. Nigel Nicolson), Collins, London, 1966.

——, *Diaries and Letters, 1945–62*, Collins, London, 1968.

Palmer, Alan, *Crowned Cousins*, Weidenfeld and Nicolson, London, 1985.

Parker, Eileen, *Step Aside For Royalty*, Bachman and Turner, London, 1982.

Parker, John, *King of Fools*, Macdonald, London, 1988.

——, *The Princess Royal*, Hamish Hamilton, London, 1989.

Pearson, John, *The Ultimate Family*, Michael Joseph, London, 1986.

Petrie, Sir Charles, *Monarchy in the Twentieth Century*, Andrew Dakers, London, 1952.

Philip, HRH Prince, Duke of Edinburgh, *Selected Speeches, 1948–55*, Oxford University Press, London, 1957.

——, *Selected Speeches, 1956–59*, Collins, London, 1960.

——, with James Fisher, *Wildlife Crisis*, Hamish Hamilton, London, 1970.

——, *Down To Earth*, Collins, London, 1989.

Pope-Hennessy, James, *Queen Mary*, Allen and Unwin, London, 1959.

Priestley, J. B., *Victoria's Heyday*, Heinemann, London, 1972.

Ribbentrop, Joachim, *Memoirs*, Weidenfeld and Nicolson, London, 1954.

Schellenberg, Walter, *Memoirs* (ed. Alan Bullock), André Deutsch, London, 1956.

Sitwell, Osbert, *Queen Mary and Others*, Michael Joseph, London, 1947.

Speer, Albert, *Inside the Third Reich*, Weidenfeld and Nicolson, London, 1970.

Stephenson, Admiral Sir Henry E., *A Royal Correspondence: Letters of King Edward VII to King George V* (ed. John Stephenson), Macmillan, London, 1938.

Summers, Anthony, and Dorrill, Stephen, *Honeytrap: the Secret Worlds of Stephen Ward*, Weidenfeld and Nicolson, London, 1987.

Templewood, Lord, *Nine Troubled Years*, Collins, London, 1954.

Thorton, Michael, *Royal Feud*, Michael Joseph, London, 1985.

Toland, John, *Adolf Hitler*, Doubleday, New York, 1976.

Townsend, Peter, *Time and Chance: an Autobiography*, Collins, London, 1978.

BIBLIOGRAPHY

Wheeler-Bennett, Sir John W., *King George VI, His Life and Reign*, Macmillan, London, 1958.

Windsor, Duchess of, *The Heart Has Its Reasons*, Michael Joseph, London, 1956.

Windsor, HRH Duke of, *A King's Story*, Cassell, London, 1951.

Ziegler, Philip, *Mountbatten*, Collins, London, 1985.

Index

INDEX

Cobbold, 1st Baron 247
Cobden, Richard MP 121-2
Colville, Commander Richard 164, 165, 172, 191, 236; and Parkers' divorce 176-7; retirement 240
Colville, Sir John 129, 133, 164, 252
Compton, Denis 211
Constantine I, King of the Hellenes 7, 8, 15-16, 17-18, 19, 24, 28; death 32, 33; ashes 60-1
Constantine II, King of the Hellenes 233
Coombe, Carol 202
Cooper, Tommy 212
Cordet, Hélène 35-6, 87-8, 120, 138, 203-5, 240
Cornwall, Duchy of 250, 253
Course, Richard 218
Coward, Noël 45, 48, 83, 154, 182n
Crawford, Marion 49, 73, 113
Crichton, Lt Cmdr Michael 137
Cripps, Sir Stafford 128, 134
Crossman, Richard MP 205-6, 251
Cudlipp, Hugh 174, 199, 205-6, 224, 240
Cunningham, Admiral Sir Andrew 82
Cunningham Reid, Captain Alex 85-6
Curzon, 1st Marquess 29

Dagmar, Tsarina of Russia 6
Dalkeith, John 100
Dalrymple-Hamilton, Admiral Sir Frederick 72, 73
Dean, John 113
Dalton, Hugh 127-8
Damaskynos, Archbishop 101
Dartmouth Naval College 71-3, 77, 238
Dawson, Geoffrey 172-3
de Laszlo, John 165
de Valera, Eamon 137n
Dean, John 129
Diana, Princess of Wales 129, 239, 242, 243, 244
Dieppe raid 109, 184
Dimbleby, Richard 163
Disraeli, Benjamin 220
Donahue, Jimmy 162
Dorothea, Princess of Hesse 134
Dorrill, Stephen 140
Douglas-Home, Sir Alec 219
Driberg, Tom 184
Duke of Edinburgh's Award Scheme 212-13
Durant, Jack 104-6
Duschene Commission 103

Ede, Chuter 114, 132
Eden, Anthony 101, 171-2; and Suez 175, 176, 177; resignation 178, 181; and name of royal family 200; memoirs 219
Edinburgh, Duchy of 119
Edrich, Bill 211
Edward, HRH Prince 236, 239

Edward VII, King of Great Britain: and Andrew of Greece's marriage 14; Coronation 13; and Cullinan diamond 248; evidence at Gordon Cumming trial 46, 56n; and Louis IV of Hesse's marriage 13n; marriage 6; visit to Fredensborg 8
Edward VIII, King of Great Britain *as Prince of Wales*; at Dartmouth 71; charitable works 209; Mountbatten's friendship 26-7, 65, 77, 154; and Nazism 55; private life 45, 47, 48, 55; shooting 216-17; tours of Dominions 26-7, 122, 151; George V's judgement of 61 *as King*; Abdication 64, 65, 110, 154, 163, 172-3; changes introduced by 133, 160, 188; and Nazism 54, 55, 62, 63-4; and royal jewellery 248; Simpson affair 47, 49, 110, 219; visit to Greece and Yugoslavia 63 *as Duke of Windsor*; excluded from Princesses' weddings 126, 203; in Bahamas 85; life in Paris 207; and Nazism 55, 70, 74, 75, 92, 107, 108; and Philip 158, 160; plans to move to Eire (1948) 137n; Queen Mother blames for George VI's ill-health 141; visits England 77, 160, 169
Edwards, Robert 184-5
Eire 137
Eisenhower, Dwight David 108
Elizabeth II, HM Queen of Great Britain: childhood 49; life during war 79, 84, 89, 100; tour of South Africa 111-12, 115; courtship and marriage *see* wedding *and under* Philip, HRH Prince; Order of Garter 122, 132; first pregnancy 134, 136; birth of Charles 141; and husband's career 145-6; and Philip's posting to Malta 146-8; second pregnancy 146; accession 152, 158, 160, 161; Coronation 162-3; tours after Coronation 168-9; and choice of successor to Eden 178; pregnancy with Andrew 200; Civil List payment 253; jewellery 249; love for Philip 136, 196, 207, 235, and media 111, 190, workload 210 *Interests*; art collection 192, 196, 249; cultural tastes 183; horse racing 161, 198; shooting 216-17
Elizabeth, HM the Queen Mother: marriage 34; married life 49; and Marina 47; war work 84, 100, 133; and Princess Elizabeth's courtship 72, 99-100; royal tour of South Africa 108-9, 111-12, 115; silver wedding anniversary 132-3; visits Northern Ireland in King's place 149; and Mountbatten 154; mourning 161-2; and Duchess of Windsor 64, 141, 161-2; 169; and Margaret and Townsend 164, 166, 171; and abolition of débutante system 190; role in family 232; and Prince Charles 237, 238; art collection 249; Civil List payment 253; cultural tastes 183; helicopter travel 254
Elizabeth, Queen of Greece 35
Elizabeth, Princess of Romania 59

275

INDEX

Philip, HRH Prince, Duke of Edinburgh:
birth 3, 15; exile 30, 32; childhood 33, 34–9,
43, 44, 49–50, 51, 67–8, (and grandmother)
36, 37, 38, 67, 68, (and Milford Haven
family) 36, 38, 56, 57, 62, 67, 68; education,
(The Elms, St Cloud) 33, 37, (Cheam
Preparatory School) 38, (Salem School) 53,
55, 56, (Gordonstoun School) 57–8, 62, 66,
68, 70–1, 99; visits Greece 59–61; meets
Princess Elizabeth 72–3; friendship
develops 78, 80, 85, 87, 89, 90, 100, 101,
109–11, 115; British naturalization 3, 30, 77,
80, 90–1, 101, 109–11, 114, 156; and
George VI 90, 130, 150, 209, 221;
engagement 116, 117–18; wedding 118–19,
121–3; honeymoon 126–7; assumes official
duties 131–2, 133–4, 143–4; resumes naval
career 131–2, 146–8; leaves Navy 149,
160, 209; and Townsend 101–2, 166,
167–8 *Interests*; carriage-driving 198, 235,
cars 175, 195, 197, 198, 199; cost of 245–54;
cultural tastes 183; flying 160, 162; gliding
187; hunting 215, 229; painting 196;
photography 196, 215–16; polo 146, 187, 195,
196, 197, 198, 236, 246, 254; publications
222–3, (*Down to Earth*) 215, 218, 223;
shooting 198, 216–18, (of wildlife) 177, 178,
183, 216; showbusiness connections 144,
195–6, 211–12; sport 129–30, 195, 196–7,
234, 236; yachting 137–8, 161, 175, 187, 196,
197, 198, 199, 246
Naval career: at Dartmouth 71–3, 77, naval
orders 77; Sub–Lt 77, 84, 86; First Lt 90;
wartime operations 77–8, 78–9, 81–3, 84,
86, 88–9, 90, 92–3, 93–4, 94–5; resumes
career after marriage 131–2, 146–8; Lt
Commander 147; leaves Navy 149, 160,
209; *see also individual ships*
Private life: marriage 136, 169, 176, 177,
179, 200, 206–7, 235; and parents (father)
61–2, 65, 77, 113, (mother) 77, 115, 116,
126; role in family 141, 167–8, 232, 233,
234–9, (and Charles) 176, 236–7, 238–9,
(and German family) 77, 105, 126, 134–5,
147–8, 162, 217, 223–5, 232–5; social life
137–41, 171, 206–7 (*see also* Thursday Club)
Public life: charity work 143–4, 208–18;
comments 219–30; as consort 129, 131–2,
139, 148, 152–3, 157–8, 159, 168, 219–21,
232; and environmental causes 214–18,
219, 222, 229–30; finances 113–14, 127–8,
158, 225, 246, 253; humour 228–9, 234;
and matters of state 219–20, 232, and
monarchy 186–92, 208, 219, 231–4, 239–44,
245; and political issues 65, 219–21, 222,
223–5; and press 126–7, 178–80, 198,
199–200, 221, 223, 225–8, 244; and protocol
117, 129, 162–3; and Royal household and
estates 159–61, 188–91, 245; speeches
143–5, 190, 219, 221–3, (on environment)

229–30, (on industry) 149–50, 195, 209,
222, 245; television appearances 190, 246;
titles 119, 122, 156, 158, 181; travels 170,
210, 234–5, (world tour) (1956) 174–6,
177–8, 180, 182, 240; workload 131–2, 134,
143–4, 160, 181, 210, 239
Philip, Prince of Hesse; marriage 54; Nazi
connections 54, 55, 74, 90–1, 91–2;
imprisonment in Dachau 92; trial 103,
106–7, 111
Phillips, Jan 229
Phillips, Mark 129, 145, 235, 242
Phillips, Zara 217
Pickering, Edward 224
Pine, L. G. 156
Plunket, Lord 167
Portal, Sir Charles 132
Portugal; official visit 181
press: changing attitude to Royal Family 174,
175, 183–8, 243–4; Philip and 126–7,
178–80, 198, 199–200, 221, 223, 225–8,
244; and Princess Margaret and Townsend
165, 174, 175; North American 151, 191–2;
public relations work on Royal Family's
image with 239–44
Priestley, Sir Raymond 182–3
Prince's Trust 211

Qatar, Emir of 249

Ramillies, HMS 77–8
Ramsey, Dr Michael 238
Rasputin 21
Rhodesia 224
Ribbentrop, Joachim von 63
Robertson, E.J. 110–11
Robeson, Paul 46–7
Robson, Dame Flora 187
Rogers, Henry 240–1
Roose, Miss (nanny) 24–5, 33
Royal Family (film) 240, 242–3
Runcie, Dr Robert 196

St Cloud; 'The Elms' (school) 33, 37
Salem School 51–3, 56
Salisbury, Lord 171, 172, 178
Sanegre, Georges 207
Sarah, Duchess of York 129, 223, 242, 253
Sargent, Orme 64
Scott, Sir Peter 137, 215–16
Seago, Edward 175
Sharples, Richard 137
Shropshire, HMS 79
Simeon, King of Bulgaria 233
Simouić, General 81
Simpson, Ernest 49
Simpson, Mrs (wife of David Milford Haven)
140
Simpson, Wallis *see* Windsor, Duchess of
Sinatra, Frank 144, 211

279